THIRTY YEARS IN THE
ARCTIC REGIONS

THIRTY YEARS IN THE
ARCTIC REGIONS

The Narrative of a Polar Explorer

By Sir John Franklin

Foreword by David Welky

Skyhorse Publishing

Visit our website at www.skyhorsepublishing.com.

10 9 8 7 6 5 4 3 2 1

Library of Congress Cataloging-in-Publication Data is available on file.

Cover design by Tom Lau
Cover photo credit: Library of Congress

Print ISBN: 978-1-5107-2385-6
Ebook ISBN: 978-1-5107-2386-3

Printed in the United States of America.

FOREWORD TO THE 2017 EDITION

Assembled from earlier writings and first released in 1859, Sir John Franklin's *Thirty Years in the Arctic Regions* captures a fascinating era of British and, indeed, world history. Not only is it an exemplary travel narrative that spans some of the most treacherous territory on Earth, it also opens a literary window onto a bygone era when brave—perhaps foolhardy—men plunged into dangerous expeditions with talk of God, country, and honor on their lips and little thought of their chances for survival in their minds. Beyond this, *Thirty Years* is a character study of its frumpy, balding, rather dowdy author, whose Arctic exploits made him famous and whose mysterious disappearance inspired a generations-long search for his final resting place.

"His countrymen, and the entire civilised world, have recognised that the great though imperfect exploits of the traveler were outshone by the heroic qualities of the man," Henry Duff Traill wrote in his 1896 hagiography *The Life of Sir John Franklin*. Nothing about Franklin's youth suggested heroism. He was born in 1786 in Spilsby, a market town 130 miles north of London. The ninth of twelve children, John entered the world with many advantages. His mother, Hannah, was the daughter of a well-to-do farmer and landholder. His father, Willingham, descended from generations of country squires, was a prosperous banker. Their combined wealth supported a rollicking household tempered by firm discipline. John's childhood hijinks brought him into frequent contact with a whip that lay curled by the staircase. Punishment, however, could not quiet his instinctive desire for adventure. Although his parents sent him to respectable schools appropriate to their status, John decided at a young age that his future lay with the Royal Navy.

Willingham Franklin disapproved but eventually gave his consent after a two-year tussle to keep his youngest son on dry land. John volunteered at the age of fourteen for service aboard the HMS *Polyphemus*. Named for the Cyclops that appears in Homer's *Odyssey*, the ship carried Franklin through the first stages of his own epic voyage. Great Britain was immersed in the Napoleonic Wars, and its navy represented both the pride and salvation of the nation. Franklin saw action at the Battle of Copenhagen and elsewhere before transferring to the old and leaky discovery ship *Investigator*, bound for Australia on a scientific mission. In 1803 he was aboard the *Porpoise* when it foundered on a reef in the South Pacific, two hundred miles from the nearest land. Franklin made it home, by way of China, in time to serve as a midshipman aboard the HMS *Bellerophan* during the 1804 Battle of Trafalgar, one of the climactic sea battles of the Napoleonic Era. A decade later Franklin was a seasoned lieutenant striding the deck of the HMS *Bedford*, part of a fleet trying to bottle up New Orleans during the War of 1812.

The Battle of New Orleans ended the War of 1812 with a thud for the British, who took solace from

Napoleon's final defeat at Waterloo three years later. With these two wars ended, the vast British navy suddenly faced a crisis of purpose. For years it had served as Albion's oceangoing shield. Now the world's most powerful military force had no apparent enemy. Lieutenant Franklin, thirty-one years old and envisioning a future without promotion or glory, was one of many fine officers searching for a new mission to justify the fleet's—and his own—existence.

The answer lay far to the north, in the Arctic Ocean. The Arctic wasn't exactly *terra incognita* to westerners. Whalers had charted some of its waters and shorelines. In the 1500s English privateer Martin Frobisher had searched the archipelago above eastern Canada for gold and a water route to China and India. He found neither, although he did carry home a hold full of worthless iron pyrite, or fool's gold. A few other expeditions sailed north over the next few centuries, most notably the HMS *Racehorse* and the unfortunately named HMS *Carcass,* which struck out for the North Pole with a crew that included the young Horatio Nelson and the former slave Olaudah Equiano, whose abolitionist autobiography is still read today. Ice quickly turned them back.

Much of the region remained a mystery in John Franklin's day. Charts reflected a combination of sketchy surveying, educated guesses, and outright speculation. Cartographers didn't even know whether Greenland was an island or a continent whose northern boundary extended beyond the North Pole. Many areas of the map were simply blank. Entire tribes of Inuit remained unknown to westerners. Some scientists believed the ocean around the North Pole was warm and free from ice. Educated men postulated that advanced civilizations lived at the pole, or within deep caverns accessible at 90 degrees north.

More important for the maritime nation of Great Britain was finding a navigable passage through the Arctic Archipelago to the Pacific Ocean and the riches of the Orient. The driving force behind this quest was Second Secretary of the Admiralty Sir John Barrow, a sharp-eyed civil servant who, besides understanding the public relations benefits of exploration, recognized the tremendous commercial potential in sending the fleet into the unknown. Discovering the fabled Northwest Passage, or better yet, a route passing directly over the pole, would shave thousands of miles from the voyage to Asia.

In 1818 the navy sent the HMS *Isabella,* under Commander John Ross, and the *Alexander,* under Lieutenant William Parry, to find the Northwest Passage. Ross's tiny fleet probed Baffin Bay before pushing west. He made it as far as Lancaster Sound before spotting a line of forbidding peaks blocking his way. He named them the Croker Mountains, in honor of First Secretary of the Admiralty John Croker, before turning around and heading home. Future expeditions proved that Ross had been deceived. The Croker Mountains were an optical illusion created by unusual atmospheric conditions. The Arctic would not yield its secrets easily.

John Franklin, in command of the *Trent,* sailed north at the same time as Ross as part of a two-ship expedition under David Buchan, who commanded the *Dorothea.* The admiralty tasked them with reaching the North Pole via Spitzbergen (present-day Svalbard), an archipelago about six hundred miles north of Norway's northernmost coast. This mission, which proved fruitless, comprises the opening pages of *Thirty Years in the Arctic Regions.*

Franklin got nowhere near the pole, but the journey, difficult as it was, aroused his passions for the extreme north. Subsequent adventurers often spoke of "Arctic Fever," which famed American explorer Robert E. Peary defined as "the lure of the North." Most people could not imagine spending years in such a barren place. But Franklin and others of his ilk saw the Arctic as neither deadly nor a wasteland. Its mysteries enticed them. Rather than something to be feared, its sparse landscapes, so unlike those of Franklin's native Lincolnshire, represented challenges to be overcome. And even though Franklin often complained of chilly hands and feet while at home in England, the Arctic cold—the unfathomably bitter, biting cold, a cold so deep it numbed you in seconds and could kill you in minutes—attracted him on some level so deep he could never quite explain it.

Franklin pushed for his own Arctic command. In response, the admiralty tasked him with an audacious mission to map Canada's northern coast by trekking overland from Hudson's Bay to the mouth of the Coppermine River, around 1,700 miles as the crow flies, then backtracking to rendezvous with ships under William Parry, whom Secretary Barrow had sent searching for the elusive Northwest Passage. Budgets were tight and supplies short. "Experience . . . has taught me never to indulge in too superior hopes either of success or reward," Franklin wrote his sister soon before leaving Britain. "May the Almighty power protect and guide us." His words suggest a man who is not entirely confident of his safe return.

The expedition sailed in May of 1819. Franklin's travails over the following three years make up the bulk of *Thirty Years in the Arctic Regions*. Although the party did manage to survey a few hundred miles of shoreline, the hardships it endured garnered far more public attention than did its scientific achievements. Neither Franklin nor his men had the requisite knowledge for survival in the Arctic, and the expedition's relationship with the natives who could have helped them was rocky at best. Bitter cold and sucking mud slowed their pace to a literal crawl. Eleven of Franklin's nineteen men died. Franklin, weak from starvation, nearly became the twelfth before he and the other survivors straggled into Fort Providence, a trading post on Great Slave Lake in Canada's Northwest Territories, in late 1821. They finally escaped the north in the summer of 1822, reaching Great Britain that October.

Franklin's account of the ordeal reads like a literary representation of the stereotypical English stiff upper lip. He recounts every painful step with a deadpan modesty that enhances the cruelty of his suffering. No matter how bad the situation gets— not even when the party is reduced to eating moldy deerskins, maggots, the barely edible fungus *tripe de roche*, or shoe leather (Franklin became known as "the man who ate his boots") —he never laments his fate, never complains, never offers any hint of dissatisfaction. Instead, he soldiers on, dragging himself through step after step of knee-deep muck.

Besides revealing Franklin's modest, forbearing character, *Thirty Years in the Arctic Regions* also shows him as a man devoted to both religion and science. Franklin was pious from a young age; as a child he spoke of fetching a ladder so he could climb to heaven. Christian devotion and confidence in divine intervention suffuse the text. At the same time, Franklin upheld his responsibilities as a seaman and an explorer by carefully surveying and measuring everything he saw. He noted the location and frequency of plant and animal species, along with anything else that might assist those who followed. His papers and journals, not his life, were his top priority.

Thirty Years in the Arctic Regions displays sides of Franklin that might offend modern sensibilities. He portrays the French Canadian *voyageurs* and the native peoples, the two communities most responsible for keeping him alive, as inferior to Englishmen. Non-Christians should be converted if at all possible. Perhaps most damaging to himself and his party, Franklin arrogantly eschewed native methods of survival in order to retain what he perceived as more civilized travel and clothing conventions.

In this he was not alone. Throughout the nineteenth century, British Arctic explorers donned woolen military uniforms instead of native furs, ate tinned food rather than fresh meat, and lived in flimsy tents rather than stone or snow houses. Even when they made some concessions, their refusal to see the north through native eyes could prove fatal. Some explorers wore coats made from deerskins but insisted on making them with button-up fronts that allowed gale-force winds to rip through the gaps. Nor did the British adopt native methods of travel. As late at the 1870s, British commanders were ordering their men to drag heavy sledges rather than let dogs pull them, as if lugging an eight-hundred-pound load through waist-deep snow proved their superior manliness. Only at the end of the nineteenth century, when Americans such as Robert E. Peary came to dominate Arctic exploration, did westerners truly embrace Inuit ways.

Franklin became a celebrated figure in London. Dark stories of murder, cannibalism, and privation followed his every step. Parents used tales of his journey as morality lessons for children needing instruction in the proper English spirit. The admiralty promoted him to captain. And remarkably, considering his sufferings, Franklin wanted another crack at the Arctic. In 1825 he sailed north again, leaving behind an eight-month-old daughter and a wife in miserable health (Eleanor Anne Porden Franklin died of tuberculosis a week after her husband left) in search of the Northwest Passage. This trip, which also features in *Thirty Years in the Arctic Regions*, was better planned and more successful than the previous one. Although the Northwest Passage remained elusive, Franklin charted several hundred miles of coastline before sailing home in 1827. His accomplishment earned him a knighthood from King George IV. He remarried in 1828, winning the hand of the bewitching Jane Griffin, a friend of his late first wife.

In 1836 the crown made Sir John the lieutenant governor of Van Dieman's Land (present-day Tasmania), where he and Lady Jane would spend a miserable six years. The colony's elites resented Franklin's modest efforts to curb their exploitation of convict labor. Their antipathy fueled a spate of bureaucratic and political warfare that devastated the Franklins' reputation. The couple limped home in 1842 humiliated and eager for redemption.

Franklin, already in his fifties and never the most fit of men, saw salvation in the north. Great Britain's interest in exploration had not dimmed since Franklin's previous trip. Sir John Ross had headed north in 1828 along with his nephew Sir James Clark Ross. Their five-year expedition reached the magnetic north pole and nearly completed the Northwest Passage. Franklin's companion George Back twice journeyed into the Canadian Arctic in the 1830s. Sir James Clark Ross took the HMS *Erebus* and HMS *Terror* to Antarctica in 1839, returning to Britain four years later after charting much of the continent's coastline.

Sir John Barrow thought one more expedition might finally crack open the passage. In 1844 he began searching for a leader. Sir William Parry was in his mid-fifties and wanted nothing more to do with the Arctic. Sir James Clark Ross was game, but his wife had extracted a promise from him to never journey into the dangerous north again. No one wanted the job except Franklin. Both he and Lady Jane lobbied hard for the opportunity, which the admiralty granted, reluctantly, in February 1845. John Franklin was fifty-eight years old, and turned fifty-nine before Sir James Ross's former ships, *Erebus* and *Terror*, pointed him north for the fourth and, as it turned out, final time.

A few days before sailing, Sir John lay shivering with the flu. Lady Jane took pity on her husband. She draped a silk Union Jack she had embroidered over his legs to warm him up. Franklin leapt to his feet. "There's a flag thrown over me!" he shouted. "Don't you know that they lay the Union Jack over a corpse?"

Dark omens aside, Franklin seemed destined for success. His expedition carried enough supplies for five years in the Arctic, and Sir John figured he could stretch them for an extra year or two if need be. His ships had already proven themselves under adverse conditions, and had recently been fitted with steam engines and top-of-the-line screw propellers. Desalinators would provide fresh water. The crew could draw from a well-stocked library or play music on a hand organ.

Erebus and *Terror* sailed on May 19, 1845. None of the 129 men on board, including Sir John Franklin, would ever see Great Britain again.

After a prolonged silence from Franklin, the admiralty pressed Arctic whalers for news of the expedition. Receiving none, and with Lady Jane urging action, the navy began dispatching relief missions in 1847, including one under Sir James Clark Ross, who overcame his wife's objections in order to search for

his friend. Between 1847 and 1859, thirty-six orga-
nized expeditions went looking for the missing party. The admiralty offered a £20,000 reward to whoever rescued the Franklin expedition, and half that
amount to anyone providing incontrovertible proof
of its fate. Lady Jane added her own £3,000 reward
and did everything possible to keep her missing husband in the public's mind. In this she was successful.
Public pressure drove the crown to send mission after mission. Lady Jane herself visited the Arctic in
the 1870s. Newspapers printed the latest speculation. Poets composed doleful lines. Clairvoyants offered search tips gleaned from helpful spirits. None
of it helped.

Many books have been written about the search
for Franklin, and *Thirty Years in the Arctic Regions*
contains some choice documents originating from
that search. Admiral Sherard Osborn called the
lost men "martyrs to science" in his *The Career, Last
Voyage and Fate of Sir John Franklin* (1860). This was
true, in a way, as the hunt for Franklin accomplished
something Franklin himself could not; Sir Robert
McClure completed the Northwest Passage in 1854
while looking for his missing compatriot. Other parties found remnants of Franklin's expedition, including the corpses of many of his crewmen, while
plying previously uncharted waters and mapping
shorelines heretofore unknown to westerners. Some
of Franklin's pursuers, particularly John Rae and the
American Charles Francis Hall, began incorporating
native survival methods, paving the way for the next
generation of explorers.

A Canadian team found *Erebus* on the bottom of
Queen Maud Gulf in 2014. *Terror* was found near
King William Island in 2016. As of 2017, Sir John
Franklin's body has not been found.

Franklin's disappearance inspired reams of tribute in both prose and verse. "His highest and truest claim to the rank of a national hero is that he was filled with that spirit which is even more national than the love of adventure, more English even than the passion for the 'great waters'—the thirst for the discovery of the unknown," biographer Henry Duff Traill wrote in 1896. Poet Algernon Charles Swinburne waxed even more rhapsodic in his 1860 "The Death of Sir John Franklin." "This England hath not made a better man," he wrote of the banker's son whose character and career inspired countless others to follow his footsteps, "More steadfast, or more wholly pure of wrong/Since the large book of English praise began."

THIRTY YEARS

IN THE ARCTIC REGIONS.

~~~~~

CHAPTER I.

S<small>IR</small> John Franklin's first expedition to the Arctic
Regions was made in the year 1816, as Lieutenant
under Captain Buchan, with the ships " Dorothea" and
" Trent."

After much difficulty, these vessels gained lat.
80 deg. 34 min., north of Spitzbergen ; but were obliged speedily to withdraw, and try their fortune off
the western edge of the pack.   Here, however, a wild
war of ice and waves prevailed, so that choice and necessity equally induced the bold experiment of dash-
ing through it, to take shelter in the pack.   First
went the " Dorothea," and then the " Trent," whose
crew seemed to a man imbued with the dauntless
spirit of the Lieutenant in command.   A dreadful
pause preceded the critical moment.   " Each person,"
says Beechey, in his narrative, " instinctively secured
his own hold, and, with his eyes fixed upon his masts,

awaited in breathless anxiety the moment of concussion. It soon arrived—the brig, cutting her way through the light ice, came in violent contact with the main body. In an instant we all lost our footing, the masts bent with the impetus, and the cracking timbers from below bespoke a pressure which was calculated to awaken our serious apprehensions." The gloominess of the scene and circumstances was not cheered by the dolorous tolling of the ship's great bell, which never sounded of itself in the roughest gale, but now was so swung by the violent motion of the ship, that its deep tones pealed forth like a death-knell, and the officers, fearing the awakened superstition of the men, ordered it to be muffled. A few hours released the vessels from their imprisonment, but the "Dorothea" was found to be completely disabled. A short time at Fairhaven in Spitzbergen was spent in necessary repairs, and even then she was unfit for any further service than the voyage to England. Franklin volunteered to prosecute the enterprise with the "Trent" alone, but the Admiralty orders opposed such a proceeding, and the vessels returned home in company.

In 1819, Sir John Franklin—then Captain Franklin—was appointed to the command of an Expedition from the shores of Hudson's Bay, to explore the Northern Coast of America, from the mouth of Copper Mine River eastward. This is probably the most thrilling Arctic Expedition on record, and we shall give it in Franklin's own words. The Expedition consisted of John Franklin, Commander ; John Richardson, Doctor ; George Bach and Robert Hood, two Admiralty Midshipmen. The agents of the Hudson's Bay Company were ordered to assist the Expedition in every possible way. The two Admiralty Midshipmen were to make drawings of the land and waters, and Doctor Richardson was naturalist as well as doctor to the Expedition.

On Sunday, the 23d of May, 1814, the party set sail from Gravesend, and arrived at Hudson's Straits August 11, and at York Factory the 30th. The Governor of the Company here received the exploring party. The Northwest Company and the Bay Company were, at this time, in violent opposition to each other, which was unfortunate for the Expedition. The Governor of the Hudson's Bay Company gave to the party one of the largest of his boats, and a crew was made up from the ship's company, with the exception of the steersman, who was furnished by the Governor.

The narrative now commences in the words of Captain Franklin.

CHAPTER II.

On the 9th of September, 1819, our boat being completed, arrangements were made for our departure as soon as the tide should serve. But, when the stores were brought down to the beach, it was found that the boat would not contain them all. The whole, therefore, of the bacon, and part of the flour, rice, tobacco, and ammunition, were returned into the store. The bacon was too bulky an article to be forwarded under any circumstances ; but the Governor undertook to forward the rest next season. In making the selection of articles to carry with us, I was guided by the judgment of Governor Williams, who assured me that tobacco, ammunition, and spirits, could be procured in the interior, otherwise I should have been very unwilling to have left these essential articles behind. We embarked at noon, and were honored with a salute of eight guns and three cheers from the Governor and all the inmates of the fort, assembled to witness our departure. We gratefully returned their cheers, and then made sail, much delighted at having now commenced our voyage into the interior of America. The wind and tide failing us at the distance of six miles above the Factory, and the current being too rapid for using oars to advantage, the crew had to commence tracking, or dragging the boat by a line, to which they were harnessed. This operation is extremely laborious in these rivers. Our men were obliged to walk along the steep declivity of a high bank, rendered at this season soft and slippery by frequent rains, and their progress was often further impeded by fallen trees, which, having slipped from the verge of the thick wood above, hung on the face of the bank in a great variety of directions. Notwithstanding these obstacles, however, we advanced at the rate of two miles an hour, one-half of the crew relieving the other at intervals of an hour and a half. The banks of the river, and its islands, composed of alluvial soil, are well covered with pines, larches, poplars, and willows. The breadth of the stream some distance above the Factory is about half a mile, and its depth during this day's voyage varied from three to nine feet.

At sunset we landed, and pitched the tent for the night, having made a progress of twelve miles. A large fire was quickly kindled, supper speedily prepared, and as readily despatched, when we retired with our buffalo robes on, and enjoyed a night of sound repose.

The next morning our camp was in motion at five
A. M., and we soon afterwards embarked with the flat-
tering accompaniment of a fair wind : it proved, however, too light to enable us to stem the stream, and
we were obliged to resume the fatiguing operation of
tracking, sometimes under cliffs so steep that the men
could scarcely find a footing, and not unfrequently
over spots rendered so miry, by the small streams that
trickled from above, as to be almost impassable.   In
the course of the day we passed the scene of a very
melancholy accident.   Some years ago two families of Indians, induced by the flatness of a small
beach, which lay betwixt the cliff and the river, chose
it as the site of their encampment.   They retired
quietly to rest, not aware that the precipice, detached
from the bank, aud urged by an accumulation of water in the crevice behind, was tottering to its base.
It fell during the night, and the whole party was buried
under its ruins.

The length of our voyage to-day was, in a direct
line, sixteen miles and a quarter, on a S. S. W. course.
We encamped soon after sunset, and the tent was
scarcely pitched when it began to rain heavily, and
continued to do so all night.

Sixteen miles on the 11th, and five on the following
morning, brought us to the commencement of Hayes'
River, which is formed by the confluence of the Sha-

mattawa and Steel Rivers. Our observations place this spot in latitude 56 deg. 22 min. 32 sec. N., longitude 93 deg. 1 min. 37 sec., W. It is forty-eight miles and a half from York Factory, including the windings of the river. Steel River, through which our course lay, is about three hundred yards wide at its mouth ; its banks have more elevation than those of Hayes' River, but they shelve more gradually down to the stream, and afford a tolerably good towing path, which compensates, in some degree, for the rapids and frequent shoals that impede its navigation. We succeeded in getting about ten miles above the mouth of the river, before the close of the day compelled us to disembark.

We made an effort, on the morning of the 13th, to stem the current under sail, but as the course of the river was very serpentine, we found that greater progress could be made by tracking. Steel River presents much beautiful scenery ; it winds through a narrow, but well-wooded valley, which, at every turn disclosed to us an agreeable variety of prospect, rendered more picturesque by the effect of the season on the foliage, now ready to drop from the trees. The light yellow of the fading poplars formed a fine contrast to the dark evergreen of the spruce, whilst the willows, of an intermediate hue, served to shade the two principal masses of color into each other. The scene was occasionally enlivened by the bright purple tints of the dogwood, blended with the browner shades of the dwarf birch, and frequently intermixed with the gay yellow flowers of the shrubby cinquefoil. With all these charms, the scene appeared desolate from the want of the human species. The stillness was so great, that even the twittering of the *Whiskey-john-eesh,* or cinereous crow, caused us to start. Our voyage to-day was sixteen miles on a S. W. course.

Sept. 14.—We had much rain during the night, and also in the morning, which detained us in our encampment later than usual. We set out as soon as the weather cleared up, and in a short time arrived at the head of Steel River, where it is formed by the junction of Fox and Hill Rivers. These two rivers are nearly of equal width, but the latter is the most rapid. Mr. M'Donald, on his way to Red River, in a small canoe, manned by two Indians, overtook us at this place. It may be mentioned as a proof of the dexterity of the Indians, and the skill with which they steal upon their game, that they had on the preceding day, with no other arms than a hatchet, killed two deer, a hawk, a curlew, and a sturgeon. Three of the Company's boats joined us in the course of the morning, and we pursued our course up Hill River in company. The water in this river was so low, and the rapids so bad, that we were obliged

several times, in the course of the day, to jump into
the water, and assist in lifting the boat over the large
stones which impeded the navigation. The length of
our voyage to-day was only six miles and three
quarters.

The four boats commenced operations together at
five o'clock the following morning ; but our boat
being overladen, we soon found that we were unable
to keep pace with the others ; and therefore proposed
to the gentlemen in charge of the Company's boats,
that they should relieve us of part of our cargo. This
they declined doing, under the plea of not having
received orders to that effect, notwithstanding that the
circular, with which I was furnished by Governor
Williams, strictly enjoined all the Company's servants
to afford us every assistance. In consequence of this
refusal we dropt behind, and our steersman, who was
inexperienced, being thus deprived of the advantage
of observing the route followed by the guide, who was
in the foremost boat, frequently took a wrong channel.
The tow-line broke twice, and the boat was only prevented from going broadside down the stream, and
breaking to pieces against the stones, by the officers
and men leaping into the water, and holding her head
to the current until the line could be carried again to
the shore. It is but justice to say, that in these
trying situations we received much assistance from

Mr. Thomas Swayne, who with great kindness waited for us with the boat under his charge, at such places as he apprehended would be most difficult to pass. We encamped at sunset, completely jaded with toil. Our distance made good this day was twelve miles and a quarter.

The labors of the 16th commenced at half-past five, and for some time the difficulty of getting the boats over the rapids was equal to what we experienced yesterday. Having passed a small brook, however, termed *Half-way Creek*, the river became deeper, and although rapid, it was smooth enough to be named by our Orkney boatmen *Still-water*. We were further relieved by the Company's clerks consenting to take a few boxes of our stores into their boats. Still we made only eleven miles in the course of the day.

The banks of Hill River are higher, and have a more broken outline, than those of Steel or Haye's Rivers. The cliffs of alluvial clay rose in some places to the height of eighty or ninety feet above the stream, and were surmounted by hills about two hundred feet high, but the thickness of the wood prevented us from seeing far beyond the mere banks of the river.

Sept. 17.—About half-past five in the morning we commenced tracking, and soon came to a ridge of rock which extended across the stream. From this place the boat was dragged up several narrow rocky channels, until we came to the Rock-Portage, where the stream, pent in by a range of small islands, forms several cascades. In ascending the river, the boats with their cargoes are carried over one of the islands, but in the descent they are shot down the most shelving of the cascades. Having performed the operations of carrying, launching and re-stowing the cargo, we plied the oars for a short distance, and landed at a depôt called Rock-House. Here we were informed that the rapids in the upper parts of Hill River were much worse and more numerons than those we had passed, particularly in the present season, owing to the unusual lowness of the water. This intelligence was very mortifying, especially as the gentlemen in charge of the Company's boats declared that they were unable to carry any part of our stores beyond this place ; and the traders, guides, and most experienced of the boatmen, were of opinion, that unless our boat was still further lightened, the winter would put a stop to our progress before we could reach Cumberland House, or any eligible post. Sixteen pieces were therefore necessarily left with Mr. Bunn, the gentleman in charge of the post, to be forwarded by the Athabasca canoes next season, this being their place of rendezvous.

After this we recommenced our voyage, and having

pulled nearly a mile, arrived at Borrowick's Fall, where the boat was dragged up with a line, after part of the cargo had been carried over a small portage. From this place to the Mud Portage, a distance of a mile and three-quarters, the boats were pushed on with poles against a very rapid stream. Here we encamped, having come seven miles during the day on a S. W. course. We had several snow showers in the course of the day, and the thermometer at bed-time stood at 30°.

On the morning of the 18th, the country was clothed in the livery of winter, a heavy fall of snow having taken place during the night. We embarked at the usual hour, and, in the course of the day, crossed the Point of Rocks, and Brassa Portages, and dragged the boats through several minor rapids. In this tedious way we only made good about nine miles.

On Sunday the 19th, we hauled the boats up several short rapids, or, as the boatmen term them, expressively enough, *spouts*, and carried them over the Portages of Lower Burntwood and Morgan's Rocks; on the latter of which we encamped, having proceeded, during the whole day, only one mile and three-quarters.

The upper part of Hill River swells out considerably, and at Morgan's Rocks, where it is three quarters of a mile wide, we were gratified with a more extensive prospect of the country than any we had enjoyed since leaving York Factory. The banks of the river here, consisting of low flat rocks with intermediate swamps, permitted us to obtain views of the interior, the surface of which is broken into a multitude of cone-shaped hills. The highest of these hills, which gives a name to the river, has an elevation not exceeding six hundred feet. From its summit, thirty-six lakes are said to be visible. The beauty of the scenery, dressed in the tints of autumn, called forth our admiration, and was the subject of Mr. Hood's accurate pencil. On the 20th we passed Upper Burntwood and Rocky Ledge Portages, besides several strong *spouts ;* and in the evening arrived at Smooth Rock Portage, where we encamped, having come three miles and a half. It is not easy for any but an eye-witness to form an adequate idea of the exertions of the Orkney boatmen in the navigation of this river. The necessity they are under of frequently jumping into the water, to lift the boats over the rocks, compels them to remain the whole day in wet clothes, at a season when the temperature is far below the freezing point. The immense loads too, which they carry over the portages, is not more a matter of surprise than the alacrity with which they perform these laborious duties.

At six on the morning of the 21st, we left our en-

:ampment, and soon after arrived at the Mossy Portage, where the cargoes were carried through a deep
bog for a quarter of a mile.   The river swells out,
above this portage, to the breadth of several miles,
and as the islands are numerous, there are a great variety of channels. Night overtook us before we arrived
at the *Second Portage,* so named from its being the
second in the passage down the river.   Our whole distance this day, was one mile and a quarter.

On the 22d, our route led us amongst many wooded
islands, which lying in long vistas, produced scenes of
much beauty.   In the course of the day we crossed
the Upper Portage, surmounted the Devil's Landing
Place, and urged the boat with poles through Ground-
water Creek.   At the upper end of this creek, our
bowman having given the boat too broad a sheer, to
avoid the rock, it was caught on the broadside by the
current, and, in defiance of our utmost exertions, hurried down the rapid.   Fortunately, however, it
grounded against a rock high enough to prevent the
current from oversetting it, and the crews of the other
boats having come to our assistance, we succeeded,
after several trials, in throwing a rope to them, with
which they dragged our almost sinking vessel stern
foremost up the stream, and rescued us from our perilous situation.

We began the ascent of Trout River early in the

morning of the 27th, and in the course of the day passed three portages and several rapids. At the first of these portages the river falls between two rocks about sixteen feet, and it is necessary to launch the boat over a precipitous rocky bank. This cascade is named the *Trout Fall*, and the beauty of the scenery afforded a subject for Mr. Hood's pencil. The rocks which form the bed of this river are slaty, and present sharp fragments, by which the feet of the boatmen are much lacerated. The Second Portage, in particular, obtains the expressive name of *Knife Portage*. The length of our voyage to-day was three miles.

On the 28th, we passed through the remainder of Trout River; and, at noon, arrived at Oxford house, on Holey Lake. This was formerly a post of some consequence to the Hudson's Bay Company, but at present it exhibits unequivocal signs of decay. The Indians have, of late years, been gradually deserting the low or swampy country, and ascending the Saskatchawan, where animals are more abundant. A few Crees were at this time encamped in front of the fort. They were suffering under the combined maladies of whooping-cough and measles, and looked miserably dejected. We endeavored in vain to prevail on one of them to accompany us for the purpose of killing ducks, which were numerous, but too shy for our sportsmen. We had the satisfaction, however, of exchanging the

mouldy pemmican, obtained at Swampy Lake, for a
better kind, and received, moreover, a small, but very
acceptable, supply of fish. Holey Lake, viewed from
an eminence behind Oxford House, exhibits a pleasing
prospect ; and its numerous islands, varying much in
shape and elevation, contribute to break that uniformity of scenery which proves so palling to a traveler in
this country. Trout of a great size, frequently exceeding forty pounds weight, abound in this lake.
We left Oxford House in the afternoon, and encamped
on an island about eight miles distant, having come,
during the day, nine miles and a quarter.

At noon, on the 29th, after passing through the
remainder of Holey Lake, we entered the Weepinap-
annis, a narrow grassy river, which runs parallel to
the lake for a considerable distance, and forms its
south bank into a narrow peninsula. In the morning
we arrived at the Swampy Portage, where two of the
boats were broken against the rocks. The length of
the day's voyage was nineteen miles and a half.

In consequence of the accident yesterday evening,
we were detained a considerable time this morning,
until the boats were repaired, when we set out, and
after ascending a strong rapid, arrived at the Portage
by John Moore's Island. Here tne river rushes with
irresistible force through the channels formed by two
rocky islands ; and we learnt, that last year a poor

man, in hauling a boat up one of these channels, was, by the breaking of the line, precipitated into the stream and hurried down the cascade with such rapidity, that all efforts to save him were ineffectual. His body was afterwards found and interred near the spot.

Oct. 1.—Hill Gates is the name imposed on a romantic defile, whose rocky walls rising perpendicularly to the height of sixty or eighty feet, hem in the stream for three-quarters of a mile, in many places so narrowly, that there is a want of room to ply the oars. In passing through this chasm we were naturally led to contemplate the mighty but, probably, slow and gradual effects of the water in wearing down such vast masses of rock ; but in the midst of our speculations, the attention was excited anew to a grand and picturesque rapid, which, surrounded by the most wild and majestic scenery, terminated the defile. The brown fishing-eagle had built its nest on one of the projecting cliffs. In the course of the day we surmounted this and another dangerous portage, called the Upper and Lower Hill Gate Portages, crossed a small sheet of water, termed the White-Fall Lake, and entering the river of the same name, arrived at the White Fall about an hour after sunset, having come fourteen miles on a S. W. course.

The whole of the 2d of October was spent in carrying the cargoes over a portage of thirteen hundred yards in length, and in launching the empty boats over three several ridges of rock which obstruct the channel and produce as many cascades. I shall long remember the rude and characteristic wildness of the scenery which surrounded these falls ; rocks piled on rocks hung in rude and shapeless masses over the agitated torrents which swept their bases, whilst the bright and variegated tints of the mosses and lichens, that covered the face of the cliffs, contrasting with the dark green of the pines, which crowned their summits, added both beauty and grandeur to the general effect of the scene. Our two companions, Back and Hood, made accurate sketches of these falls. At this place we observed a conspicuous *lop-stick,* a kind of land-mark, which I have not hitherto noticed, notwithstanding its great use in pointing out the frequented routes. It is a pine-tree divested of its lower branches, and having only a small tuft at the top remaining. This operation is usually performed at the instance of some individual emulous of fame. He treats his companions with rum, and they in return, strip the tree of its branches, and ever after designate it by his name.

In the afternoon, whilst on my way to superintend the operations of the men, a stratum of loose moss gave way under my feet, and I had the misfortune to slip from the summit of a rock into the river, betwixt two of the falls. My attempts to regain the bank were, for a time, ineffectual, owing to the rocks within my reach having been worn smooth by the action of the water, but after I had been carried a considerable distance down the stream, I caught hold of a willow, by which I held until two gentlemen of the Hudson's Bay Company came in a boat to my assistance. The only bad consequence of this accident was an injury sustained by a very valuable chronometer, (No. 1733,) belonging to Daniel Moore, Esq., of Lincoln's Inn One of the gentlemen, to whom I delivered it immediately on landing, in his agitation let it fall, whereby the minute-hand was broken, but the works were not in the smallest degree injured, and the loss of the hand was afterwards supplied.

During the night the frost was severe, and at sunrise, on the 3d, the thermometer stood at 25°. After leaving our encampment at the White Fall, we passed through several small lakes connected with each other by narrow, deep, grassy streams, and at noon arrived at the Painted Stone. Numbers of musk-rats frequent these streams, and we observed, in the course of the morning, many of their mud-houses rising in a conical form to the height of two or three feet above the grass of the swamps in which they are built.

Having launched the boats over the rock, we commenced the descent of the Echemamis. This small stream has its course through a morass, and in dry seasons its channel contains, instead of water, merely a foot or two of thin mud. On these occasions it is customary to build dams, that it may be rendered navigable by the accumulation of its waters. As the beavers perform this operation very effectually, endeavors have been made to encourage them to breed in this place, but it has not hitherto been possible to restrain the Indians from killing that useful animal whenever they discover its retreats. On the present occasion there was no want of water, the principal impediment we experienced being from the narrowness of the channel, which permitted the willows of each bank to meet over our heads, and obstruct the men at the oars. After proceeding down the stream for some time, we came to a recently constructed beaver-dam through which an opening was made sufficient to admit the boat to pass. We were assured that the beach would be closed by the industrious creature in a single night. We encamped about eight miles from the source of the river, having come during the day seventeen miles and a half.

On the 4th we embarked amidst a heavy rain, and pursued our route down the Echemamis. In many parts the morass, by which the river is nourished, and through which it flows, is intersected by ridges of rock which cross the channel, and require the boat to be lifted over them. In the afternoon we passed through a shallow piece of water overgrown with bulrushes, and hence named Hairy Lake; and in the evening, encamped on the banks of Blackwater-Creek, by which this lake empties itself into Sea River; having come during the day twenty miles and three-quarters.

On the morning of the 5th, we entered Sea River, one of the many branches of Nelson River. It is about four hundred yards wide, and its waters are of a muddy white color. After ascending the stream for an hour or two, and passing through Carpenter's Lake, which is merely an expansion of the river to about a mile in breadth, we came to the Sea River Portage, where the boat was launched across a smooth rock, to avoid a fall of four or five feet. Re-embarking at the upper end of the portage, we ran before a fresh gale through the remainder of Sea River, the lower part of Play Greene Lake, and entering Little Jack River, landed and pitched our tents. Here there is a small log-hut, the residence of a fisherman, who supplies Norway House with trout and sturgeon. He gave us a few of these fish. which afforded an acceptable supper. The length of our voyage this day was thirty-four miles.

We left Norway House soon after noon of the 7th,
and the wind being favorable, sailed along the northern shore of Lake Winipeg the whole of the ensuing
night ; and on the morning of the 8th landed on a
narrow ridge of sand, which, running out twenty miles
to the westward, separates Limestone Bay from the
body of the Lake.　When the wind blows hard from
the southward, it is customary to carry boats across
this isthmus, and to pull up under its lee.　From
Norwegian Point to Limestone Bay the shore consists
of high clay cliffs against which the waves beat with
much violence during strong southerly winds.　When
the wind blows from the land, and the waters of the
lake are low, a narrow, sandy beach is uncovered, and
affords a landing-place for boats.　The shores of
Limestone Bay are covered with small fragments of
calcareous stones.　During the night the Aurora Borealis was quick in its motions, and various and vivid
in its colors.　After breakfasting we re-embarked, and
continued our voyage until three P. M., when a strong
westerly wind arising, we were obliged to shelter ourselves on a small island, which lies near the extremity
of the above-mentioned peninsula.　This island is
formed of a collection of small rolled pieces of limestone, and was remembered by some of our boatmen
to have been formerly covered with water.　For the
last ten or twelve years the waters of the lake have

been low, but our information did not enable us to judge whether the decrease was merely casual, or going on continually, or periodical. The distance of this island from Norway House is thirty-eight miles and a half.

The westerly winds detained us all the morning of the 9th, but, at two P. M., the wind chopped round to the eastward : we immediately embarked, and the breeze afterwards freshening, we reached the mouth of the Saskatchawan at midnight, having run thirty-two miles

Sunday, Oct. 10.—The whole of this day was occupied in getting the boats from the mouth of the river to the foot of the grand rapid, a distance of two miles. There are several rapids in this short distance during which the river varies its breadth from five hundred yards to half a mile. Its channel is stony. At the grand rapid, the Saskatchawan forms a sudden bend, from south to east, and works its way through a narrow channel, deeply worn into the limestone strata. The stream, rushing with impetuous force over a rocky and uneven bottom, presents a sheet of foam, and seems to bear with impatience the straitened confinement of its lofty banks. A flock of pelicans, and two or three brown fishing eagles, were fishing in its agitated waters, seemingly with great success. There is a good sturgeon fishery at the foot of the

rapid.   Several golden plovers, Canadian gros-beaks,
cross-bills, wood-peckers, and pin-tailed grouse, were
shot to-day ; and Mr. Back killed a small striped
marmot.   This beautiful little animal was busily employed in carrying in its distended pouches the seeds of
the American vetch to its winter hoards.

The portage is eighteen hundreds yards long, and
its western extremity was found to be in 53 deg. 08
min. 25 sec. North latitude, and 99 deg. 28 min. 02
sec. West longitude.   The route from Canada to the
Athabasca joins that from York Factory at the mouth
of the Saskatchawan, and we saw traces of a recent
encampment of the Canadian voyagers.   Our companions in the Hudson's Bay boats, dreading an attack
from their rivals in trade, were on the alert at this
place.   They examined minutely the spot of encampment, to form a judgment of the number of canoes
that had preceded them ; and they advanced, armed,
and with great caution, through the woods.   Their
fears, however, were fortunately, on this occasion,
groundless.

By noon, on the 12th, the boats and their cargoes
having been conveyed across the portage, we embarked and pursued our course.   The Saskatchawan be-
comes wider above the Grand Rapid, and the scenery
improves.   The banks are high, composed of white
clay and limestone, and their summits are richly

clothed with a variety of firs, poplars, birches, and willows. The current runs with great rapidity, and the channel is, in many places, intricate and dangerous, from broken ridges of rock jutting into the stream. We pitched our tents at the entrance of Cross Lake, having advanced only five miles and a half.

Cross Lake is extensive, running towards the N. E., it is said, for forty miles. We crossed it at the narrow part, and pulling through several winding channels, formed by a group of islands, entered Cedar Lake, which, next to Lake Winneipeg, is the largest sheet of fresh water we had hitherto seen. Ducks and geese resort hither in immense flocks in the spring and autumn. These birds are now beginning to go off, owing to its muddy shores having become quite hard through the nightly frosts. At this place the Aurora Borealis was extremely brilliant in the night, its coruscations darting, at times, over the whole sky, and assuming various prismatic tints, of which the violet and yellow were predominant.

After pulling, on the 14th, seven miles and a quarter on the lake, a violent wind drove us for shelter to a small island, or rather a ridge of rolled stones, thrown up by the frequent storms which agitate this lake. The weather did not moderate the whole day, and we were obliged to pass the night on this exposed spot. The delay, however, enabled us to obtain some lunar observations. The wind having subsided, we left our resting-place the following morning, crossed the remainder of the lake, and, in the afternoon, arrived at Muddy Lake, which is very appropriately named, as it consists merely of a few channels, winding amongst extensive mud banks, which are overflowed during the spring floods. We landed at an Indian tent, which contained two numerous families, amounting to thirty souls. These poor creatures were badly clothed, and reduced to a miserable condition by the ravages of the whooping-cough and measles. At the time of our arrival they were busy in preparing a sweating-house for the sick. This is a remedy, which they consider, with the addition of singing and drumming, to be the grand specific for all diseases. Our companions having obtained some geese, in exchange for rum and tobacco, we proceeded a few more miles and encamped on Devil's Drum Island, having come, during the day, twenty miles and a half. A second party of Indians were encamped on an adjoining island, a situation chosen for the purpose of killing geese and ducks.

On the 16th we proceeded eighteen miles up the Saskatchawan. Its banks are low, covered with willows, and lined with drift timber. The surrounding country is swampy, and intersected by the numerous arms of the river. After passing for twenty or thirty yards through the willow thicket on the banks of the stream, we entered upon an extensive marsh, varied only by a distant line of willows, which marks the course of a creek or branch of the river. The branch we navigated to-day is almost five hundred yards wide. The exhalations from the marshy soil produced a low fog, although the sky above was perfectly clear. In the course of the day we passed an Indian encampment of three tents, whose inmates appeared to be in a still more miserable condition than those we saw yesterday. They had just finished the ceremony of conjuration over some of their sick companions ; and a dog, which was recently killed as a sacrifice to some deity, was hanging to a tree, where it would be left (I was told) when they moved their encampment.

We continued our voyage up the river, to the 20th, with little variation of scenery or incident, traveling in that time about thirty miles. The near approach of winter was marked by severe frosts, which continued all day, unless when the sun chanced to be unusually bright, and the geese and ducks were observed to take a southerly course in large flocks. On the morning of the 20th we came to a party of Indians, encamped behind the bank of the river, on the borders of a small marshy lake, for the purpose of killing water-fowl. Here we were gratified with the view of a very large tent. Its length was about forty feet, its breadth

eighteen, and its covering was moose deer leather,
with apertures for the escape of the smoke from the
fires which were placed at each end ; a ledge of wood
was placed on the ground on both sides of the whole
length of the tent, within which were the sleeping
places, arranged probably according to families ; and
the drums and other instruments of enchantment were
piled up in the centre.   Amongst the Indians there
were a great many half-breeds, who lead an Indian
life. Governor Williams gave a dram and a piece of
tobacco to each of the males of the party.

On the morning of the 21st, a heavy fall of snow
took place, which lasted until two in the afternoon.
In the evening we left the Saskatchawan, and entered
the Little River, one of the two streams by which
Pine Island Lake discharges its waters. We advanced
to-day fourteen miles and a quarter.   On the 22d, the
weather was extremely cold and stormy, and we had
to contend against a strong head wind.   The spray
froze as it fell, and the oars were so loaded with ice
as to be almost unmanageable.   The length of our
voyage this day was eleven miles.

The following morning was very cold ; we embarked
at daylight, and pulled across a part of Pine Island
Lake, about three miles and a half to Cumberland
House. The margin of the lake was so encrusted
with ice, that we had to break through a considerable

space of it to approach the landing place. When we considered that this was the effect of only a few days' frost at the commencement of winter, we were convinced of the impracticability of advancing further by water this season, and, therefore, resolved on accepting Governor Williams's kind invitation to remain with him at this post. We immediately visited Mr. Connolly, the resident partner of the North-West Company, and presented to him Mr. M'Gillivray's circular letter. He assured us that he should be most desirous to forward our progress by every means in his power, and we subsequently had ample proofs of his sincerity and kindness. The unexpected addition of our party to the winter residents at this post, rendered an increase of apartments necessary; and our men were immediately appointed to complete and arrange an unfinished building as speedily as possible.

Nov. 8.—Some mild weather succeeded to the severe frosts we had at our arrival; and the lake had not been entirely frozen before the 6th; but this morning the ice was sufficiently firm to admit of sledges crossing it. The dogs were harnessed at a very early hour, and the winter operations commenced by sending for a supply of fish from Swampy River, where men had been stationed to collect it, just before the frost set in. Both men and dogs seemed to enjoy the change; they started in full glee, and drove rapidly along. An Indian, who had come to the house on the preceding evening, to request some provision for his family, whom he represented to be in a state of star-vation, accompanied them. His party had been suffering greatly under the epidemic diseases of the whooping-cough and measles ; and the hunters were still in too debilitated a state to go out and provide them with meat. A supply was given to him, and the men were directed to bring his father, an old and faithful hunter, to the house, that he might have the comforts of nourishment and warmth. He was brought accordingly, but these attentions were unavailing, as he died a few days afterwards. Two days before his death, I was surprised to observe him sitting for near three hours, in a piercingly sharp day, in the saw-pit, employed in gathering the dust, and throwing it by handfuls over his body, which was naked to the waist. As the man was in possession of his mental faculties, I conceived he was performing some devotional act preparatory to his departure, which he felt approaching ; and, induced by the novelty of the incident, I went twice to observe him more closely ; but when he perceived that he was noticed, he immediately ceased his operation, hung down his head, and by his demeanor, intimated that he considered my appearance an intrusion. The residents at the fort could give me no information on the subject, and I could not learn that the Indians in general observe any particular ceremony on the approach of death.

Nov. 15.—The sky had been overcast during the last week ; the sun shone forth once only, and then not sufficiently for the purpose of obtaining observations. Faint coruscations of the Aurora Borealis appeared one evening, but their presence did not in the least affect the electrometer nor the compass. The ice daily became thicker in the lake, and the frost had now nearly overpowered the rapid current of the Saskatchawan River ; indeed, parties of men who were sent from both the forts to search for the Indians, and procure whatever skins and provisions they might have collected, crossed that stream this day on the ice; the white partridges made their first appearance near to the house. These birds are considered as the infallible harbingers of severe weather.

Monday, Nov. 22.—The Saskatchawan, and every other river, were now completely covered with ice, except a small stream near to the fort through which the current ran very powerfully. In the course of the week we removed into the house our men had been preparing for us since our arrival. We found it at first extremely cold, notwithstanding a good fire was kept in each apartment, and we frequently experienced the extremes of heat and cold on opposite sides of the body.

Nov. 24.—We this day obtained observations for the dip of the needle and intensity of the magnetic force in a spare room. The dip was 83° 9' 45", and the difference produced by reversing the face of the instrument, 13° 3' 6". When the needle was faced to the west, it hung nearly perpendicular. The Aurora Borealis was faintly visible for a short time last evening. Some Indians arrived in search of provision, having been totally incapacitated from hunting by sickness ; the poor creatures looked miserably ill, and they represented their distress to have been extreme. Few recitals are more affecting than those of their sufferings during unfavorable seasons, and in bad situations for hunting and fishing. Many assurances have been given me that men and women are yet living who have been reduced to feed upon the bodies of their own family, to prevent actual starvation ; and a shocking case was cited to us of a woman who had been principal agent in the destruction of several persons, and amongst the number her husband and nearest relatives, in order to support life.

Nov. 28.—The atmosphere had been clear every day during the last week, about the end of which snow fell, when the thermometer rose from 20° below to 16° above zero. The Aurora Borealis was twice visible, but faint on both occasions. Its appearance did not affect the electrometer, nor could we perceive the compass to be disturbed.

The men brought supplies of moose meat from the
hunter's tent, which is pitched near the Basquiau
Hill, at the distance of forty or fifty miles from the
house, and from whence the greatest part of the meat
is procured. The residents have to send nearly the
same distance for their fish, and on this service horse-
sledges are used. Nets are daily set in Pine Island
Lake, which occasionally procure some fine sturgeon,
tittameg and trout, but not more than sufficient to
supply the officers' table.

Dec. 1.—This day was so remarkably fine, that we
procured another set of observations for the dip of the
needle in the open air; the instrument being placed
firmly on a rock, the results gave 83° 14' 22". The
change produced by reversing the face of the instrument
was 12° 50' 55".

There was a determined thaw during the last three
days, which caused the Saskatchawan River, and some
parts of the lake, to break up, and rendered the traveling across either of them dangerous. On this account the absence of Wilkes, one of our men, caused
no small anxiety. He had incautiously undertaken
the charge of conducting a sledge and dogs, in company with a person, going to Swampy River for fish.
On their return, being unaccustomed to driving, he
became fatigued, and seated himself on his sledge, in
which situation his companion left him, presuming

that he would soon rise and hasten to follow his track.
He however returned safe in the morning, and reported that, foreseeing night would set in before he could
get across the lake, he prudently retired into the
woods before dark, where he remained until daylight ;
when the men, who had been despatched to look for
him, met him returning to the house, shivering with
cold, he having been unprovided with the materials
for lighting a fire ; which an experienced voyager never
neglects to carry.

We had mild weather until the 20th of December.
On the 13th there had been a decided thaw, which
caused the Saskatchawan, which had again frozen, to
re-open, and the passage across it was interrupted for
two days.   We now received more agreeable accounts
from the Indians, who are recovering strength, and
beginning to hunt a little ; but it is generally feared
that their spirits have been so much depressed by the
loss of their children and relatives, that the season will
be far advanced before they can be roused to any exertion in searching for animals beyond what may be
necessary for their own support.   It is much to be regretted that these poor men, during their long intercourse with Europeans, have not been taught how
pernicious is the grief which produces total inactivity,
and that they have not been furnished with any of the
consolations which the Christian religion never fails to

afford. This, however, could hardly have been expected from persons who have permitted their own offspring, the half-casts, to remain in lamentable ignorance on a subject of such vital importance. It is probable, however, that an improvement will soon take place among the latter class, as Governor Williams proposes to make the children attend a Sunday school, and has already begun to have divine service performed at his post.

The conversations which I have had with the gentlemen in charge of these posts, convinced me of the necessity of proceeding during the winter into the Athabasca department, the residents of which are best acquainted with the nature and resources of the country lying to the north of the Great Slave Lake; and from whence only guides, hunters, and interpreters can be procured. I had previously written to the partners of the North-West Company in that quarter, requesting their assistance in forwarding the Expedition, and stating what we should require of them; but, on reviewing the matter, and reflecting upon the accidents that might delay these letters on the road, I determined on proceeding to the Athabasca as soon as I possibly could, and communicated my intention to Governor Williams and Mr. Connolly, with a request that I might be furnished, by the middle of January, with the means of conveyance for three persons, intending that Mr. Back and Hepburn should accompany me, whilst Dr. Richardson and Mr. Hood remained till the spring at Cumberland House.

After the 20th December the weather became cold, the thermometer constantly below zero. Christmas-day was particularly stormy; but the gale did not prevent the full enjoyment of the festivities which are annually given at Cumberland House on this day. All the men who had been despatched to different parts in search of provision or furs returned to the fort on the occasion, and were regaled with a substantial dinner and a dance in the evening.

1820. January 1. The new year was ushered in by repeated discharges of musketry; a ceremony which has been observed by the men of both the trading Companies for many years. Our party dined with Mr. Connolly, and were regaled with a beaver, which we found extremely delicate. In the evening his men were entertained with a dance, in which the Canadians exhibited some grace and much agility; and they contrived to infuse some portion of their activity and spirits into the steps of their female companions. The half-breed women are passionately fond of this amusement, but a stranger would imagine the contrary on witnessing their apparent want of animation. On such occasions they affect a sobriety of demeanor which I understand to be the very opposite of their general character.

CHAPTER IV.

January 18.
     1820. THIS day we set out from Cumberland House for Carlton House ; but previously to detailing the events of the journey, it may be proper to describe the necessary equipments of a winter traveler in this region, which I cannot do better than by extracting the following brief, but accurate, account of it from Mr. Hood's journal :—

"A snow-shoe is made of two light bars of wood, fastened together at their extremities, and projected into curves by transverse bars. The side bars have been so shaped by a frame, and dried before a fire, that the front part of the shoe turns up, like the prow of a boat, and the part behind terminates in an acute angle ; the spaces between the bars are filled up with a fine netting of leathern thongs, except that part behind the main bar, which is occupied by the feet ; the netting is there close and strong, and the foot is attached to the main bar by straps passing round the heel, but only fixing the toes, so that the heel rises after each step, and the tail of the shoe is dragged on

the snow.   Between the main bar and another in front
of it, a small space is left, permitting the toes to
descend a little in the act of raising the heel to make
the step forward, which prevents their extremities from
chafing.   The length of a snow-shoe is from four to six
feet, and the breadth one foot and a half, or one foot
and three-quarters, being adapted to the size of the
wearer.   The motion of walking in them is perfectly
natural, for one shoe is level with the snow, when the
edge of the other is passing over it.   It is not easy to
use them among bushes, without frequent overthrows,
nor to rise afterwards without help.   Each shoe weighs
about two pounds when unclogged with snow.   The
northern Indian snow-shoes differ a little from those
of the southern Indians, having a greater curvature on
the outside of each shoe ; one advantage of which is,
that when the foot rises the over-balanced side
descends and throws off the snow.   All the superiority
of European art has been unable to improve the native
contrivance of this useful machine.

   " Sledges are made of two or three flat boards,
curving upwards in front, and fastened together by
transverse pieces of wood above.   They are so thin
that, if heavily laden, they bend with the inequalities
of the surface over which they pass.   The ordinary
dog-sledges are eight or ten feet long, and very
narrow, but the lading is secured to a lacing round

the edges. The cariole used by the traders is merely a covering of leather for the lower part of the body, affixed to the common sledge, which is painted and ornamented according to the taste of the proprietor. Besides snow-shoes, each individual carries his blanket, hatchet, steel, flint, and tinder, and generally fire-arms."

The general dress of the winter traveler is a *capot*, having a hood to put up under the fur cap in windy weather, or in the woods, to keep the snow from his neck ; leathern trowsers and Indian stockings, which are closed at the ankles, round the upper part of his *moccasins*, or Indian shoes, to prevent the snow from getting into them. Over these he wears a blanket, or leathern coat, which is secured by a belt round his waist, to which his fire-bag, knife, and hatchet are suspended.

Mr. Beck and I were accompanied by the seaman, John Hepburn ; we were provided with two carioles and two sledges ; and their drivers and dogs were furnished in equal proportions by the two Companies. Fifteen days' provision so completely filled the sledges, that it was with difficulty we found room for a small sextant, one suit of clothes, and three changes of linen, together with our bedding. Notwithstanding we thus restricted ourselves, and even loaded the carioles with part of the luggage, instead of embarking

in them ourselves, we did not set out without
considerable grumbling from the voyagers of both
Companies, respecting the overlading of their dogs.
However, we left the matter to be settled by our
friends at the fort, who were more conversant with
winter traveling than ourselves.   Indeed, the loads
appeared to us so great that we should have been
inclined to listen to the complaints of the drivers.
The weight usually placed upon a sledge, drawn by
three dogs, cannot, at the commencement of a journey,
be estimated at less than three hundred pounds, which,
however, suffers a daily diminution from the consumption of provisions.   The sledge itself weighs
about thirty pounds.   When the snow is hard frozen,
or the track well trodden, the rate of traveling is
about two miles and a half an hour, including rests,
or about fifteen miles a day.   If the snow is loose,
the speed is necessarily much less and the fatigue
greater.

At eight in the morning of the 18th, we quitted the
fort, and took leave of our hospitable friend, Governor
Williams, whose kindness and attention I shall ever
remember with gratitude.   Dr. Richardson, Mr. Hood,
and Mr. Connolly, accompanied us along the Saskatchawan, until the snow became too deep for their
walking without snow-shoes.   We then parted from
our associates, with sincere regret at the prospect of a

long separation. Being accompanied by **Mr. Mac-**
kenzie, of the Hudson's Bay Company, who was going
to Isle à la Crosse, with four sledges under his charge,
we formed quite a procession, keeping in an Indian
file, in the tract of the man who preceded the foremost
dogs ; but, as the snow was deep, we proceeded
slowly on the surface of the river, which is about three
hundred and fifty yards wide, for the distance of six
miles, which we went to-day. Its alluvial banks and
islands are clothed with willows. At the place of our
encampment we could scarcely find sufficient pine
branches to floor " the hut," as the Orkney men term
the place where travelers rest. Its preparation, however, consists only in clearing away the snow to the
ground, and covering that space with pine branches,
over which the party spread their blankets and coats,
and sleep in warmth and comfort, by keeping a good
fire at their feet, without any other canopy than the
heaven, even though the thermometer should be far
below zero.

The arrival at the place of encampment gives immediate occupation to every one of the party ; and it is
not until the sleeping-place has been arranged, and a
sufficiency of wood collected as fuel for the night, that
the fire is allowed to be kindled. The dogs alone
remain inactive during this busy scene, being kept
harnessed to their burdens until the men have leisure

to unstow the sledges, and hang upon the trees every species of provision out of the reach of these rapacious animals. We had ample experience, before morning, of the necessity of this precaution, as they contrived to steal a considerable part of our stores, almost from underneath Hepburn's head, notwithstanding their having been well-fed at supper.

This evening we found the mercury of our thermometer had sunk into the bulk, and was frozen. It arose again into the tube on being held to the fire, but quickly re-descended into the bulb on being removed into the air ; we could not, therefore, ascertain by it the temperature of the atmosphere, either then or during our journey. The weather was perfectly clear.

Jan. 19.—We arose this morning after the enjoyment of a sound and comfortable repose, and recommenced our journey at sun-rise, but made slow progress through the deep snow. The task of beating the track for the dogs was so very fatiguing, that each of the men took the lead in turn, for an hour and a half. The scenery of the banks of the river improved as we advanced to-day ; some firs and poplars were intermixed with the willows. We passed through two creeks, formed by islands, and encamped on a pleasant spot on the north shore, having only made six miles and three-quarters actual distance.

The next day we pursued our course along the river ; the dogs had the greatest difficulty in dragging their heavy burdens through the snow. We halted to refresh them at the foot of Sturgeon River, and obtained the latitude 53° 51' 41" N. This is a small stream, which issues from a neighboring lake. We encamped near to Musquito Point, having walked about nine miles. The termination of the day's journey was a great relief to me, who had been suffering during the greater part of it, in consequence of my feet having been galled by the snow-shoes; this, however, is an evil which few escape on their initiation to winter traveling. It excites no pity from the more experienced companions of the journey, who travel on as fast as they can, regardless of the pain of the sufferer.

Mr. Isbester, and an Orkney man, joined us from Cumberland House, and brought some pemmican which we had left behind ; a supply which was seasonable after our recent loss. The general occupation of Mr. Isbester during the winter, is to follow or find out the Indians, and collect their furs, and his present journey will appear adventurous to persons accustomed to the certainty of traveling on a well-known road. He is going in search of a band of Indians, of whom no information had been received since last October, and his only guide for finding them was their promise to hunt in a certain quarter ; but he looked at the jaunt with indifference, and calculated on meeting them in six or seven days, for which time only he had provision. Few persons in this country suffer more from want of food than those occasionally do who are employed on this service. They are furnished with a sufficiency of provision to serve until they reach the part where the Indians are expected to be ; but it frequently occurs that, on their arrival at the spot, they have gone elsewhere, and that a recent fall of snow has hidden their track, in which case the voyagers have to wander about in search of them ; and it often happens, when they succeed in finding the Indians, that they are unprovided with meat. Mr. Isbester had been placed in this distressing situation only a few weeks ago, and passed four days without either himself or his dogs tasting food. At length, when he had determined on killing one of the dogs to satisfy his hunger, he happily met with a beaten track, which led him to some Indian lodges, where he obtained a supply of food.

The morning of the 21st was cold, but pleasant for traveling. We left Mr. Isbester and his companion, and crossed the peninsula of Musquito Point, to avoid a detour of several miles which the river makes. Though we put up at an early hour, we gained eleven miles this day. Our encampment was at the lower extremity of Tobin's Falls. The snow being less deep on the rough ice which enclosed this rapid, we proceeded, on the 22d, at a quicker pace than usual, though at the expense of great suffering to Mr. Back, myself, and Hepburn, all our feet being much galled. After passing Tobin's Falls, the river expands to the breadth of five hundred yards, and its banks are well wooded with pines, poplars, birch, and willows. Many tracks of moose-deer and wolves were observed near the encampment.

On the 23d the sky was generally overcast, and there were several snow showers. We saw two wolves and some foxes cross the river in the course of the day, and passed many tracks of the moose and red deer. Soon after we had encamped the snow fell heavily, which was an advantage to us after we had retired to rest, by its affording an additional covering to our blankets. The next morning, whilst at breakfast, two men arrived from Carlton on their way to Cumberland. Having the benefit of their track, we were, to our great joy, able to get on at a quick pace without snow-shoes. My only regret was, that the party proceeded too fast to allow Mr. Black's halting occasionally, to note the bearings of the points, and delineate the course of the river,* without being left behind. As

* This was afterwards done by Dr. Richardson during a voyage to Carlton in the spring

the provisions were getting short, I could not, therefore, with propriety, check the progress by interrupt-
ing the party ; and, indeed, it appeared to me less
necessary, as I understood the river had been carefully
surveyed.   In the afternoon, we had to resume the in-
cumbrance of the snow-shoes, and to pass over a rugged part where the ice had been piled over a collection
of stones.   The tracks of animals were very abundant
on the river, particularly near the remains of an old
establishment, called the Lower Nippéween.

So much snow had fallen on the night of the 24th,
that the track we intended to follow was completely
covered, and our march to-day was very fatiguing.
We passed the remains of two red-deer, lying at the
basis of perpendicular cliffs, from the summits of which
they had, probably, been forced by the wolves.   These
voracious animals, who are inferior in speed to the
moose and red-deer, are said frequently to have recourse to this expedient in places where extensive
plains are bounded by precipitous cliffs.   Whilst the
deer are quietly grazing, the wolves assemble in great
numbers, and, forming a crescent, creep slowly towards
the herd so as not to alarm them much at first, but
when they perceive that they have fairly hemmed in
the unsuspecting creatures, and cut off their retreat
across the plain, they move more quickly, and with
hideous yells terrify their prey and urge them to flight

by the only open way, which is that towards the precipice ; appearing to know, that when the herd is once
at full speed, it is easily driven over the cliff, the rear-
most urging on those that are before. The wolves
then descend at their leisure, and feast on the mangled
carcasses. One of these ferocious animals passed close
to the person who was beating the track, but did not
offer any violence. We encamped at sunset, after
walking thirteen miles.

On the 26th, we were rejoiced at passing the half-
way point, between Cumberland and Carlton. The
scenery of the river was less agreeable beyond this
point, as there was a scarcity of wood. One of our
men was despatched after a red-deer that appeared on
the bank. He contrived to approach near enough to
fire twice, though without success, before the animal
moved away. After a fatiguing march of seventeen
miles, we put up at the upper Nippéween, a deserted
establishment ; and performed the comfortable operations of shaving and washing for the first time since
our departure from Cumberland, the weather having
been hitherto too severe. We passed an uncomfortable and sleepless night, and agreed next morning to
encamp in future in the open air, as preferable to the
imperfect shelter of a deserted house without doors or
windows.

The morning was extremely cold, but fortunately

the wind was light, which prevented our feeling it severely ; experience indeed had taught us that the sensation of çold depends less upon the state of temperature, than the force of wind.   An attempt was made
to obtain the latitude, which failed in consequence of
the screw, which adjusts the telescope of the sextant,
being immovably fixed, from the moisture upon it
having frozen.   The instrument could not be replaced
in its case before the ice was thawed by the fire in the
evening.

In the course of the day we passed the confluence
of the south branch of the Saskatchawan, which rises
from the rocky mountains near the sources of the
northern branch of the Missouri.   At Coles Falls,
which commences a short distance from the branch, we
found the surface of the ice very uneven, and many
spots of open water.

We passed the ruins of an establishment, which the
traders had been compelled to abandon, in consequence
of the intractable conduct and pilfering habits of the
Assinéboine Indians ; and we learnt that all the residents at a post on the south branch, had been cut off
by the same tribe some years ago.   We traveled
twelve miles to-day.   The wolves serenaded us through
the night with a chorus of their agreeable howling,
but none of them ventured near the encampment.
Mr. Back's repose was disturbed by a more serious

evil ; his buffalo robe caught fire, and the shoes on his feet, being contracted by the heat, gave him such pain, that he jumped up in the cold, and ran into the snow as the only means of obtaining relief.

On the 28th we had a strong and piercing wind from N. W. in our faces, and much snow-drift ; we were compelled to walk as quick as we could, and to keep constantly rubbing the exposed parts of the skin, to prevent their being frozen, but some of the party suffered in spite of every precaution. We descried three red-deer on the banks of the river, and were about to send the best marksmen after them, when they espied the party and ran away. A supply of meat would have been very seasonable, as the men's provision became scanty, and the dogs were without food, except a little burnt leather. Owing to the scarcity of wood, we had to walk until a late hour, before a good spot for an encampment could be found, and had then come only eleven miles. The night was miserably cold ; our tea froze in the tin pots before we could drink it, and even a mixture of spirits and water became quite thick by congelation ; yet, after we lay down to rest, we felt no inconvenience, and heeded not the wolves, though they were howling within view.

The 29th was also very cold, until the sun burst forth, when the traveling became pleasant. The

banks of the river are very scantily supplied with
wood through the part we passed to-day. A long
track on the south shore, called Holms Plains, is destitute of anything like a tree, and the opposite bank
has only stunted willows ; but after walking sixteen
miles, we came to a spot better wooded, and encamped opposite to a remarkable place, called by the voyagers " The Neck of Land."

On the thirtieth we directed our course round The
Neck of Land, which is well clothed with pines and
firs ; though the opposite or western bank is nearly
destitute of wood. This contrast between the two
banks continued until we reached the commencement
of what our companions called the barren grounds,
when both the banks were alike bare. Vast plains
extend behind the southern bank, which afford excellent pasturage for the buffalo, or other grazing animals.
In the evening we saw a herd of the former, but could
not get near to them. After walking fifteen miles we
encamped. The men's provision having been entirely
expended last night, we shared our small stock with
them. The poor dogs had been toiling some days on
the most scanty fare ; their rapacity, in consequence,
was unbounded ; they forced open a deal box, containing tea, &c., to get at a small piece of meat which had
been incautiously placed in it.

As soon as daylight permitted, the party commenced their march, in the expectation of reaching Carlton House to breakfast, but we did not arrive until noon, although the track was good. We were received by Mr. Prudens, the gentleman in charge of the post, with that friendly attention which Governor Williams' circular was calculated to insure at every station ; and were soon afterwards regaled with a substantial dish of buffalo steaks, which would have been thought excellent under any circumstances, but were particularly relished by us, though eaten without either bread or vegetables, after our traveling fare of dried meat and pemmican. After this repast, we had the comfort of changing our traveling dresses, which had been worn for fourteen days. This was a gratification which can only be truly estimated by those who may have been placed under similar circumstances.

Feb. 8.—Having recovered from the swellings and pains which our late march from Cumberland had occasioned, we prepared for the commencement of our journey to Isle à la Crosse, and requisitions were made on both the establishments for the means of conveyance, and the necessary supply of provisions for the party, which was readily furnished. On the 9th, the carioles and sledges were loaded, and sent off after breakfast ; but Mr. Back and I remained till the afternoon, as Mr. Prudens had offered that his horses should convey us to the encampment. At 3 P.M. we parted from our kind host, and in passing through the gate were honored with a salute of musketry. After riding six miles, we joined the men at their encampment, which was made under the shelter of a few poplars. The dogs had been so much fatigued in wading through the very deep snow with their heavy burdens, having to drag upwards of ninety pounds weight each, that they could get no farther. Soon after our arrival the snow began to fall heavily, and it continued through the greater part of the night.

Our next day's march was therefore particularly tedious, the snow being deep, and the route lying across an unvarying level, destitute of wood, except one small cluster of willows. In the afternoon we reached the end of the plain, and came to an elevation, on which poplars, willows, and some pines grew, where we encamped, having traveled ten miles. We crossed three small lakes, two of fresh water, and one of salt, near the latter of which we encamped, and were, in consequence, obliged to use for our tea, water made from snow, which has always a disagreeable taste.

We had scarcely ascended the hill on the following morning, when a large herd of red deer was perceived grazing at a little distance ; and, though we were amply supplied with provision, our Canadian companions could not resist the temptation of endeavoring to add to our stock. A half-breed hunter was therefore sent after them. He succeeded in wounding one, but not so as to prevent its running off with the herd, in a direction wide of our course. A couple of rabbits and a brace of wood partridges were shot in the afternoon. There was an agreeable variety of hill and dale in the scenery we passed through to-day ; and sufficient wood for ornament, but not enough to crowd the picture. The valleys were intersected by several small lakes and pools, whose snowy covering was happily contrasted with the dark green of the pine trees which surrounded them. After ascending a moderately high hill by a winding path through a close wood, we opened suddenly upon Lake Iroquois, and had a full view of its picturesque shores. We crossed it and encamped.

Though the sky was cloudless, yet the weather was warm. We had the gratification of finding a beaten track soon after we started on the morning of the 12th, and were thus enabled to walk briskly. We crossed at least twenty hills, and found a small lake or pool at the foot of each. The destructive ravages of fire were visible during the greater part of the day. The only wood we saw for miles together consisted of pine trees, stript of their branches and bark by this element: in other parts poplars alone were growing, which we have remarked invariably to succeed the pine after a conflagration. We walked twenty miles to-day, but the direct distance was only sixteen miles.

The remains of an Indian hut were found in a deep glen, and close to it was placed a pile of wood, which our companions supposed to cover a deposit of provision. Our Canadian voyagers, induced by an insatiable desire of procuring food, proceeded to remove the upper pieces, and examine its contents ; when to their surprise, they found the body of a female, clothed in leather, which appeared to have been recently placed there. Her former garments, the materials for making a fire, a fishing line, a hatchet, and a bark dish, were laid beside the corpse. The wood was carefully replaced. A small owl, perched on a tree near the spot, called forth many singular remarks from our companions, as to its being a good or bad omen.

We walked the whole of the 13th over flat meadow land, which is much resorted to by the buffalo at all seasons. We saw some herds, but our hunters were too unskilful to get within shot. In the afternoon we reached Stinking Lake, which is nearly of an oval form. Its shores are very low and swampy, to which circumstances, and not to the bad quality of the waters, it owes its Indian name. Our observations place its western part in latitude 53° 25' 24" N., longitude 107° 18' 58" W., variation 20° 32' 10" E.

After a march of fifteen miles and a half, we encamped among a few pines, at the only spot at which we saw sufficient wood for making our fire during the

day. The next morning, about an hour after we had
commenced our march, we came upon a beaten track,
and perceived recent marks of snow-shoes. In a short
time an Iroquois joined us, who was residing with a
party of Cree Indians, to secure the meat and furs
they should collect, for the North-West Company.
He accompanied us as far as the stage on which his
meat was placed, and then gave us a very pressing invitation to halt for the day and partake of his fare;
which, as the hour was too early, we declined, much
to the annoyance of our Canadian companions, who
had been cherishing the prospect of indulging their
amazing appetites at this well-furnished store, ever
since the man had been with us. He gave them,
however, a small supply previous to our parting. The
route now crossed some ranges of hills, on which fir,
birch, and poplar, grew so thickly, that we had much
difficulty in getting the sledges through the narrow
pathway between them. In the evening we descended from the elevated ground, crossed three swampy
meadows, and encamped at their northern extremity,
within a cluster of large pine-trees, the branches of
which were elegantly decorated with abundance of a
greenish yellow lichen. Our march was ten miles.
The weather was very mild, almost too warm for the
exercise we were taking.

We had a strong gale from the N. W. during the

night, which subsided as the morning opened. One
of the sledges had been so much broken yesterday
amongst the trees, that we had to divide its cargo
among the others. We started after this had been
arranged, and finding almost immediately a firm track,
we soon arrived at some Indian lodges to which it led.
The inhabitants were Crees, belonging to the posts on
the Saskatchawan, from whence they had come to hunt
beaver. We made but a short stay, and proceeded
through a Swamp to Pelican Lake. Our view to the
right was bounded by a range of lofty hills, which extended for several miles in a north and south direction, which, it may be remarked, has been that of
all the hilly land we have passed since quitting the
plain.

Pelican Lake is of an irregular form, about six miles
from east to west, and eight from north to south ; it
decreases to the breadth of a mile towards the northern extremity, and is there terminated by a creek.
We went up this creek for a short distance, and then
struck into the woods, and encamped among a cluster
of the firs, which the Canadians term cyprès (*pinus
inops*) ; having come fourteen miles and a half.

Feb. 16.—Shortly after commencing the journey to-
day, we met an Indian and his family who had come
from the houses at Green Lake ; they informed us
the track was well beaten the whole way. We, there-

fore, put forth our utmost speed in the hope of reaching them by night ; but were disappointed, and had
to halt at dark, about twelve miles from them, in a
fisherman's hut, which was unoccupied. Frequent
showers of snow fell during the day, and the atmosphere was thick and gloomy.

We started at an early hour the following morning,
and reached the Hudson's Bay Company's post to
breakfast, and were received very kindly by Mr. Mac-
Farlane, the gentleman in charge. The other establishment, situated on the opposite side of the river,
was under the direction of Mr. Dougal Cameron, one
of the partners of the North-West Company, on whom
Mr. Back and I called soon after our arrival, and were
honored with a salute of musketry.

These establishments are small, but said to be well
situated for the procuring of furs ; as the numerous
creeks in their vicinity are much resorted to by the
beaver, otter, and musquash. The residents usually
obtain a superabundant supply of provision. This
season, however, they have barely had sufficient for
their own support, owing to the epidemic which has
incapacitated the Indians for hunting. The Green
Lake lies nearly north and south, is eighteen miles in
length, and does not exceed one mile and a half of
breadth in any part. The water is deep, and it is in
consequence one of the last lakes in the country that

is frozen. Excellent tittameg and trout are caught in it from March to December, but after that time most of the fish remove to some larger lake.

We remained two days, awaiting the return of some men who had been sent to the Indian lodges for meat, and who were to go on with us. Mr. Back and I did not need this rest, having completely surmounted the pain which the walking in snow-shoes had occasioned. We dined twice with Mr. Cameron, and received from him many useful suggestions respecting our future operations. This gentleman having informed us that provisions would, probably, be very scarce next spring in the Athabasca department, in consequence of the sickness of the Indians during the hunting season, undertook at my request to cause a supply of pemmican to be conveyed from the Saskatchawan to Isle a la Crosse for our use during the winter, and I wrote to apprize Dr. Richardson and Mr. Hood, that they would find it at the latter post when they passed ; and also to desire them to bring as much as the canoes would stow from Cumberland.

The atmosphere was clear and cold during our stay ; observations were obtained at the Hudson Bay fort, lat. 54° 16' 10" N., long. 107° 29' 52" W., var. 22° 6' 36" E.

Feb. 20.—Having been equipped with carioles, sledges, and provisions, from the two posts, we this day recommenced our journey, and were much amused by the novelty of the salute given at our departure, the guns being principally fired by the half-breed women in the absence of the men. Our course was directed to the end of the lake, and for a short distance along a small river ; we then crossed the woods to the Beaver River, which we found to be narrow and very serpentine, having moderately high banks. We encamped about one mile and a half further up among poplars. The next day we proceeded along the river ; it was winding, and about two hundred yards broad. We passed the mouths of two rivers whose waters it receives ; the latter one, we were informed, is a channel by which the Indians go to the Lesser Slave Lake. The banks of the river became higher as we advanced, and were furnished with pines, poplars, and willows.

Though the weather was very cold, we traveled more comfortably than at any preceding time since our departure from Cumberland, as we were enabled, by having light carioles, to ride nearly the whole day, and to be warmly covered up with a buffalo robe. Mr. M'Leod, of the North-West Company, joined us. He had kindly brought some things from Green Lake, which our sledges could not carry. Pursuing our route along the river, we reached at an early hour the upper extremity of the " Grand Rapid," where the ice was so rough that the carioles and sledges had to be conveyed across a point of land. Soon after noon we left the river, inclining N. E., and directed our course N. W., until we reached Long Lake, and encamped at its northern extremity, having come twenty-three miles. This lake is about fourteen miles long, and from three-quarters to one mile and a half broad ; its shores and islands low, but well wooded. There were frequent snow-showers during the day.

Feb. 23.—The night was very stormy, but the wind became more moderate in the morning. We passed to-day through several nameless lakes and swamps before we came to Train Lake, which received its name from being the place where the traders procured the birch to make the sledges, or traineaux ; but this wood has been all used, and there only remain pines and a few poplars. We met some sledges laden with fish, kindly sent to meet us by Mr. Clark, of the Hudson's Bay Company, directly he heard of our approach. Towards the evening the weather became much more unpleasant ; we were exposed to a piercingly cold wind, and much snow-drift, in traversing Isle à la Crosse Lake ; we were, therefore, highly pleased at reaching the Hudson's Bay House by six P. M. We were received in the most friendly manner by Mr. Clark, and honored by volleys of musketry on our arrival. Similar marks of attention were shewn to us on the following day by Mr. Bethune, the partner in charge of the North-West Company's fort. I found here the letters which I had addressed to the partners of the North-West Company, in the Athabasca, from Cumberland, in November last. This circumstance convinced us of the necessity of our present journey.

These establishments are situated on the southern side of the lake, and close to each other. They are forts of considerable importance, being placed at a point of communication with the English River, the Athabasca, and Columbia Districts. The country around them is low, and intersected with water, and was formerly much frequented by beavers and otters, which, however, have been so much hunted by the Indians, that their number is greatly decreased. The Indians frequenting these forts are the Crees and some Chipewyans; they scarcely ever come except in the spring and autumn; in the former season to bring their winter's collection of furs, and in the latter to get the stores they require.

Three Chipewyan lads came in during our stay, to report what furs the band to which they belonged had collected, and to desire they might be sent for; the Indians having declined bringing either furs or meat themselves, since the opposition between the Companies commenced. Mr. Back drew the portrait of one of the boys.

Isle à la Crosse Lake receives its name from an island

situated near the forts, on which the Indians formerly
assembled annually to amuse themselves at the game
of the Cross.   It is justly celebrated for abundance of
the finest tittameg, which weigh from five to fifteen
pounds.   The residents live principally upon this most
delicious fish, which fortunately can be eaten a long
time without producing any disrelish.   They are plentifully caught with nets throughout the year, except
for two or three months.

March 4.—We witnessed the Aurora Borealis very
brilliant, for the second time since our departure from
Cumberland.   A winter encampment is not a favorable situation for viewing this phenomenon, as the
trees in general hide the sky.   Arrangements had been
made for recommencing our journey to-day, but the
wind was stormy, and the snow had drifted too much
for traveling with comfort; we therefore stayed and
dined with Mr. Bethune, who promised to render every
assistance in getting pemmican conveyed to us from
the Saskatchawan, to be in readiness for our canoes
when they might arrive in the spring; Mr. Clark has
also engaged to procure six bags for us, and to furnish
our canoes with any other supplies which may be
wanted, and can be spared from his post, and to contribute his aid in forwarding the pemmican to the
Athabasca, if our canoes cannot carry it all.

I feel greatly indebted to Mr. Clark, for much valuable information respecting the country and the Indians residing to the north of the Slave Lake, and for furnishing me with a list of stores he supposed we should require. This gentleman had resided some years on the Mackensie's River, and had been once so far towards its mouth as to meet the Esquimaux in great numbers. But they assumed such a hostile attitude, that he deemed it unadvisable to attempt opening any communication with them, and retreated as speedily as he could.

The observations we obtained here shewed that the chronometers had varied their rates a little, in consequence of the jolting of the carioles in which we rode ; but their errors and rates were ascertained previous to our departure. We observed the position of this fort to be latitude 55° 25' 35" N., longitude 107° 51' 00" W., by lunars reduced back from Fort Chipewyan, variation 22° 15' 48" W., dip 84° 13' 35"

March 5.—We recommenced our journey this morning, having been supplied with the means of conveyance by both the companies in equal proportions. Mr. Clark accompanied us with the intention of going as far as the boundary of his district. This gentleman was an experienced winter traveler, and we derived much benefit from his suggestions ; he caused the men to arrange the encampment with more attention to comfort and shelter than our former companions had done. After marching eighteen miles we put up on Gravel Point, in the Deep River.

At nine the next morning, we came to the commencement of Clear Lake. We crossed its southern extremes, and then went over a point of land to Buffalo Lake, and encamped after traveling twenty-six miles. After supper we were entertained until midnight with paddling songs, by our Canadians, who required very little stimulus beside their natural vivacity, to afford us this diversion. The next morning we arrived at the establishments which are situated on the western side of the lake, near to a small stream, called the Beaver River. They were small log buildings, hastily erected last October, for the convenience of the Indians who hunt in the vicinity. Mr. MacMurray, a partner in the N. W. Company, having sent to Isle à la Crosse an invitation to Mr. Back and me, our carioles were driven to his post, and we experienced the kindest reception. These posts are frequented by only a few Indians, Crees and Chipewyans. The country round is not sufficiently stocked with animals to afford support to many families, and the traders almost entirely subsist on fish caught in the autumn, prior to the lake being frozen. The water being shallow, the fish remove to a deeper part, as soon as the lake is covered with ice. The Aurora Borealis was brilliantly displayed on both the nights we remained here, but particularly on the 7th, when its appearances were most diversified, and the motion extremely rapid. Its coruscations occasionally concealed from sight stars of the first magnitude in passing over them, at other times these were faintly discerned through them; once I perceived a stream of light to illumine the under surface of some clouds as it passed along. There was no perceptible noise.

Mr. MacMurray gave a dance to his voyagers and the half breed women; this is a treat which they expect on the arrival of any stranger at the post.

We were presented by this gentleman, with the valuable skin of a black fox, which he had entrapped some days before our arrival; it was forwarded to England with other specimens.

Our observations place the North-West Company's house in latitude 55° 53' 00" N., longitude 108° 51' 10" W.; variation 22° 33' 22" E.

The shores of Buffalo Lake are of moderate height, and well wooded, but immediately beyond the bank the country is very swampy, and intersected with water in every direction. At some distance from the western side there is a conspicuous hill, which we hailed with much pleasure, as being the first interruption to the tedious uniform scene we had for some time passed through.

On the 10th we recommenced our journey after

breakfast and traveled quickly, as we had the advantage of a well beaten track. At the end of eighteen miles we entered upon the river " Loche," which has a serpentine course, and is confined between alluvial banks that support stunted willows and a few pines ; we encamped about three miles further on ; and in the course of the next day's march perceived several holes in the ice, and many unsafe places for the sledges. Our companions said the ice of this river is always in the same insecure state, even during the most severe winter, which they attribute to warm springs. Quitting the river we crossed a portage and came upon the Methye Lake, and soon afterwards arrived at the trading posts situated on the western side of it. These were perfect huts, which had been hastily built after the commencement of the last winter. We here saw two hunters who were Chipewyan half-breeds, and made many inquiries of them respecting the countries we expected to visit, but we found them quite ignorant of every part beyond the Athabasca Lake. They spoke of Mr. Hearne and of his companion Matonnabee, but did not add to our stock of information respecting that journey. It had happened before their birth, but they remembered the expedition of Sir Alexander Mackenzie towards the sea.

This is a picturesque lake, about ten miles long and six broad, and receives its name from a species of fish

caught in it. This fish, the methye, is not much esteemed ; the residents never eat any part but the liver
except through necessity, the dogs dislike even that.
The tittameg and trout are also caught in the fall of
the year.

On the 13th we renewed our journey, and parted
from Mr. Clark, to whom we were much obliged for
his hospitality and kindness. We soon reached the
Methye Portage, and had a very pleasant ride across
it in our carioles. The track was good, and led
through groups of pines, so happily placed that it
would not have required a great stretch of imagination to fancy ourselves driving through a well arranged park. We had now to cross a small lake, and
then gradually ascended hills beyond it, until we arrived at the summit of a lofty chain of mountains,
commanding the most picturesque and romantic prospect we had yet seen in this country. Two ranges of
high hills run parallel to each other for several miles,
until the faint blue haze hides their particular characters, when they slightly change their course, and are
lost to the view. The space between them is occupied by nearly a level plain, through which a river
pursues a meandering course, and receives supplies
from the creeks and rills issuing from the mountains
on each side. The prospect was delightful even amid
the snow, and though marked with all the cheerless

characters of winter ; how much more charming must
it be when the trees are in leaf, and the ground is ar-
rayed in summer verdure ! Some faint idea of the
difference was conveyed to my mind by witnessing the
effect of the departing rays of a brilliant sun. The
distant prospect, however, is surpassed in grandeur by
the wild scenery which appeared immediately below
our feet. There the eye penetrates into vast ravines
from two to three hundred feet in depth, that are
clothed with trees, and lie on either side of the narrow pathway descending to the river over eight suc-
cessive ridges of hills. At one spot, termed the Cocks-
comb, the passenger stands insulated as it were on a
small slip, where a false step might precipitate him
into the glen. From this place Mr. Back took an interesting and accurate sketch of the view, to enable
him to do which, we encamped early, having come
twenty-one miles.

The Methye Portage is about twelve miles in extent,
and over this space the canoes and all their cargoes
are carried, both in going to and from the Athabasca
department. It is part of the range of mountains
which separates the waters flowing south from those
flowing north. According to Sir Alexander Mackenzie, " this range of hills continues in a S. W. direction
until its local height is lost between the Saskatchawan and Elk Rivers, close on the banks of the former,

in latitude 53° 36′ N., longitude 113° 45′ W., when
it appears to take its course due north.

At daylight on the 14th we began to descend the
range of hills leading towards the river, and no small
care was required to prevent the sledges from being
broken in going down these almost perpendicular
heights, or being precipitated into the glens on each
side. As a precautionary measure the dogs were taken
off, and the sledges guided by the men, notwithstanding which they descended with amazing rapidity, and
the men were thrown into the most ridiculous attitudes
in endeavoring to stop them. When we had arrived
at the bottom I could not but feel astonished at the
laborious task which the voyagers have twice in the
year to encounter at this place, in conveying their
stores backwards and forwards. We went across the
Clear Water River, which runs at the bases of these
hills, and followed an Indian track along its northern
bank, by which we avoided the White Mud and Good
Portages. We afterwards followed the river as far as
the Pine Portage, when we passed through a very romantic defile of rocks, which presented the appearance
of Gothic ruins, and their rude characters were happily contrasted with the softness of the snow, and the
darker foliage of the pines which crowned their summits. We next crossed the Cascade Portage, which
is the last on the way to the Athabasca Lake, and we

soon afterwards came to some Indian tents, containing
five families, belonging to the Chipewyan tribe.   We
smoked the calumet in the Chief's tent, whose name was
the Thumb, and distributed some tobacco and a weak
mixture of spirits and water among the men.   They
received this civility with much less grace than the
Crees, and seemed to consider it a matter of course.
There was an utter neglect of cleanliness, and a total
want of comfort in their tents ; and the poor creatures
were miserably clothed.   Mr. Frazer, who accompanied
us from the Methye Lake, accounted for their being
in this forlorn condition by explaining, that this band
of Indians had recently destroyed every thing they
possessed, as a token of their great grief for the loss of
their relatives in the prevailing sickness.   It appears
that no article is spared by these unhappy men when
a near relative dies ; their clothes and tents are cut to
pieces, their guns broken, and every other weapon
rendered useless, if some person do not remove these articles from their sight, which is seldom done.   Mr. Back
sketched one of the children.   This delighted the
father very much, who charged the boy to be very
good now, since his picture had been drawn by a great
Chief.   We learned that they prize pictures very
highly, and esteem any they can get, however badly
executed, as efficient charms.   They were unable to
give us any information respecting the country beyond

the Athabasca Lake, which is the boundary of their peregrinations to the northward. Having been apprized of our coming, they had prepared an encampment for us; but we had witnessed too many proofs of their importunity to expect that we could pass the night near them in any comfort, whilst either spirits, tobacco, or sugar, remained in our possession; and therefore preferred to go about two miles further along the river, and to encamp among a cluster of fine pine trees, after a journey of sixteen miles.

On the morning of the 15th, in proceeding along the river, we perceived a strong smell of sulphur, and on the north shore found a quantity of it scattered, which seemed to have been deposited by some spring in the neighborhood : it appeared very pure and good. We continued our course the whole day along the river, which is about four hundred yards wide, has some islands, and is confined between low land, extending from the bases of the mountains on each side. We put up at the end of thirteen miles, and were then joined by a Chipewyan, who came, as we supposed, to serve as our guide to Pierre au Calumet, but as none of the party could communicate with our new friend, otherwise than by signs, we waited patiently until the morning to see what he intended to do. The wind blew a gale during the night, and the snow fell heavily. The next day our guide led us to the

Pembina River, which comes from the southward, where we found traces of Indians, who appeared to have quitted this station the day before ; we had, therefore, the benefit of a good track, which our dogs much required, as they were greatly fatigued, by having dragged their loads through very deep snow for the last two days. A moose deer crossed the river just before the party : this animal is plentiful in the vicinity. We encamped in a pleasant, well sheltered place, having traveled fourteen miles.

We had made but a short distance the following morning, when we came to some Indian lodges, which belonged to an old Chipewyan chief, named the Sun, and his family, consisting of five hunters, their wives, and children. They were delighted to see us, and when the object of our expedition had been explained to them, expressed themselves much interested in our progress ; but they could give no particle of information respecting the countries beyond the Athabasca Lake. We smoked with them, and gave each person a glass of mixed spirits and some tobacco. We learned from a Canadian servant of the North-West Company, who was residing with them, that this family had lost numerous relatives, and that the destruction of property, which had been made after their deaths, was the only cause for the pitiable condition in which we saw them. He said the whole were industrious hunters, and, therefore, were usually better provided with clothes, and other useful articles, than most of the Indians. We purchased from them a pair of snow-shoes, in exchange for some ammunition. The Chipewyans are celebrated for making them good and easy to walk in; we saw some here upwards of six feet long, and three broad; with these unwieldy clogs an active hunter, in the spring, when there is a crust on the surface of the snow, will run down a moose or red deer.

We made very slow progress after leaving this party, on account of the deep snow, but continued along the river until we reached its junction with the Athabasca, or Elk River. Very little wood has been seen during this day's march. The western shore, near the Forks, is destitute of trees; it is composed of lofty perpendicular cliffs, which are now covered with snow. The eastern shore supports a few pines.

March 18.—Soon after our departure from the encampment we met two men, from the establishment at Pierre au Calumet, who gave us correct information of the situation and distance. Having the benefit of their track, we marched at a tolerably quick pace, and made twenty-two miles in the course of the day, though the weather was very disagreeable for traveling, being stormy, with constant snow. We kept along the river the whole time; its breadth is

about two miles.   The islands appear better furnished with wood than its banks, the summits of which
are almost bare.   Soon after we had encamped our
Indian guide rejoined us ; he had remained behind
yesterday, to accompany a friend on a hunting excursion, without consulting us.   On his return this evening he made no endeavor to explain the reason of his
absence, but sat down coolly, and began to prepare his
supper.

Showers of snow fell until noon on the following
day, but we continued our journey along the river,
whose banks and islands became gradually lower as we
advanced, and less abundantly supplied with wood,
except willows.   We came up with an old Canadian,
who was resting his wearied dogs during the heat of
the sun.   He was carrying meat from some Indian
lodges to Fort Chipewyan, having a burden exceeding
two hundred and fifty pounds on his sledge, which
was dragged by two miserable dogs.   He came up to
our encampment after dark.   We were much amused
by the altercation that took place between him and our
Canadian companions as to the qualifications of their
respective dogs.   This, however, is such a general topic
of conversation among the voyagers in the encampment,
that we should not probably have remarked it, had
not the old man frequently offered to bet the whole of
his wages that his two dogs, poor and lean as they

were, would drag their load to the Athabasca Lake in less time than any three of theirs could. Having expressed our surprise at his apparent temerity, he coolly said the men from the lower countries did not understand the management of their dogs, and that he depended on his superior skill in driving ; and we soon gathered from his remarks, that the voyagers of the Athabasca department consider themselves as very superior to any other. The only reasons which he could assign were, that they had borne their burdens across the terrible Methye Portage, and that they were accustomed to live harder and more precariously.

March 25.—Having now the guidance of an old Canadian, we sent forward the Indian, and one of our men, with letters to the gentleman at the Athabasca Lake. The rest of the party set off afterwards, and kept along the river until ten, when we branched off by portages into the Embarrass River, the usual channel of communication in canoes with the lake. It is a narrow and serpentine stream, confined between alluvial banks which support pines, poplars, and willows. We had not advanced far before we came up with the two men despatched by us this morning. The stormy weather had compelled them to encamp, as there was too much drifting of the snow for any attempt being made to cross the lake. We were obliged, though most reluctantly, to follow their example ; but we com-

forted ourselves with the reflection that this was the
first time we had been stopped by the weather during
our long journey, which was so near at an end. The
gale afterwards increased, the squalls at night became
very violent, disburthened the trees of the snow, and
gave us the benefit of a continual fall of patches from
them, in addition to the constant shower. We therefore quickly despatched our suppers, and retired under
the shelter of our blankets.

March 26.—The boisterous weather continued
through the night, and it was not before six this morning, that the wind became apparently moderate, and the
snow ceased. Two of the Canadians were immediately
sent off with letters to the gentlemen at Fort Chipewyan. After breakfast we also started, but our Indian
friend, having a great indisposition to move in such
weather, remained by the fire. We soon quitted the
river, and after crossing a portage, a small lake, and a
point of land, came to the borders of the Mam-ma-
wee Lake. We then found our error as to the strength
of the wind; and that the gale still blew violently,
and there was so much drifting of the snow as to
cover the distant objects by which our course could be
directed. We fortunately got a glimpse through this
cloud of a cluster of islands in the direction of the
houses, and decided on walking towards them; but in
doing this we suffered very much from the cold, and

were obliged to halt under the shelter of them, and await the arrival of our Indian guide. He conducted us between these islands, over a small lake, and by a swampy river, into the Athabasca Lake, from whence the establishments were visible. At four P. M. we had the pleasure of arriving at Fort Chipewyan, and of being received by Messrs. Keith and Black, the partners of the North-West Company in charge, in the most kind and hospitable manner. Thus has terminated a winter's journey of eight hundred and fifty-seven miles, in the progress of which there has been a great intermixture of agreeable and disagreeable circumstances. Could the amount of each be ballanced, I suspect the latter would much preponderate ; and amongst these the initiation into the practice of walking in snow-shoes must be considered as prominent. The suffering it occasions can be but faintly imagined by a person who thinks upon the inconvenience of marching with a weight of between two and three pounds constantly attached to galled feet, and swelled ankles. Perseverance and practice only will enable the novice to surmount this pain.

The next evil is the being constantly exposed to witness the wanton and unnecessary cruelty of the men to their dogs, especially those of the Canadians, who beat them unmercifully, and habitually vent on them the most dreadful and disgusting imprecations.

There are other inconveniences which, though keenly
felt during the day's journey, are speedily forgotten,
when stretched out in the encampment before a large
fire, you enjoy the social mirth of your companions,
who usually pass the evening in recounting their former feats in traveling. At this time the Canadians
are always cheerful and merry, and the only bar to
their comfort arises from the frequent interruption occasioned by the dogs, who are constantly prowling
about the circle, and snatching at every kind of food
that happens to be within their reach. These useful
animals are a comfort to them afterwards, by the
warmth they impart when lying down by their side or
feet, as they usually do. But the greatest gratifica-
tions a traveler in these regions enjoys, are derived
from the hospitable welcome he receives at every
trading post, however poor the means of the host may
be ; and from being disrobed even for a short time of
the trappings of a voyager, and experiencing the pleasures of cleanliness.

The following are the estimated distances, in statute miles, which Mr. Back and I have traveled since
our departure from Cumberland :

From Cumberland House to Carlton House - - - -	263
From Carlton to Isle a la Crosse - - - - - - -	230
From Isle a la Crosse to North side of the Methyo Portage	124
From the Methye Portage to Fort Chipewyan - - -	240
	857 Miles

CHAPTER IV.

1820.
March 26. ON the day of our arrival at Fort Chipewyan we called upon Mr. MacDonald, the gentleman
in charge of the Hudson's Bay Establishment, called
Fort Wedderburne, and delivered to him Governor
Williams's circular letter, which desired that every assistance should be given to further our progress, and a
statement of the requisitions which we should have to
make on his post.

Our first object was to obtain some certain information respecting our future route ; and accordingly we
received from one of the North-West Company's interpreters, named Beaulieu, a half-breed, who had
been brought up amongst the Dog-ribbed and Copper
Indians, some satisfactory information, which we afterwards found tolerably correct, respecting the mode of
reaching the Copper-mine River, which he had descended a considerable way, as well as of the course of
that river to its mouth. The Copper Indians, however, he said, would be able to give us more accurate

information as to the latter part of its course, as they
occasionally pursue it on the sea. He sketched on the
floor a representation of the river, and a line of coast
according to his idea of it. Just as he had finished,
an old Chipewyan Indian, named Black Meat, unexpectedly came in, and instantly recognized the plan.
He then took the charcoal from Beaulieu, and inserted
a track along the sea-coast, which he had followed in
returning from a war excursion, made by his tribe
against the Esquimaux. He detailed several particulars of the coast and the sea, which he represented as
studded with well-wooded islands, and free from ice,
close to the shore, but not to a great distance, in the
month of July. He described two other rivers to the
eastward of Copper-mine River, which also fall into
the Northern Ocean. The Anatessy, which issues from
the Contway-to or Rum Lake, and the Thloueea-tessy
or Fish River, which rises near the eastern boundary
of the Great Slave Lake ; but he represented them
both as being shallow, and too much interrupted by
barriers for being navigated in any other than small
Indian canoes.

Having received this satisfactory intelligence, I
wrote immediately to Mr. Smith, of the North-West
Company, and Mr. M'Vicar, of the Hudson's Bay
Company, the gentlemen in charge of the posts at the
Great Silver Lake, to communicate the object of the

Expedition, and our proposed route ; and to solicit
any information they possessed, or could collect, from
the Indians, relative to the countries we had to pass
through, and the best manner of proceeding. As the
Copper Indians frequent the establishment on the
north side of the lake, I particularly requested them
to explain to that tribe the object of our visit, and
to endeavor to procure from them some guides and
hunters to accompany our party. Two Canadians
were sent by Mr. Keith with these letters.

The month of April commenced with fine and clear
but extremely cold weather ; unfortunately we were
still without a thermometer, and could not ascertain
the degrees of temperature. The coruscations of the
Aurora were very brilliant almost every evening of the
first week, and were generally of the most variable
kind. On the 3d, they were particularly changeable.
The first appearance exhibited three illuminated beams
issuing from the horizon in the north, east, and west
points, and directed towards the zenith ; in a few
seconds these disappeared, and a complete circle was
displayed, bounding the horizon at an elevation of
fifteen degrees. There was a quick lateral motion in
the attenuated beams of which this zone was composed. Its color was a pale yellow, with an occasional
tinge of red.

On the 8th of April the Indians saw some geese in

the vicinity of this lake, but none of the migratory
birds appeared near to the houses before the 15th, when
some swans flew over. These are generally the first
that arrive ; the weather had been very stormy for the
four preceding days, and this in all probability kept
the birds from venturing farther north than where the
Indians had first seen them.

In the middle of the month the snow began to waste
daily, and by degrees it disappeared from the hills and
the surface of the lake. On the 17th and 19th the
Aurora appeared very brilliant in patches of light,
bearing N.W. An old Cree Indian having found a
beaver lodge near to the fort, Mr. Keith, Back, and I,
accompanied him to see the method of breaking into
it, and their mode of taking those interesting animals. The lodge was constructed on the side of a
rock in a small lake, having the entrance into it beneath the ice. The frames were formed of layers of
sticks, the interstices being filled with wood, and the
outside was plastered with earth and stones, which
the frost had so completely consolidated, that to break
through required great labor, with the aid of the ice
chisel, and the other iron instruments which the beaver hunters use. The chase, however, was unsuccessful, as the beaver had previously evacuated the
lodge.

The first geese we observed flying near to the fort

were seen on the 21st, and some were brought to the house on the 30th, but they were very lean ; on the 25th flies were seen sporting in the sun, and on the 26th the ice on the lake, near the channel of the river, was overflowed, in consequence of the Athabasca river having broken up ; but except where this water spread, there was no appearance of decay in the ice.

May.—During the first part of this month, the wind blew from the N.W., and the sky was cloudy. It generally thawed during the day, but froze through the night. On the 2d the Aurora faintly gleamed through very dense clouds.

We had a long conversation with Mr. Dease of the North-West Company, who had recently arrived from his station at the bottom of the Athabasca Lake. This gentleman, having passed several winters on the Mackenzie's River, and at the posts to the northward of Slave Lake, possessed considerable information respecting the Indians, and those parts of the country to which our inquiries were directed, which he very promptly and kindly communicated. During our conversation, an old Chipewyan Indian, named the Rabbit's Head, entered the room, to whom Mr. Dease referred for information on some point. We found from his answer that he was a step son of the late Chief Matonnabee, who had accompanied Mr. Hearne on his journey to the sea, and that he had himself been of the party, but being then a mere boy, he had forgotten many of the circumstances. He confirms, however, the leading incidents related by Hearne, and was positive he reached the sea, though he admitted that none of the party had tasted the water. He represented himself to be the only survivor of that party. As he was esteemed a good Indian, I presented him with a medal, which he received gratefully, and concluded a long speech upon the occasion, by assuring me he should preserve it carefully all his life.

On the 10th of May we were gratified by the appearance of spring, though the ice remained firm on the lake. The anemone (pulsatilla, pasque flower,) appeared this day in flower, the trees began to put forth their leaves, and the musquitoes visited the warm rooms. On the 17th and 18th there were frequent showers of rain, and much thunder and lightning. This moist weather caused the ice to waste so rapidly, that by the 24th it had entirely disappeared from the lake. The gentlemen belonging to both the Companies quickly arrived from the different posts in this department, bringing their winter's collection of furs, which are forwarded from these establishments to the dcpòts.

July 2.—The canoe, which was ordered to be built for our use, was finished. As it was constructed after the manner, which has been accurately described by

Hearne, and several of the American travelers, a detail of the process will be unnecessary. Its extreme length was thirty-two feet six inches, including the bow and stern pieces ; its greatest breadth was four feet ten inches, but it was only two feet nine inches forward where the bowman sat, and two feet four inches behind where the steersman was placed ; and its depth was one foot eleven and a quarter inches.* There were seventy-three hoops of thin cedar, and a layer of slender laths of the same wood within the frame. These feeble vessels of bark will carry twenty-five pieces of goods, each weighing ninety pounds, exclusive of the necessary provision and baggage for the crew of five or six men, amounting in the whole to about three thousand three hundred pounds' weight. This great lading they annually carry between the depôts and the posts, in the interior ; and it rarely happens that any accidents occur, if they are managed by experienced bowmen and steersmen, on whose skill the safety of the canoe entirely depends in the rapids and difficult places. When a total portage is made, these two men carry the canoe, and they often run with it, though its weight is estimated at about three hundred pounds, exclusive of the poles and oars, which are occasionally left in where the distance is short.

July 13.—This morning Mr. Back and I had the sincere gratification of welcoming our long separated friends, Dr. Richardson and Mr. Hood, who arrived in perfect health with two canoes, having made a very expeditious journey from Cumberland, notwithstanding they were detained near three days in consequence of the melancholy loss of one of their bowmen, by the upsetting of a canoe in a strong rapid ; but, as the occurrences of this journey, together with the mention of some other circumstances that happened previous to their departure from Cumberland, which have been extracted from Mr. Hood's narrative, will appear in the following chapter, it will be unnecessary to enter farther into these points now.

The zeal and talent displayed by Dr. Richardson and Mr. Hood in the discharge of their several duties, since my separation from them, drew forth my highest approbation. These gentlemen had brought all the stores they could procure from the establishments at Cumberland and at Isle à la Crosse ; and at the latter place they had received ten bags of pemmican from the North-West Company, which proved to be mouldy and so totally unfit for use that it was left at the Methye portage. They got none from the Hudson's Bay post. The voyagers belonging to that Company, being destitute of provisions, had eaten what was intended for us. In consequence of these untoward circumstances, the canoes arrived with only one's day supply of this most essential article. The prospect of having to commence our journey from hence, almost destitute of provision, and scantily supplied with stores, was distressing to us, and very discouraging to the men. It was evident, however, that any unnecessary delay here would have been very imprudent, as Fort Chipewyan did not, at the present time, furnish the means of subsistence for so large a party, much less was there a prospect of our receiving any supply to carry with us. We, therefore, hastened to make the necessary arrangements for our speedy departure. All the stores were demanded that could possibly be spared from both the establishments ; and we rejoiced to find, that when this collection was added to the articles that had been brought up by the canoes, that we had a sufficient quantity of clothing for the equipment of the men who had been engaged here, as well as to furnish a present to the Indians, besides some few goods for the winter's consumption ; but we could not procure any ammunition, which was the most essential article, or spirits, and but little tobacco.

We then made a final arrangement respecting the voyagers, who were to accompany the party ; and fortunately, there was no difficulty in doing this, as Dr. Richardson and Mr. Hood had taken the very judicious precaution of bringing up ten men from Cumberland, who were engaged to proceed forward if their services were required. The Canadians, whom they brought,

were most desirous of being continued, and we felt sincere pleasure in being able to keep men who were so
zealous in the cause, and who had given proofs of their
activity on their recent passage to this place, by discharging those men who were less willing to undertake
the journey ; of these three were Englishman, one
American, and three Canadians.   When the numbers
were completed, which we had been recommended by
the traders to take as a protection against the Esquimaux, we had sixteen Canadian-voyagers, and our
worthy and only English attendant John Hepburn,
besides the two interpreters whom we were to receive
at the Great Slave Lake ; we were also accompanied
by a Chipewyan woman.   An equipment of-goods
was given to each of the men who had been engaged
at this place, similar to what had been furnished to the
others at Cumberland ; and when this distribution
had been.made, the remainder were made up into
bales, preparatory to our departure on the following
day.   We were cheerfully assisted in these and all our
occupations by Mr. Smith, who evinced an anxious
desire to supply our wants as far as his means permitted.

CHAPTER V.

July 18. 1820. EARLY this morning the stores were distributed to the three canoes. Our stock of provision unfortunately did not amount to more than sufficient for one day's consumption, exclusive of two barrels of flour, three cases of preserved meats, some chocolate, arrow-root, and portable soup, which we had brought from England, and intended to reserve for our journey to the coast next season. Seventy pounds of moose meat and a little barley-were all that Mr. Smith was enabled to give us. It was gratifying, however, to perceive that this scarcity of food did not depress the spirits of our Canadian companions, who cheerfully loaded their canoes, and embarked in high glee after they had received the customary dram. At noon we bade farewell to our kind friend Mr. Smith. The crews commenced a lively paddling song on quitting the shore, which was continued until we had lost sight of the houses. We soon reached the western boundary of the lake, and at two entered the Stoney River, one of the discharges of the Athabasca Lake,

into the Slave River, and having a favoring current
passed swiftly along. This narrow stream is confined
between low swampy banks, which support willows,
dwarf birch, and alder. At five we passed its conflux
with Peace River. The Slave River, formed by the
union of these streams, is about three-quarters of a
mile wide. We descended this magnificent river with
much rapidity, and after passing through several narrow channels, formed by an assemblage of islands,
crossed a spot where the waters had a violent whirl-
ing motion, which, when the river is low, is said to
subside into a dangerous rapid ; on the present occasion, no other inconvenience was felt than the inability of steering the canoes, which were whirled about in
every direction by the eddies, until the current carried
them beyond their influence. We encamped at seven,
on the swampy bank of the river, but had scarcely
pitched the tents before we were visited by a terrible
thunder-storm ; the rain fell in torrents, and the violence of the wind caused the river to overflow its
banks, so that we were completely flooded. Swarms
of musquitoes succeeded the storm, and their tormenting stings, superadded to other inconveniences, induced
us to embark, and, after taking a hasty supper, to
pursue our voyage down the stream during the night.

At six on the following morning we passed the
Reindeer Islands, and at ten reached the entrance of

the Dog River, where we halted to set the fishing nets. These were examined in the evening, but to our mortification we obtained only four small trout, and were compelled to issue part of our preserved meats for supper. The latitude of the mouth of Dog River, was observed 59° 52′ 16″ N.

The nets were taken up at daylight, but they furnished only a solitary pike. We lost no time in embarking, and crossed the crooked channel of the Dog Rapid, when two of the canoes came in such violent contact with each other, that the sternmost had its bow broken off. We were fortunately near to the shore, or the disabled canoe would have sunk. The injury being repaired in two hours, we again embarked, and having descended another rapid, arrived at the Cassette Portage of four hundred and sixty paces, over which the cargoes and canoes were carried in about twenty-six minutes. We next passed through a narrow channel full of rapids, crossed the Portage d'Embarras of seventy yards; and the portage of the Little Rock, of three hundred yards, at which another accident happened to one of the canoes, by the bowman slipping and letting it fall upon a rock, and breaking it in two. Two hours were occupied in sewing the detached pieces together, and covering the seam with pitch; but this being done, it was as effective as before. After leaving this place we soon came to the

next portage, of two hundred and seventy-three paces ;
and shortly afterwards to the Mountain Portage, of one
hundred and twenty : which is appropriately named,
as the path leads over the summit of a high hill.
This elevated situation commands a very grand and
picturesque view, for some miles along the river, which
at this part is about a mile wide.

We next crossed a portage of one hundred and
twenty yards ; and then the Pelican portage of eight
hundred paces.   Mr. Back took an accurate sketch of
the interesting scenery which the river presents at this
place.   After descending six miles further we came to
the last portage on the route to Slave Lake, which we
crossed, and encamped at its lower end.   It is called
"The Portage of the Drowned," and it received that
name from a melancholy accident which took place
many years ago.   Two canoes arrived at the upper
end of the portage, in one of which there was an experienced guide.   This man, judging from the height
of the river, deemed it practicable to shoot the rapid,
and determined upon trying it.   He accordingly
placed himself in the bow of his canoe, having previously agreed, that if the passage was found easy, he
should, on reaching the bottom of the rapid, fire a
musket, as a signal for the other canoe to follow.
The rapid proved dangerous, and called forth all the
skill of the guide, and the utmost exertion of his

crew, and they narrowly escaped destruction. Just as they were landing, an unfortunate fellow, seizing the loaded fowling-piece, fired at a duck which rose at the instant. The guide anticipating the consequences, ran with the utmost haste to the other end of the portage, but he was too late : the other canoe had pushed off, and he arrived only to witness the fate of his comrades. They got alarmed in the middle of the rapid, the canoe was upset, and every man perished.

The various rapids we have passed to-day, are produced by an assemblage of islands and rocky ledges, which obstruct the river, and divide it into many narrow channels. Two of these channels are rendered still more difficult by accumulations of drift timber ; a circumstance which has given a name to one of the portages. The rocks which form the bed of the river, and the numerous islands, belong to the granite formation. The distance made to-day was thirteen miles.

July 21.---We embarked at four A.M., and pursued our course down the river. The rocks cease at the last portage ; and below it the banks are composed of alluvial soil, which is held together by the roots of the trees and shrubs that crown their summits. The river is about a mile wide, and the current is greatly diminished. At eight we landed at the mouth of the

Salt River, and pitched our tents, intending to remain here this and the next day for the purpose of fishing. After breakfast, which made another inroad on our preserved meats, we proceeded up the river in a light canoe, to visit the salt springs, leaving a party behind to attend the nets. This river is about one hundred yards wide at its mouth. Its waters did not become brackish until we had ascended it seven or eight miles ; but when we had passed several rivulets of fresh water which flowed in, the main stream became very salt, at the same time contracting to the width of fifteen or twenty yards. At a distance of twenty-two miles, including the windings of the river, the plains commence. Having pitched the tent at this spot, we set out to visit the principal springs, and walked about three miles when the musquitoes compelled us to give up our project. We did not see the termination of the plains towards the east, but on the north and west they are bounded by an even ridge, about six or seven hundred feet in height. Several salt springs issue from the foot of this ridge, and spread their waters over the plain, which consists of tenacious clay. During the summer much evaporation takes place, and large heaps of salt are left behind crystalized in the form of cubes. Some beds of greyish compact gypsum were exposed on the sides of the hills.

The next morning after filling some casks with salt for our use during winter, we embarked to return, and had descended the rrver a few miles, when turning round a point, we perceived a buffalo plunge into the river before us. Eager to secure so valuable a prize, we instantly opened a fire upon him from four muskets, and in a few minutes he fell, but not before he had received fourteen balls. The carcass was towed to the bank, and the canoe speedily laden with meat. After this piece of good fortune, we descended the stream merrily, our voyagers chanting their liveliest songs. On arrival at the mouth of the river, we found that our nets had not produced more than enough to supply a scanty meal to the men whom we had left behind, but this was now of little importance as the acquisition of meat we had made, would enable us to proceed without more delay to Slave Lake. In the evening, a violent thunder-storm came on with heavy rain ; thermometer 70°.

At a very early hour on the following morning, we embarked, and continued to paddle against a very strong wind and high waves, under the shelter of the bank of the rivers, until two P. M., when having arrived at a more exposed part of the stream, the canoes took in so much water that we were obliged to disembark on a small island. The river here is from one mile and a quarter to one mile and three-quarters

wide.   Its banks are of moderate height, sandy, and
well wooded.

July 24.—We made more progress notwithstanding
the continuance of the wind.   The course of the river
is very winding, making in one place a circuit of seven
or eight miles round a peninsula, which is joined to
the west bank by a narrow isthmus.   Near the foot
of this elbow, a long island occupies the centre of the
river, which it divides into two channels.

Soon after landing, I visited the Hudson's Bay post
on the same island, and engaged Pierre St. German,
an interpreter for the Copper Indians.   We regretted
to find the posts of both the Companies extremely
bare of provision ; but as the gentleman in charge had
despatched men on the preceding evening, to a band
of Indians, in search of meat, and they promised to
furnish us with whatever should be brought, it was
deemed advisable to wait for their return, as the smallest supply was now of importance to us.   Advantage
was taken of the delay to repair effectually the canoe,
which had been broken in the Dog Rapid.   On the next
evening, the men arrived with the meat, and enabled
Mr. M'Cleod, of the North-West Company, to furnish
us with four hundred pounds of dried provisions.   Mr.
M'Vicar, of the Hudson's Bay Company, also supplied
one hundred and fifty pounds.   This quantity we considered would be sufficient, until we could join the hun-

ters. We also obtained three fishing nets, a gun, and a pair of pistols, which were all the stores these posts could furnish, although the gentlemen in charge were much disposed to assist us.

On the 27th of July we embarked at four Λ. M., and proceeded along the south shore of the lake, through a narrow channel, formed by some islands, beyond the confluence of the principal branch of the Slave River ; and as far as Stoney Island, where we breakfasted. This island is merely a rock of gneiss, that rises forty or fifty feet above the lake, and is precipitous on the north side. As the day was fine, and the lake smooth, we ventured upon paddling across to the Reindeer Islands, which were distant about thirteen miles in a northern direction, instead of pursuing the usual track by keeping further along the south shore, which inclines to the eastward from this point. These islands are numerous, and consist of granite, rising from one hundred to two hundred feet above the water. They are for the most part naked ; but towards the centres of the larger ones, there is a little soil, and a few groves of pines. At seven in the evening we landed upon one of them, and encamped. On the following morning we ran before a strong breeze and a heavy swell, for some hours, but at length were obliged to seek shelter on a large island adjoining to Isle à la Cache of Mackenzie.

The wind and swell having subsided in the afternoon, we re-embarked, and steered towards the western
point of the Big Island of Mackenzie, and when four
miles distant from it, had forty-two fathoms soundings.
Passing between this island and a promontory of the
main shore, termed Big Cape, we entered into a deep
bay, which receives the waters from several rivers that
come from the northward ; and we immediately perceived a decrease in the temperature of the water,
from 59° to 48°.   We coasted along the eastern side
of the day, its western shore being always visible, but
the canoes were exposed to the hazard of being broken
by the numerous sudden rocks, which were scattered
in our track.   We encamped for the night on a rocky
island, and by eight A. M. on the following morning,
arrived at Fort Providence, which is situated twenty-
one miles from the entrance of the bay.   The post is
exclusively occupied by the North-West Company,
the Hudson's Bay Company having no settlement to
the northward of Great Slave Lake.   We found Mr.
Wentzel and our interpreter Jean Baptiste Adam
here, with one of the Indian guides : but the chief of
the tribe and his hunters were encamped with their
families, some miles from the fort, in a good situation
for fishing.   Our arrival was announced to him by a
fire on the top of a hill, and before night a messenger
came to communicate his intention of seeing us next

morning. The customary present, of tobacco and some other articles, was immediately sent to him.

Mr. Wentzel prepared me for the first conference with the Indians, by mentioning all the information they had already given to him. The duties allotted to this gentleman were, the management of the Indians, the superintendence of the Canadian voyagers, the obtaining, and the general distribution, of the provision, and the issue of the other stores. These services he was well qualified to perform, having been accustomed to execute similar duties, during a residence of upwards of twenty years in this country. We also deemed Mr. Wentzel to be a great acquisition to our party, as a check upon the interpreters, he being one of the few traders who speak the Chipewyan language.

As we were informed that external appearances made lasting impressions upon the Indians, we prepared for the interview by decorating ourselves in uniform, and suspending a medal round each of our necks. Our tents had been previously pitched, and over one of them a silken union flag was hoisted. Soon after noon, on July 30th, several Indian canoes were seen advancing in a regular line, and on their approach, the chief was discovered in the headmost, which was paddled by two men. On landing at the fort, the chief assumed a very grave aspect, and walked up to

Mr. Wentzel with a measured and dignified step, looking neither to the right nor to the left, at the persons who had assembled on the beach to witness his debarkation, but preserving the same immovability of countenance until he reached the hall, and was introduced to the officers. When he had smoked his pipe, drank a small portion of spirits and water himself, and issued a glass to each of his companions, who had seated themselves on the floor, he commenced his harangue, by mentioning the circumstances that led to his agreeing to accompany the expedition, an engagement which he was quite prepared to fulfil. He was rejoiced, he said, to see such great chiefs on his lands, his tribe were poor, but they loved white men who had been their benefactors ; and he hoped that our visit would be productive of much good to them. The report which preceded our arrival, he said, had caused much grief to him. It was at first rumored that a great medicine chief accompanied us, who was able to restore the dead to life ; at this he rejoiced, the prospect of again seeing his departed relatives had enlivened his spirits, but his first communication with Mr. Wentzel had removed these vain hopes, and he felt as if his friends had a second time been torn from him. He now wished to be informed exactly of the nature of our expedition.

In reply to this speech, which I understood had

been prepared for many days, I endeavored to explain
the objects of our mission in a manner best calculated
to ensure his exertions in our service. With this view,
I told him that we were sent out by the greatest chief
in the world, who was the sovereign also of the trading companies in the country ; that he was the friend
of peace, and had the interest of every nation at heart.
Having learned that his children in the north, were
much in want of articles of merchandize, in consequence of the extreme length and difficulty of the
present route ; he had sent us to search for a passage
by the sea, which, if found, would enable large vessels
to transport great quantities of goods more easily to
their lands. That we had not come for the purpose of
traffic, but solely to make discoveries for their benefit,
as well as that of every other people. That we had
been directed to inquire into the nature of all the pro-
ductions of the countries we might pass through, and
particularly respecting their inhabitants. That we
desired the assistance of the Indians in guiding us,
and providing us with food ; finally, that we were
most positively enjoined by the great chief to recom-
mend that hostilities should cease throughout this
country ; and especially between the Indians and Esquimaux, whom he considered his children, in common with other natives ; and by way of enforcing
the latter point more strongly, I assured him that a

forfeiture of all the advantages which might be anticipated from the expedition would be a certain consequence, if any quarrel arose between his party and the
Esquimaux. I also communicated to him that owing
to the distance we had traveled, we had now few more
stores than were necessary for the use of our own
party, a part of these, however, should be forthwith
presented to him ; on his return, he and his party
should be remunerated with cloth, ammunition, tobacco, and some useful iron materials, besides having
their debts to the North-West Company discharged.

The chief, whose name is Akaitcho or Big-foot,
replied by a renewal of his assurances, that he and his
party would attend us to the end of our journey, and
that they would do their utmost to provide us with
the means of subsistence. He admitted that his tribe
made war upon the Esquimaux, but said they were
now desirous of peace, and unanimous in their opinion
as to the necessity of all who accompanied us abstaining from every act of enmity against that nation.
He added, however, that the Esquimaux were very
treacherous, and therefore recommended that we should
advance towards them with caution.

The communication which the chief and the guides
then gave respecting the route to the Copper-Mine
River, and its course to the sea, coincided in every
material point with the statements which were made

by Boileau and Black-meat at Chipewyan, but they differed in the descriptions of the coast. The information, however, collected from both sources was very vague and unsatisfactory. None of his tribe had been more than three days' march along the sea-coast to the eastward of the river's mouth.

As the water was unusually high this season, the Indian guides recommended our going by a shorter route to the Copper-Mine River than that they had first proposed to Mr. Wentzel, and they assigned as a reason for the change, that the rein-deer would be sooner found upon this tract. They then drew a chart of the proposed route on the floor with charcoal, exhibiting a chain of twenty-five small lakes extending towards the north, about one-half of them connected by a river which flows into Slave Lake, near Fort Providence. One of the guides, named Keskarrah, drew the Copper-Mine River, running through the Upper Lake in a westerly direction towards the Great Bear Lake, and then northerly to the sea. The other guide drew the river in a straight line to the sea from the above mentioned place, but after some dispute, admitted the correctness of the first delineation. The latter was elder brother to Akaitcho, and he said that he had accompanied Mr. Hearne on his journey, and though very young at the time, still remembered many of the circumstances, and particularly the mas-

sacre committed by the Indians on the Esquimaux.
They pointed out another lake to the southward of
the river, about three days' journey distant from it,
on which the chief proposed the next winter's establishment should be formed, as the rein-deer would pass
there in the autumn and spring.   Its waters contained fish, and there was a sufficiency of wood for
building as well as for the winter's consumption.
These were important considerations, and determined
me in pursuing the route they now proposed.   They
could not inform us what time we should take in
reaching the lake, until they saw our manner of
traveling in the large canoes, but they supposed we
might be about twenty days, in which case I entertained the hope that if we could then procure provision we should have time to descend the Copper-
Mine River for a considerable distance, if not to the
sea itself, and return to the lake before the winter
set in.

It may here be proper to mention that it had been
my original plan to descend the Mackenzie's River,
and to cross the Great Bear Lake, from the eastern
side of which, Boileau informed me, there is a communication with the Copper-Mine River by four small
lakes and portages; but, under our present circumstances, this course could not be followed, because it
would remove us too far from the establishments, at

the Great Slave Lake, to receive the supplies of ammunition and some other stores in the winter which were absolutely necessary for the prosecution of our journey, or to get the Esquimaux interpreter, whom we expected. If I had not deemed these circumstances paramount I should have preferred the route by Bear Lake.

Akaitcho and the guides having communicated all the information they possessed on the different points to which our questions had been directed, I placed my medal round the neck of the chief, and the officers presented theirs to an elder brother of his and the two guides, communicating to them that these marks of distinction were given as tokens of our friendship and as pledges of the sincerity of our professions. Being conferred in the presence of all the hunters, their acquisition was highly gratifying to them, but they studiously avoided any great expression of joy, because such an exposure would have been unbecoming the dignity which the senior Indians assume during a conference. They assured us, however, of their being duly sensible of these tokens of our regard, and that they should be preserved during their lives with the utmost care. The chief evinced much penetration and intelligence during the whole of this conversation, which gave us a favorable opinion of his intellectual powers. He made many inquiries respecting the

Discovery ships, under the command of Captain Parry, which had been mentioned to him, and asked why a passage had not been discovered long ago, if one existed. It may be stated that we gave a faithful explanation to all his inquiries, which policy would have prompted us to do if a love of truth had not ; for whenever these northern nations detect a falsehood in the dealings of the traders, they make it an unceasing subject of reproach, and their confidence is irrecoverably lost.

We presented to the chief, the two guides, and the seven hunters, who had engaged to accompany us, some cloth, blankets, tobacco, knives, daggers, besides other useful iron materials, and a gun to each ; also a keg of very weak spirits and water, which they kept until the evening, as they had to try their guns before dark, and make the necessary preparations for commencing the journey on the following day. The Indians, however, did not leave us on the next day, as the chief was desirous of being present, with his party, at the dance, which was given in the evening to our Canadian voyagers. They were highly entertained by the vivacity and agility displayed by our companions in their singing and dancing : and especially by their imitating the gestures of a Canadian, who placed himself in the most ludicrous postures ; and, whenever this was done, the gravity of the chief gave way to violent bursts of laughter. In return for the gratification Akaitcho had enjoyed, he desired his young men to exhibit the Dog-Rib Indian dance ; and immediately they ranged themselves in a circle, and keeping their legs widely separated, began to jump simultaneously sideways ; their bodies were bent, their hands placed on their hips, and they uttered forcibly the interjection *tsa* at each jump. Devoid as were their attitudes of grace, and their music of harmony, we were much amused by the novelty of the exhibition.

In the midst of this scene an untoward accident occurred, which for a time interrupted our amusements. The tent in which Dr. Richardson and I lodged having caught fire from some embers that had been placed in it to expel the musquitoes, was entirely burnt. Hepburn, who was sleeping within it, close to some powder, most providentially awoke in time to throw it clear of the flame, and rescue the baggage, before any material injury had been received. We dreaded the consequences of this disaster upon the fickle minds of the Indians, and wished it not to be communicated to them. The chief, however, was soon informed of it by one of his people, and expressed his desire that no future misfortune should be concealed from him. We found he was most concerned to hear that the flag had been burnt, but we removed his anxiety on that point by the assurance that it could easily be repaired. We

were advised by Mr. Wentzel to recommence the
dancing after this event, lest the Indians should imagine, by our putting a stop to it, that we considered
the circumstance as an unfavorable commencement of
our undertaking. We were, however, deeply impressed with a grateful sense of the Divine Providence, in
averting the threatened destruction of our stores,
which would have been fatal to every prospect of proceeding forward this season.

August 1.—This morning the Indians set out, intending to wait for us at the mouth of the Yellow-
Knife River.   We remained behind to pack our stores,
in bales of eighty pounds each, an operation which
could not be done in the presence of these Indians, as
they are in the habit of begging for every thing they
see.   Our stores consisted of two barrels of gunpow-
der, one hundred and forty pounds of ball and small
shot, four fowling pieces, a few old trading guns, eight
pistols, twenty-four Indian daggers, some packages of
knives, chisels, axes, nails, and fastenings for a boat ;
a few yards of cloth, some blankets, needles, looking-
glasses, and beads ; together with nine fishing nets,
having meshes of different sizes. ⸱ Our provision was
two casks of flour, two hundred dried reindeer tongues,
some dried moose meat, portable soup, and arrow-root,
sufficient in the whole for ten days' consumption, besides two cases of chocolate, and two canisters of tea.

We engaged another Canadian voyager at this place, and the expedition then consisted of twenty-eight persons, including the officers, and the wives of three of the voyagers, who were brought for the purpose of making shoes and clothes for the men at the winter establishment ; there were also three children, belonging to two of these women.*

* The following is the list of the officers and men who composed the expedition on its departure from Fort Providence :

John Franklin, Lieutenant of the Royal Navy and Commander.
John Richardson, M. D., Surgeon of the Royal Navy.
Mr. George Back, of the Royal Navy, Admiralty Midshipman.
Mr. Robert Hood, of the Royal Navy, Admiralty Midshipman.
Mr. Frederic Wentzel, Clerk to the North-West Company.
John Hepburn, English seaman.

CANADIAN VOYAGERS.

John Peltier,	Gabriel Beauparlant,
Mathew Pelonquin, dit Credit,	Vincenza Fontano,
Solomon Belanger,	Registe Vaillant,
Joseph Bennoit,	Jean Baptiste Parent,
Joseph Gagne,	Jean Baptiste Belanger,
Pierre Dumas,	Jean Baptiste Belleau,
Joseph Forcier,	Emanuel Cournoyee,
Ignace Perrault,	Michel Teroahaute an Troquois,
Francais Samandre.	

INTERPRETERS.

Pierre St. German,	Chipewyan Bois Brules,
Jean Baptiste Adam.	

Our observations place Fort Providence in latitude 62° 17' 19" N., longitude 114° 9' 28" W.; the variation of the compass is 33° 35' 55" E., and the dip of the needle 86° 38' 02". It is distant from Moose-Deer Island sixty-six geographic miles. This is the last establishment of the traders in this direction, but the North-West Company have two to the northward of it, on the Mackenzie River. It has been erected for the convenience of the Copper and Dog-rib Indians, who generally bring such a quantity of reindeer meat that the residents are enabled, out of their superabundance, to send annually some provision to the fort at Moose-Deer Island. They also occasionally procure moose and buffalo meat, but these animals are not numerous on this side of the lake. Few furs are collected. *Les poissons inconnus*, trout, pike, carp, and white fish, are very plentiful, and on these the residents principally subsist. Their great supply of fish is procured in the latter part of September and the beginning of October, but there are a few taken daily in the nets during the winter. The surrounding country consists almost entirely of coarse grained granite, frequently enclosing large masses of reddish felspar. These rocks form hills which attain an elevation of three hundred or four hundred feet, about a mile behind the house; their surface is generally naked, but in the valleys between them a few spruces, aspens, and birches grow, together with a variety of shrubs and berry-bearing plants.

On the afternoon of the 2d of August we commenced our journey, having, in addition to our three canoes, a smaller one to convey the women ; we were all in high spirits, being heartily glad that the time had at length arrived when our course was to be directed towards the Copper-Mine River, and through a line of country which had not been previously visited by any European. We proceeded to the northward, along the eastern side of a deep bay of the lake, passing through various channels, formed by an assemblage of rocky islands ; and, at sunset, encamped on a projecting point of the north main shore, eight miles from Fort Providence. To the westward of this arm, or bay, of the lake, there is another deep bay, that receives the waters of a river, which communicates with great Marten Lake, where the North-West Company had once a post established.

Aug. 3.—We embarked at three A. M. and proceeded to the entrance of the Yellow-Knife River of the traders, which is called by the Natives Beg-ho-lo-dessy ; or, River of the Toothless Fish. We found Akaitcho, and the hunters with their families, encamped here. There were also several other Indians of his tribe, who intended to accompany us some distance into the interior. This party was quickly in motion

after our arrival, and we were soon surrounded by a
fleet of seventeen Indian canoes. In company with
them we paddled up the river, which is one hundred
and fifty yards wide, and, in an hour, came to a cascade of five feet, where we were compelled to make a
portage of one hundred and fifty-eight yards. We
next crossed a dilatation of the river, about six miles
in length, upon which the name of Lake Prosperous
was bestowed. Its shores, though scantily supplied
with wood, are very picturesque.

Akaitcho caused himself to be paddled by his slave,
a young man, of the Dog-rib nation, whom he had
taken by force from his friends; when he thought himself, however, out of reach of our observation, he laid
aside a good deal of his state, and assisted in the labor; and after a few days' further acquaintance with
us, he did not hesitate to paddle in our presence, or
even carry his canoe on the portages. Several of the
canoes were managed by women, who proved to be
noisy companions, for they quarrelled frequently, and
the weakest was generally profuse in her lamentations,
which were not at all diminished, when the husband
attemped to settle the difference by a few blows with
his paddle.

Leaving the lake, we ascended a very strong rapid,
and arrived at a range of three steep cascades, situated in the bend of the river. Here we made a portage

of one thousand three hundred yards over a rocky hill, which received the name of the Bowstring Portage, from its shape. We found that the Indians had greatly the advantage of us in this operation ; the men carried their small canoes, the women and children the clothes and provisions, and at the end of the portage they were ready to embark ; whilst it was necessary for our people to return four times, before they could transport the weighty cargo with which we were burthened. After passing through another expansion of the river, and over the steep portage of one hundred and fifteen yards, we encamped on a small rocky isle, just large enough to hold our party, and the Indians took possession of an adjoining rock. We were now distant thirty miles from Fort Providence.

As soon as the tents were pitched, the officers and men were divided into watches for the night ; a precaution intended to be taken throughout the journey, not merely to prevent our being surprised by strangers, but also to show our companions that we were constantly on our guard. The chief, who suffered nothing to escape his observation, remarked, " that he should sleep without anxiety among the Esquimaux, for he perceived no enemy could surprise us."

After supper we retired to rest, but our sleep was soon interrupted by the Indians joining in loud lamentations over a sick child, whom they supposed to be dying.　Dr. Richardson, however, immediately went to the boy, and administered some medicine which relieved his pain, and put a stop to their mourning. The temperatures, this day, were at 4 A.M. 54°, three P.M. 72°, at seven P.M. 65°.

On the 4th we crossed a small lake, and passed over in succession the Blue Berry Cascade, and Double Fall Portages, where the river falls over ridges of rocks that completely obstruct the passage for canoes. We came to three strong rapids beyond these barriers, which were surmounted by the aid of the poles and lines, and then to a bend of the river in which the cascades were so frequent, that to avoid them we carried the canoes into a chain of small lakes. We entered them by a portage of nine hundred and fifty paces, and during the afternoon traversed three other grassy lakes, and encamped on the banks of the river, at the end of the Yellow-Knife Portage, of three hundred and fifty paces. This day's work was very laborious to our men. Akaitcho, however, had directed his party to assist them in carrying their burdens on the portages, which they did cheerfully. This morning Mr. Back caught several fish with a fly, a method of fishing entirely new to the Indians; and they were not more delighted than astonished at his skill and success. The extremes of temperature to-day were 54° and 65°

On August 5th, we continued the ascent of the river which varied much in breadth as did the current in
rapidity.   It flows between high rocky banks on which
there is sufficient soil to support pines, birch, and poplars.   Five portages were crossed, then the Rocky
Lake, and we finished our labors at the end of the
sixth portage.   The issue of dried meat for breakfast
this morning had exhausted all our stock ; and no
other provision remained but the portable soups, and
a few pounds of preserved meat.   At the recommen-
dation of Akaitcho, the hunters were furnished with
ammunition, and desired to go forward as speedily as
possible, to the part where the reindeer were expect-
to be found ; and to return to us with any provision
they could procure.   He also assured us that in our
advance towards them we should come to lakes abounding in fish.   Many of the Indians, being also in distress for food, decided on separating from us, and
going on at a quicker pace than we could travel.

Akaitcho himself was always furnished with a portion at our meals, as a token of regard which the traders have taught the chiefs to expect, and which we
willingly paid.

The next morning we crossed a small lake and a
portage, before we entered the river ; shortly afterwards, the canoes and cargoes were carried a mile along
its banks to avoid three very strong rapids, and over

another portage into a narrow lake ; we encamped on
an island in the middle of it, to set the nets ; but
they only yielded a few fish, and we had a very scanty
supper ; as it was necessary to deal out our provision
sparingly.

We had the mortification of finding the nets entirely empty next morning, an untoward circumstance
that discouraged our voyagers very much ; and they
complained of being unable to support the fatigue to
which they were daily exposed, on their present scanty
fare.   We had seen with regret that the portages were
more frequent as we advanced to the northward, and
feared that their strength would fail, if provision were
not soon obtained.   We embarked at six, proceeded
to the head of the lake, and crossed a portage of two
thousand five hundred paces, leading over ridges of
sand-hills, which nourished pines of a larger size than
we had lately seen.   This conducted us to Mossy
Lake, from whence we regained the river, after traversing another portage.   The Birch and Poplar Portages next followed, and beyond these we came to a part
where the river takes a great circuit, and its course is
interrupted by several heavy falls.   The guide, therefore, advised us to quit it, and proceed through a
chain of nine lakes extending to the north-east, which
we did, and encamped on Icy Portage, where the nets
were set.   The bottom of the valley, through which

the track across this portage led, was covered with ice four or five feet thick, the remains of a large iceberg, which is annually formed there, by the snow drifting into the valley, and becoming consolidated into ice by the overflowing of some springs that are warm enough to resist the winter's cold.

We were alarmed in the night by our fire communicating to the dry moss, which spreading by the force of a strong wind, encircled the encampment and threatened destruction to our canoes and baggage. The watch immediately aroused all the men, who quickly removed whatever could be injured to a distant part, and afterward succeeded in extinguishing the flame.

Aug. 8.—During this day we crossed five portages, passing over a very bad road. The men were quite exhausted with fatigue by five P.M., when we were obliged to encamp on the borders of the fifth lake, in which the fishing-nets were set. We began this evening to issue some portable soup and arrow-root, which our companions relished very much; but this food is too unsubstantial to support their vigor under their daily exhausting labor, and we could not furnish them with a sufficient quantity even of this to satisfy their desires. We commenced our labors on the next day in a very wet, uncomfortable state, as it had rained through the night until 4 A.M. The fifth

grassy lake was crossed, and four others, with their intervening portages, and we returned to the river by a
portage of one thousand four hundred and fifteen
paces. The width of the stream here is about one
hundred yards, its banks are moderately high, and
scantily covered with wood. We afterwards twice
carried the cargoes along its banks to avoid a very
stony rapid, and then crossed the first Carp portage,
and encamped on the borders of Lower Carp Lake.

The chief having told us that this was a good lake
for fishing, we determined on halting for a day or two
to recruit our men, of whom three were lame, and several others had swelled legs. The chief himself went
forward to look after the hunters, and he promised to
make a fire as a signal if they had killed any reindeer.
All the Indians had left us in the course of yesterday
and to-day to seek these animals, except the guide
Keskarrah.

Aug. 10.—The nets furnishing only four carp, we
embarked for the purpose of searching for a better spot,
and encamped again on the shores of the same lake.
The spirits of the men were much revived by seeing
some recent traces of reindeer at this place, which
circumstance caused them to cherish the hope of soon
getting a supply of meat from the hunters. They
were also gratified by finding abundance of blue berries near to the encampment, which made an agreeable

and substantial addition to their otherwise scanty fare. We were teased by the sand-flies this evening, although the thermometer did not rise above 45°. The country through which we have traveled for some days consists principally of granite, intermixed in some spots with mica slate, often passing into clay-slate. But the borders of Lower Carp Lake, where the gneiss formation prevails, are composed of hills, having less altitude, fewer precipices, and more rounded summits. The valleys are less fertile, containing a gravelly soil and fewer trees ; so that the country has throughout a more barren aspect.

Aug. 11.—Having caught sufficient trout, white fish, and carp, yesterday and this morning, to afford the party two hearty meals, and the men being recovered of their fatigue, we proceeded on our journey, crossed the Upper Carp Portage, and embarked on the lake of that name, where we had the gratification of paddling for ten miles. We put up at its termination to fish, by the advice of our guide. At this place we first perceived the north end of our dipping-needle to pass the perpendicular line when the instrument was faced to the west.

We had scarcely quitted the encampment next day before an Indian met us, with the agreeable communication, that the hunters had made several fires, which were certain indications of their having killed

reindeer.   This intelligence inspired our companions
with fresh energy, and they quickly traversed the next
portage, and paddled through the Reindeer Lake ;
at the north side of it we found the canoes of our
hunters, and learned from our guide that the Indians
usually leave their canoes here, as the water communication on their hunting grounds is bad.   The Yellow-Knife River has now dwindled into an insignificant
rivulet, and we could not trace it beyond the next
lake, except as a mere brook.   The latitude of its
source 64° 1' 30" N., longitude 113° 36' W., and its
length is one hundred and fifty-six statute miles.
Though this river is of· sufficient breadth and depth
for navigating in canoes, yet I conceive its course is
too much interrupted· by cascades and rapids. for its
ever being used as a channel for the conveyance ot
merchandize.   Whilst the crews were employed in
making a portage over the foot of Prospect Hill, we
ascended ·to the top of it, and as it is the highest
ground in the neighborhood, its summit, which is
about five hundred feet above the water, commands
an extensive view.

Akaitcho, who was here with his family, pointed
out to us the smoke of the distant fires which the
hunters had made.   The prospect from the hill is
agreeably diversified by an intermixture of hill and
valley, and the appearance of twelve lakes in different

directions. On the borders of these lakes a few thin pine groves occur, but the country in general is destitute of almost every vegetable, except a few berry-bearing shrubs and lichens, and has a very barren aspect. The hills are composed of gneiss, but their acclivities are covered with a coarse gravelly soil. There are many loose stones both on their summits and acclivities, composed of the same materials as solid rock.

We crossed another lake in the evening, encamped, and set the nets. The chief made a large fire to announce our situation to the hunters.

August 13.—We caught twenty fish this morning, but they were small, and furnished but a scanty breakfast for the party. Whilst this meal was preparing, our Canadian voyagers, who had been for some days past murmuring at their meagre diet, and striving to get the whole of our little provision to consume at once, broke out into open discontent, and several of them threatened they would not proceed forward unless more food was given to them. This conduct was the more unpardonable, as they saw we were rapidly approaching the fires of the hunters, and that provision might soon be expected. I therefore felt the duty incumbent on me, to address them in the strongest manner on the danger of insubordination, and to assure them of my determination to inflict the

heaviest punishment on any that should persist in
their refusal to go on, or in any other way attempt to
retard the Expedition.   I considered this decisive
step necessary, having learned from the gentlemen
most intimately acquainted with the character of the
Canadian voyagers, that they invariably try how far
they can impose upon every new master with whom
they may serve, and that they will continue to be
disobedient and intractable if they once gain any
ascendency over him.   I must admit, however, that
the present hardships of our companions were of a kind
which few could support without murmuring, and no
one could witness without feeling a sincere pity for
their sufferings.

After this discussion we went forward until sunset.
In the course of the day we crossed seven lakes and
as many portages.   Just as we had encamped, we
were delighted to see four of the hunters arrive, with
the flesh of two reindeer.   This seasonable supply,
though only sufficient for this evening's and the next
day's consumption, instantly revived the spirits of our
companions, and they immediately forgot all their
cares.   As we did not, after this period, experience
any deficiency of food during this journey, they worked
extremely well, and never again reflected upon us as
they had done before, for rashly bringing them into an
inhospitable country, where the means of subsistence
could not be procured.

Several blue fish, resembling the grayling, were caught in a stream which flows out of Hunter's Lake. It is remarkable for the largeness of its dorsal fins, and the beauty of its colors.

August 14.—Having crossed the Hunter's Portage, we entered the lake of the same name, but soon quitted it by desire of the Indian guide, and diverged more to the eastward, that we might get into the line upon which our hunters had gone. This was the only consideration that could have induced us to remove to a chain of small lakes, connected by long portages. We crossed three of these, and then were obliged to encamp to rest the men.

After starting we first crossed the Orkney Lake, then a portage which brought us to Sandy Lake, and here we missed one of our barrels of powder, which the steersman of the canoe then recollected had been left yesterday. He and two other men were sent back to search for it, in the small canoe. The rest of the party proceeded to the portage on the north side of the Grizzle-Bear Lake, where the hunters had made a deposit of meat, and there encamped to await their return, which happened at nine P. M. with the powder.

On August the 17th, having finished drying the meat, which had been retarded by the heavy showers of rain that fell in the morning, we embarked at one

P. M. and crossed two lakes and two portages. The
last of these was two thousand and sixty-six paces
long, and very rugged, so that the men were much
fatigued. On the next day we received the flesh of
four reindeer by the small canoe which had been sent
for it yesterday, and heard that the hunters had killed several more deer on our route. We saw many of
those animals as we passed along to-day; and our
companions, delighted with the prospect of having
food in abundance, now began to accompany their paddling with singing, which they had discontinued ever
since our provisions became scarce.

Aug. 19.—After crossing a portage of five hundred
and ninety-five paces, a small lake and another portage
of two thousand paces, which occupied the crews seven
hours, we embarked on a small stream, running towards the north-west, which carried us to the lake,
where Akaitcho proposed that we should pass the winter. The officers ascended several of the loftiest hills
in the course of the day, prompted by a natural
anxiety to examine the spot which was to be their
residence for many months. The prospect, however,
was not then the most agreeable, as the borders of
the lake seemed to be scantily furnished with wood,
and that of a kind too small for the purposes of
building.

We perceived the smoke of a distant fire which the

Indians supposed had been made by some of the Dog-ribbed tribe, who occasionally visit this part of the country.

Embarking at seven next morning, we paddled to the western extremity of the lake, and there found a small river, which flows out of it to the S.W. To avoid a strong rapid at its commencement, we made a portage, and then crossed to the north bank of the river, where the Indians recommended that the winter establishment should be erected, and we soon found that the situation they had chosen possessed all the advantages we could have desired. The trees were numerous, and of a far greater size than we had sup-posed them to be yesterday—some of the pines being thirty or forty feet high, and two feet in diameter at the root. We determined on placing the house on the summit of the bank, which commands a beautiful prospect of the surrounding country. The view in the front is bounded at the distance of three miles, by round-backed hills ; to the eastward and westward lie the Winter and round-rock Lakes, which are connect-ed by the Winter River, whose banks are well clothed with pines, and ornamented with a profusion of mos-ses, lichens, and shrubs.

In the afternoon we read divine service, and offered our thanksgiving to the Almighty for his goodness in having brought us thus far on our journey ; a duty which we never neglected, when stationary on the sabbath.

The united length of the portages we have crossed, since leaving Fort Providence, is twenty-one statute miles and a half; and as our men had to traverse each portage four times, with a load of one hundred and eighty pounds, and return three times light, they walked in the whole upwards of one hundred and fifty miles. The total length of our voyage from Chipewyan is five hundred and fifty three-miles.*

A fire was made on the south side of the river to inform the chief of our arrival, which spreading before a strong wind, caught the whole wood, and we were completely enveloped in a cloud of smoke for the three following days.

On the next morning our voyagers were divided into two parties, the one to cut the wood for the building of a store house, and the other to fetch the meat as fast as the hunters procured it. An interpreter was sent with Keskarrah, the guide, to search for the Indians who had made the fire seen on Saturday, from whom we might obtain some supplies of provision.

	Statute Miles.
* Stony and Slave Rivers - - - - -	260
Slave Lake - - - - - - - -	107
Yellow-Knife River - - - - - -	156.5
Barren country between the source of the Yellow-Knife River and Fort Enterprize - - -	29.5
	553

An Indian was also despatched to Akaitcho, with directions for him to come hither directly, and bring whatever provision he had, as we were desirous of proceeding, without delay, to the Copper-Mine River. In the evening our men brought in the carcasses of seven reindeer, which two hunters had shot yesterday, and the women commenced drying the meat for our journey. We also obtained a good supply of fish from our nets to-day.

A heavy rain, on the 23d, prevented the men from working, either at the building, or going for meat; but on the next day the weather was fine, and they renewed their labors. The thermometer, that day, did not rise higher than 42°, and it fell to 31° before midnight. On the morning of the 25th, we were surprised by some early symptoms of the approach of winter; the small pools were frozen over, and a flock of geese passed to the southward. In the afternoon, however, a fog came on, which afterwards changed into rain, and the ice quickly disappeared. We suffered great anxiety all the next day respecting John Hepburn, who had gone to hunt before sunrise on the 25th, and been absent ever since. About four hours after his departure the wind changed, and a dense fog obscured every mark by which his course to the tents could be directed, and we thought it probable he had been wandering in an opposite direction to our situation, as the two hunters, who had been sent out to look for him, returned at sunset without having seen him. Akaitcho arrived with his party, and we were greatly disappointed at finding they had stored up only fifteen reindeer for us. St. Germain informed us, that having heard of the death of the chief's brother-in-law, they had spent several days in bewailing his loss, instead of hunting. We learned also, that the decease of this man had caused another party of the tribe, who had been sent by Mr. Wentzel to prepare provision for us on the banks of the Copper-Mine River, to remove to the shores of the Great Bear Lake, distant from our proposed route. Mortifying as these circumstances were, they produced less painful sensations than we experienced in the evening, by the refusal of Akaitcho to accompany us in the proposed descent of the Copper Mine River. When Mr. Wentzel, by my direction, communicated to him my intention of proceeding at once on that service, he desired a conference with me upon the subject, which being immediately granted, he began by stating, that the very attempt would be rash and dangerous, as the weather was cold, the leaves were falling, some geese had passed to the southward, and the winter would shortly set in ; and that, as he considered the lives of all who went on such a journey would be forfeited, he neither would go himself, nor permit his hunters to accompany us. He said there was no wood within eleven days' march, during which time we could not have any fire, as the moss, which the Indians use in their summer excursions, would be too wet for burning, in consequence of the recent rains ; that we should be forty days in descending the Copper-Mine River, six of which would be expended in getting to its banks, and that we might be blocked up by the ice in the next moon ; and during the whole journey the party must experience great suffering for want of food, as the reindeer had already left the river.

He was now reminded that these statements were very different from the account he had given, both at Port Providence and on the route hither ; and that up to this moment, we had been encouraged by his conversation to expect that the party might descend the Copper-Mine River, accompanied by the Indians. He replied, that at the former place he had been unacquainted with our slow mode of traveling, and that the alteration, in his opinion, arose from the advance of winter.

We now informed him, that we were provided with instruments by which we could ascertain the state of the air and water, and that we did not imagine the winter to be so near as he supposed ; however, we promised to return on discovering the first change in the season. He was also told that all the

baggage being left behind, our canoes would now, of
course, travel infinitely more expeditiously than any
thing he had hitherto witnessed.   Akaitcho appeared
to feel hurt, that we should continue to press the
matter further, and answered with some warmth :
" Well, I have said everything I can urge, to dissuade
you from going on this service, on which it seems, you
wish to sacrifice your own lives, as well as the Indians
who might attend you : however, if after all I have
said, you are determined to go, some of my young men
shall join the party, because it shall not be said, that
we permitted you to die alone after having brought
you hither ; but from the moment they embark in the
canoes, I and my relatives shall lament them as dead."

We could only reply to this forcible appeal, by
assuring him and the Indians who were seated around
him, that we felt the most anxious solicitude for the
safety of every individual, and that it was far from
our intention to proceed without considering every
argument for and against the proposed journey.

We next informed him, that it would be very de-
sirable to see the river at any rate, that we might
give some positive information about its situation and
size, in our next letters to the great chief ; and that
we were very anxious to get on its banks for the purpose of observing an eclipse of the sun, which we
described to him, and said would happen in a few

days. He received this communication with more temper than the preceding, though he immediately assigned as a reason for his declining to go, that " the Indians must now procure a sufficient quantity of deer-skins for winter clothing for themselves, and dresses for the Canadians, who would need them if they had to travel in the winter." Finding him so averse to proceed, and feeling, at the same time, how essential his continuance with us was, not only to our future success, but even to our existence during the winter; I closed the conversation here, intending to propose to him next morning some modification of the plan, which might meet his approbation. Soon after we were gone, however, he informed Mr. Wentzel, with whom he was in the habit of speaking confidentially, that as his advice was neglected, his presence was useless, and he should, therefore, return to Fort Providence with his hunters, after he had collected some winter provision for us. Mr. Wentzel having reported this to me, the night was passed in great anxiety, and after weighing all the arguments that presented themselves to my mind, I came reluctantly to the determination of relinquishing the intention of going any distance down the river this season.

` The month of September commenced with very disagreeable weather. The temperature of the atmosphere ranged between 39° and 31° during the first three days, and that of the water in the river decreased from 49° to 44°.

In the afternoon of September the 6th, we removed our tent to the summit of a hill, about three miles distant, for the better observing the eclipse, which was calculated to occur on the next morning. We were prevented, however, from witnessing it by a heavy snow-storm, and the only observation we could then make was to examine whether the temperature of the atmosphere altered during the eclipse, but we found that both the mercurial and spirit thermometers remained steadily at 30° for a quarter of an hour previous to its commencement, during its continuance, and for half an hour subsequent to its termination ; we remarked the wind increased very much, and the snow fell in heavier flakes just after the estimated time of its commencement. This boisterous weather continued until three P.M., when the wind abated, and the snow changed to rain.

The men continued to work diligently at the house, and by the 30th of September had nearly completed it for our reception, when a heavy fall of rain washed the greater part of the mud off the roof. This rain was remarked by the Indians as unusual, after what they had deemed so decided a commencement of winter in the early part of the month. The mean temperature for the month was 33¾°, but the thermometer had sunk as low as 16°. and on one occasion risen to 53°.

CHAPTER VI.

ON the 6th of October, the house being completed, we struck our tents, and removed into it. It was merely a log building, fifty feet long, and twenty-four wide, divided into a hall, three bed-rooms, and a kitchen. The walls and roof were plastered with clay, the floors laid with planks rudely squared with the hatchet, and the windows closed with parchment of deerskin. The clay, which, from the coldness of the weather, required to be tempered before the fire with hot water, froze as it was daubed on, and afterwards cracked in such a manner as to admit the wind from every quarter ; yet, compared with the tents, our new habitation appeared comfortable ; and having filled our capacious clay-built chimney with fagots, we spent a cheerful evening before the invigorating blaze. The change was peculiarly beneficial to Dr. Richardson, who having, in one of his excursions, incautiously laid down on the frozen side of a hill when heated with walking, had caught a severe inflammatory sore throat, which became daily worse whilst we remained in the tents, but began to amend soon after he was enabled to confine himself to the more equable warmth of the house. We took up our abode at first on the floor, but our working party, who had shewn such skill as house-carpenters, soon proved themselves to be, with the same tools, the hatchet and crooked knife, excellent cabinet-makers, and daily added a table, a chair, or bedstead, to the comforts of our establishment.

On the 1st of December the sky was clear, a slight appearance of stratus only being visible near the horizon; but a kind of snow fell at intervals in the forenoon, its particles so minute as to be observed only in the sunshine. Towards noon the snow became more apparent, and the two limbs of a prismatic arch were visible, one on each side of the sun near its place in the heavens, the centre being deficient. We have frequently observed this descent of minute icy spiculæ when the sky appears perfectly clear, and could even perceive that its silent, but continued action, added to the snowy covering of the ground.

Having received one hundred balls from Fort Providence by Belanger, we distributed them among the Indians, informing the leader at the same time, that the residence of so large a party as his at the house, amounting, with women and children, to forty souls, was producing a serious reduction in our stock of provisions.

As it may be interesting to the reader to know how we passed our time at this season of the year, I shall mention briefly, that a considerable portion of it was occupied in writing up our journals. Some newspapers and magazines, that we had received from England with our letters, were read again and again, and commented upon, at our meals ; and we often exercised ourselves with conjecturing the changes that might take place in the world before we could hear from it again. The probability of our receiving letters, and the period of their arrival, were calculated to a nicety. We occasionally paid the woodmen a visit, or took a walk for a mile or two on the river.

In the evenings we joined the men in the hall, and took a part in their games, which generally continued to a late hour ; in short, we never found the time to hang heavy upon our hands ; and the peculiar occupations of each of the officers afforded them more employment than might at first be supposed. I re-calculated the observations made on our route ; Mr. Hood protracted the charts, and made those drawings of birds, plants, and fishes, which cannot appear in this work, but which have been the admiration of every one who has seen them. Each of the party sedulously and separately recorded their observations on the aurora, and Dr. Richardson contrived to obtain from under the snow specimens of most of the lichens in the neighborhood, and to make himself acquainted with the mineralogy of the surrounding country.

The Sabbath was always a day of rest with us; the woodmen were required to provide for the exigencies of that day on Saturday, and the party were dressed in their best attire. Divine service was regularly performed, and the Canadians attended, and behaved with great decorum, although they were all Roman Catholics, and but little acquainted with the language in which the prayers were read. I regretted much that we had not a French prayer-book, but the Lord's Prayer and Creed were always read to them in their own language.

Our diet consisted almost entirely of the reindeer meat, varied twice a week by fish, and occasionally by a little flour, but we had no vegetables of any description. On the Sunday mornings we drank a cup of chocolate, but our greatest luxury was tea (without sugar), of which we regularly partook twice a day. With reindeer's fat, and strips of cotton shirts, we formed candles; and Hepburn acquired considerable skill in the manufacture of soap, from wood-ashes, fat, and salt. The formation of soap was considered as rather a mysterious operation by our Canadians, and, in their hands, was always supposed to fail if a woman approached the kettle in which the ley was boiling. Such are our simple domestic details.

On the 30th, two hunters came from the leader, to convey ammunition to him, as soon as our men should bring it from Fort Providence.

The men, at this time, coated the walls of the house on the outside, with a thin mixture of clay and water, which formed a crust of ice, that, for some days, proved impervious to the air ; the dryness of the atmosphere, however, was such, that the ice in a short time evaporated, and gave admission to the wind as before.   It is a general custom at the forts to give this sort of coating to the walls at Christmas time. When it was gone we attempted to remedy its defect, by heaping up snow against the walls.

1821. Jan. 1. This morning our men collected, and greeted us with the customary salutation on the commencement of the New Year.   That they might enjoy a holiday, they had yesterday collected double the usual quantity of fire-wood, and we anxiously expected the arrival of the men from Fort Providence, with some additions to their comforts.   We were led the more readily to hope for their arrival before the evening, as we knew that every voyager uses his utmost endeavor to reach a post upon, or previous to, the *jour de l'an*, that he may partake of the wonted festivities.   It forms the theme of their conversation for months before and after the period of its arrival. On the present occasion we could only treat them with a little flour and fat; these were both considered as great luxuries, but still the feast was defective from the want of rum, although we promised them a little when it should arrive.

The early part of January proved mild, the thermometer rose to 20° above zero, and we were surprised by the appearance of a kind of damp fog approaching very nearly to rain. The Indians expressed their astonishment at this circumstance, and declared the present to be one of the warmest winters they had ever experienced. Some of them reported that it had actually rained in the woody parts of the country. In the latter part of the month, however, the thermometer again descended to — 49°, and the mean temperature for the month proved to be — 15.6°. Owing to the fogs that obscured the sky, the aurora was visible only upon eighteen nights in the month.

On the 15th seven of our men arrived from Fort Providence with two kegs of rum, one barrel of powder, sixty pounds of ball, two rolls of tobacco, and some clothing. They had been twenty-one days on their march from Slave Lake, and the labor they underwent was sufficiently evinced by their sledge-collars having worn out the shoulders of their coats. Their loads weighed from sixty to ninety pounds each, exclusive of their bedding and provisions, which at start-

ing must have been at least as much more. We were
much rejoiced at their arrival, and proceeded forthwith
to pierce the spirit cask, and issue to each of the
household the portion of rum which had been promised to them on the first day of the year. The spirits,
which were proof, were frozen, but after standing at
the fire for some time, they flowed out of the consis-
tency of honey. The temperature of the liquid, even
in this state, was so low as instantly to convert into
ice the moisture which condensed on the surface of the
dram-glass. The fingers also adhered to the glass,
and would, doubtless, have been speedily frozen had
they been kept in contact with it, yet each of the
voyagers swallowed his dram without experiencing the
slightest inconvenience, or complaining even of the
tooth-ach.

The temperature in February was considerably lower than in the preceding month, although not so low
as in December, the mean being — 25.3°. The greatest temperature was 1° above zero, and the lowest 51°
below.

On the 5th of March the people returned from Slave
Lake, bringing the remainder of our stores, consisting
of a cask of flour, thirty-six pounds of sugar, a roll of
tobacco, and forty pounds of tobacco. I received a
letter from Mr. Weeks, wherein he denied that he had
ever circulated any reports to our disadvantage ; and

stated that he had done every thing in his power to assist us, and even discouraged Akaitcho from leaving us, when he had sent him a message, saying, that he wished to do so, if he was sure of being well received at Fort Providence.

On the 29th Akaitcho arrived at the house, having been sent for to make some arrangements respecting the procuring of provision, and that we might learn from him what his sentiments were with regard to accompanying us on our future journey. Next morning we had a conference, which I commenced by shewing him the charts and drawings that were prepared to be sent to England, and explaining fully our future intentions. He appeared much pleased at this mark of attention, and, when his curiosity was satisfied, began his speech by saying, that " although a vast number of idle rumors had been floating about the barren grounds during the winter," yet he was convinced that the representations that had been made to him at Fort Providence regarding the purport of the Expedition were perfectly correct. I next pointed out to him the necessity of our proceeding with as little delay as possible during the short period of the year that was fit for our operations, and that to do so it was requisite we should have a large supply of provisions at starting.

On the 7th of May, Dr. Richardson returned from his excursion. He informed me that the reindeer were again advancing to the northward, but that the leader had been joined by several families of old people, and that the daily consumption of provision at the Indian tents was consequently great. This information excited some painful apprehensions of being very scantily provided when the period for our departure should arrive.

The weather in the beginning of May was fine and warm. On the 2d some patches of sandy ground near the house were cleared of snow. On the 7th the sides of the hills began to appear bare, and on the 8th a large house fly was seen. This interesting event spread cheerfulness through our residence and formed a topic of conversation for the rest of the day.

Dr. Richardson and Mr. Back having visited the country to the northward of the Slave Rock, and reported that they thought we might travel over it, I signified my intention of sending the first party off on Monday the 4th of June. I was anxious to get the Indians to move on before, but they lingered about the house, evidently with the intention of picking up such articles as we might deem unnecessary to take. When Akaitcho was made acquainted with my purpose of sending away a party of men, he came to inform me that he would appoint two hunters to accompany them, and at the same time requested that Dr. Richardson, or as he called him, the Medicine Chief, might be sent with his own band.

On the 7th the wind changing to the southward, dispersed the clouds which had obscured the sky for several days, and produced a change of temperature under which the snow rapidly disappeared. The thermometer rose to 73°, many flies came forth, musquitoes shewed themselves for the first time, and one swallow made its appearance. We were the more gratified with these indications of summer, that St. Germain was enabled to commence upon the repair of the canoes, and before night had completed the two which had received the least injury. Augustus killed two deer to-day.

On the 10th the dip of the magnetic needle being observed, shewed a decrease of 22' 44", since last autumn. The repairs of the third canoe were finished this evening.

The snow was now confined to the bases of the hills, and our Indian hunter told us the season was early. The operations of nature, however, seemed to us very tardy. We were eager to be gone, and dreaded the lapse of summer, before the Indians would allow it had begun.

On the 11th the geese and ducks had left the vicinity of Fort Enterprize, and proceeded to the northward. Some young ravens and whiskey-johns made their appearance at this time.

On the 12th, Winter-River was nearly cleared of

ice, and on the 13th the men returned, having left Dr. Richardson on the borders of Point Lake. Dr. Richardson informed me by letter that the snow was deeper in many parts near his encampment than it had been at any time last winter near Fort Enterprize, and that the ice on Point Lake had scarcely begun to decay. Although the voyagers were much fatigued on their arrival, and had eaten nothing for the last twenty-four hours, they were very cheerful, and expressed a desire to start with the remainder of the stores next morning.

CHAPTER VII.

1821. June 14. The trains for the canoes having been finished during the night, the party attached to them commenced their journey at ten this morning. Each canoe was dragged by four men assisted by two dogs. They took the route of Winter Lake, with the intention of following, although more circuitous, the watercourse as far as practicable, it being safer for the canoes than traveling over land. After their departure, the remaining stores, the instruments, and our small stock of dried meat, amounting only to eighty pounds, were distributed equally among Hepburn, three Canadians, and the two Esquimaux; with this party and two Indian hunters, we quitted Fort Enterprize, most sincerely rejoicing that the long-wished for day had arrived, when we were to proceed towards the final object of the Expedition.

We left in one of the rooms a box, containing a journal of the occurrences up to this date, the charts, and some drawings, which was to be conveyed to Fort

Chipewyan by Mr. Wentzel, on his return from the sea, and from thence to be sent to England. The room was blocked up, and, by the advice of Mr. Wentzel, a drawing representing a man holding a dagger in a threatening attitude, was affixed to the door, to deter any Indians from breaking it open. We directed our course towards the Dog-rib Rock, but as our companions were loaded with the weight of near one hundred and eighty pounds weight each, we of necessity proceeded at a slow pace. The day was extremely warm, and the musquitoes, whose attacks had hitherto been feeble, issued forth in swarms from the marshes, and were very tormenting. Having walked five miles we encamped near a small cluster of pines about two miles from the Dog-rib Rock. The canoe party had not been seen since they set out. Our hunters went forward to Marten Lake, intending to wait for us at a place where two deer were deposited. At nine P. M. the temperature of the air was 63°.

We resumed our march at an early hour, and crossed several lakes which lay in our course, as the ice enabled the men to drag their burdens on trains formed of sticks and deers' horns, with more ease than they could carry them on their backs. We were kept constantly wet by this operation, as the ice had broken near the shores of the lakes, but this incon-

venience was not regarded, as the day was unusually
warm ; the temperature at two P. M. being 82½°.
At Marten Lake we joined the canoe party, and encamped with them. We had the mortification of
learning from our hunters that the meat they had put
en cache here, had been destroyed by the wolverenes,
and we had in consequence, to furnish the supper
from our scanty stock of dried meat. The wind
changed from S.E. to N.E. in the evening, and the
weather became very cold, the thermometer being 43°
at nine P.M. The few dwarf birches we could collect
afforded fire insufficient to keep us warm, and we
retired under the covering of our blankets as soon as
the supper was despatched. The N.E. breeze rendered the night so extremely cold, that we procured
but little sleep, having neither fire nor shelter, for
though we carried our tents, we had been forced to
leave the tent poles which we could not now replace ;
we therefore gladly recommenced the journey at five
in the morning, and traveled through the remaining
part of the lake on the ice. Its surface being quite
smooth, the canoes were dragged along expeditiously
by the dogs, and the rest of the party had to walk
very quick to keep pace with them, which occasioned
them to get many heavy falls. By the time we had
reached the end of the lake, the wind had increased to
a perfect gale, and the atmosphere was so cold that

we could not proceed with the canoes further without the risk of breaking the bark and seriously injuring them, we therefore crossed Winter River in them, and put up on a ridge of sand hills in a well sheltered place. But as the stock of provision was scanty, we determined on proceeding as quick as possible, and leaving the canoe party under the charge of Mr. Wentzel. We parted from them in the afternoon, and first directed our course towards a range of hills, where we expected to find Antonio Fontano, who had separated from us in the morning. In crossing towards these hills I fell through the ice into the lake, with my bundle on my shoulders, but was soon extricated without receiving any injury; and Mr. Back, who left us to go in search of the straggler, met with a similar accident in the evening. We put up on a ridge of sand hills, where we found some pines, and made a large fire to apprise Mr. Back and Fontano of our situation. St. Germain having killed a deer in the afternoon, we received an acceptable supply of meat. The night was stormy and very cold.

At five next morning our men were sent in different directions after our absent companions, but as the weather was foggy, we despaired of finding them unless they should chance to hear the muskets our people were desired to fire. They returned, however, at ten, bringing intelligence of them. I went immediately

with Heburn to join Mr. Back, and directed Mr. Hood
to proceed with the Canadians, and halt with them at
a spot where the hunters had killed a deer. Though
Mr. Back was much fatigued, he set off with me immediately, and in the evening we rejoined our friends
on the borders of the Big Lake. The Indians informed us that Fontano only remained a few hours with
them, and then continued his journey. We had to
oppose a violent gale and frequent snow storms
through the day, which unseasonable weather caused
the temperature to descend below the freezing point
this evening. The situation of our encampment being
bleak, and our fuel stunted green willows, we passed
a very cold and uncomfortable night.

June 18.—Though the breeze was moderate this
morning, the atmosphere was piercingly keen. When
on the point of starting, we perceived Mr. Wentzel's
party coming, and awaited his arrival to learn whether
the canoes had received any injury during the severe
weather of yesterday. Finding that they had not, we
proceeded to get upon the ice on the lake, which could
not be effected without walking up to the waist in
water, for some distance from its borders. We had
not the command of our feet in this situation, and the
men fell often ; poor Junius broke through the ice
with his heavy burden on his back, but fortunately
was not hurt.

This lake is extensive, and large arms branch from its main course in different directions. At these parts we crossed the projecting points of land, and on each occasion had to wade as before, which so wearied every one, that we rejoiced when we reached its north side and encamped, though our resting-place was a bare rock. We had the happiness of finding Fontano at this place. The poor fellow had passed the three preceding days without tasting food, and was exhausted by anxiety and hunger. His sufferings were considered to have been a sufficient punishment for his imprudent conduct in separating from us, and we only admonished him to be more cautious in future.

Having received information that the hunters had killed a deer, we sent three men to fetch the meat, which was distributed between our party, and the canoe men who had been encamped near to us. The thermometer at three P.M. was 46°, and at nine 34°.

We commenced the following day by crossing a lake about four miles in length, and then passed over a succession of rugged hills for nearly-the same distance. The men being anxious to reach some pine trees, which they had seen on their former journey, walked a quick pace, though they were suffering from swelled legs and rheumatic pains ; we could not, however, attain the desired point, and therefore encamped on the declivity of a hill, which sheltered us from the

wind ; and used the reindeer moss for fuel, which afforded us more warmth than we expected.   We perceived several patches of snow yet remaining on the
surrounding hills.   The thermometer varied to-day
between 55° and 45°.

On the 20th of June we began our march by crossing a small lake, not without much risk, as the surface of the ice was covered with water to the depth of
two feet, and there were many holes into which we
slipped, in spite of our efforts to avoid them.   A few
of the men being fearful of attempting the traverse
with their heavy loads, walked round the eastern end
of the lake.   The parties met on the sandy ridge,
which separates the streams that fall into Winter
Lake from those that flow to the northward ; and here
we killed three deer.   Near the base of this ridge we
crossed a small but rapid stream, in which there is a
remarkable cascade of about fifty feet descent.   Some
Indians joined us here, and gave us information respecting the situation of Dr. Richardson's tent, which
our hunters considered was sufficient for our guidance,
and therefore proceeded as quickly as they could.
We marched a few miles farther in the evening, and
encamped among some pines ; but the comfort of a
good fire did not compensate for the torment we suffered from the host of musquitoes we found at this spot
The temperature was 52°.

We set off next morning at a very early hour. The men took the course of Point Lake, that they might use their sledges, but the officers pursued the nearest route by land to Dr. Richardson's tent, which we reached at eleven A. M. It was situated on the western side of an arm of the lake, and near to the part through which the Copper-Mine River runs. Our men arrived soon after us, and in the evening Mr. Wentzel and his party, with the canoes in excellent condition. They were much jaded by their fatiguing journey, and several were lame from swellings of the lower extremities. The ice on the lake was still six or seven feet thick, and there was no appearance of its decay except near the edges ; and as it was evident that, by remaining here until it should be removed, we might lose every prospect of success in our undertaking, I determined on dragging our stores along its surface, until we should come to a part of the river where we could embark ; and directions were given this evening for each man to prepare a train for the conveyance of his portion of the stores. I may remark here, as a proof of the strong effect of radiation from the earth in melting the ice, that the largest holes in the ice were always formed at the base of the high and steep cliffs, which abound on the borders of this lake.

We found Akaitcho and the hunters encamped here, but their families, and the rest of the tribe, had gone off two days before to the Beth-see-to, a large lake to the northward, where they intended passing the summer. Long-legs and Keskarrah had departed, to desire the Hook to collect as much meat as he could against our arrival at his lodge. We were extremely distressed to learn from Dr. Richardson, that Akaitcho and his party had expended all the ammunition they had received at Fort Enterprize, without having contributed any supply of provision. The Doctor had, however, through the assistance of two hunters he kept with him, prepared two hundred pounds of dried meat, which was now our sole dependence for the journey. On the following morning I represented to Akaitcho that we had been greatly disappointed by his conduct, which was so opposite to the promise of exertion he had made, on quitting Fort Enterprize. He offered many excuses, but finding they were not satisfactory, he admitted that the greater part of the ammunition had been given to those who accompanied the women to the Beth-see-to, and promised to behave better in future. I then told him, that I intended in future to give them ammunition only in proportion to the meat which was brought in, and that we should commence upon that plan, by supplying him with fifteen balls, and the hunters with ten each.

The number of our hunters was now reduced to five, as two of the most active declined going any further, their father, who thought himself dying, having solicited them to remain and close his eyes. These five were furnished with ammunition, and sent forward to hunt on the south border of the lake, with directions to place any meat they might procure near to the edge of the lake, and set up marks to guide us to the spots. Akaitcho, his brother, the guide, and three other men, remained to accompany us. We were much surprised to perceive an extraordinary difference in climate in so short an advance to the northward as fifty miles. The snow here was lying in large patches on the hills. The dwarf-birch and willows were only just beginning to open their buds, which had burst forth at Fort Enterprize many days previous to our departure. Vegetation seemed to be three weeks or a month later here than at that place. We had heavy showers of rain through the night of the 22d, which melted the snow, and visibly wasted the ice.

On the 23d, the men were busily employed in making their trains, and in pounding the meat for pemmican. The arrangements being completed, we purposed commencing our journey next morning, but the weather was too stormy to admit of our venturing upon the lake with the canoes. In the afternoon a heavy fall of snow took place, which was succeeded by sleet and rain. The north-east gale continued, but the thermometer rose to 39°.

June 25.—The wind having abated during the night, we prepared for starting at an early hour. The three canoes were mounted on sledges, and nine men were appointed to conduct them, having the assistance of two dogs to each canoe. The stores and provisions were distributed equally among the rest of our men, except a few small articles which the Indians carried. The provision consisted of only two bags of pemmican, two of pounded meat, five of suet, and two small bundles of dried provision, together with fresh meat sufficient for our supper at night. It was gratifying to witness the readiness with which the men prepared for and commenced the journey, which promised to be so very laborious, as each of them had to drag upwards of one hundred and eighty pounds on his sledge.

Our course led down the main channel of the lake, which varied in breadth from half a mile to three miles ; but we proceeded at a slow pace, as the snow which fell last night, and still lay on the lake, very much impeded the sledges. Many extensive arms branched off on the north side of this channel, and it was bounded on the south by a chain of lofty islands. The hills on both sides rose to the height of six hundred or seven hundred feet, and high steep cliffs are numerous. Clusters of pines were occasionally seen in the valleys. We put up, at eight P.M., in a spot

which afforded us but a few twigs for fuel. The party
was much fatigued, and several of the men were affected by an inflammation on the inside of the thigh,
attended with hardness and swelling. The distance
made to-day was six miles.

We started at ten next morning. The day was extremely hot, and the men were soon jaded; their lameness increased very much, and some not previously affected began to complain. The dogs too shewed
symptoms of great weakness, and one of them stretched himself obstinately on the ice, and was obliged to
be released from the harness. Under these circumstances we were compelled to encamp at an early hour,
having come only four miles. The sufferings of the
people in this early stage of our journey were truly
discouraging to them, and very distressing to us, whose
situation was comparatively easy. I, therefore, determined on leaving the third canoe, which had been
principally carried to provide against any accident
happening to the others. By this we gained three
men, to lighten the loads of those who were most
lame, and an additional dog for each of the other canoes. It was accordingly properly secured on a stage
erected for the purpose near the encampment. Dried
meat was issued for supper, but in the course of the
evening the Indians killed two deer, which were immediately sent for.

The channel of the lake through which we had passed to-day was bounded on both sides by islands of
considerable height, presenting bold and rugged
scenery. We were informed by our guide, that a large
body of the lake lies to the northward of a long island
which we passed.

Another deer was killed next morning, but as the
men breakfasted off it before they started, the additional weight was not materially felt. The burthens
of the men being considerably lightened by the arrangements of last evening, the party walked at the
rate of one mile and three-quarters an hour until the
afternoon, when our pace was slackened, as the surface of the ice was more rough, and our lame companions felt their sores very galling. At noon we
passed a deep bay on the south side, which is said to
receive a river. Throughout the day's march the
hills on each side of the lake bore a strong resemblance, in height and form, to those about Fort Enterprise. We encamped on the north main shore,
among some spruce trees, having walked eight miles
and a half. Three or four fish were caught with lines
through holes, which the water had worn in the ice.
We perceived a slight westerly current at those places.

It rained heavily during the night, and this was
succeeded by a dense fog on the morning of the 28th.
Being short of provisions we commenced our journey,

though the points of land were not discernible beyond
a short distance. The surface of the ice, being honey-
combed by the recent rains, presented innumerable
sharp points, which tore our shoes, and lacerated the
feet at every step. The poor dogs, too, marked their
path with their blood.

In the evening the atmosphere became clear, and,
at five P.M., we reached the rapid by which Point
Lake communicates with Red-Rock Lake. This rapid
is only one hundred yards wide, and we were much
disappointed at finding the Copper-Mine River such
an inconsiderable stream. The canoes descended the
rapid, but the cargoes were carried across the peninsula, and placed again on the sledges, as the next lake
was still frozen. We passed an extensive arm,
branching to the eastward, and encamped just below
it, on the western bank, among spruce pines, having
walked six miles of direct distance. The rolled stones
on the beach are principally red clay slate, hence its
Indian appellation, which we have retained.

We continued our journey at the usual hour next
morning. At noon the variation was observed to be
47° east. Our attention was afterwards directed to
some pine branches, scattered on the ice, which proved to be marks placed by our hunters, to guide us to
the spot where they had deposited the carcasses of two
small deer. This supply was very seasonable, and the

men cheerfully dragged the additional weight. Akait-cho, judging from the appearance of the meat, thought it had been placed here three days ago, and that the hunters were considerably in advance. We put up at six P.M., near the end of the lake, having come twelve miles and three-quarters, and found the channel open by which it is connected with the Rock-nest Lake. A river was pointed out, bearing south from our encamp-ment, which is said to rise near Great Marten Lake. Red-rock Lake is in general narrow, its shelving banks are well clothed with wood, and even the hills, which attain an elevation of four hundred or five hundred feet, are ornamented, half way up, with stunted pines.

On June 30, the men having gummed the canoes, embarked with their burdens to descend the river; but we accompanied the Indians about five miles across a neck of land, when we also embarked. The river was about two hundred yards wide, and its course being uninterrupted, we cherished a sanguine hope of now getting on more speedily, until we per-ceived that the waters of Rock-nest Lake were still bound by ice, and that recourse must again be had to the sledges. The ice was much decayed, and we were exposed to great risk of breaking through in making the traverse. In one part we had to cross an open channel in the canoes, and in another were compelled to quit the lake, and make a portage along the land. When the party had got upon the ice again, our guide evinced much uncertainty as to the route. He first directed us towards the west end of the lake ; but when we had nearly gained that point, he discovered a remarkable rock to the north-east, named by the Indians the Rock-nest, and then recollected that the River ran at its base. Our course was immediately changed to that direction, but the traverse we had then to make was more dangerous than the former one. The ice cracked under us at every step, and the party were obliged to separate themselves widely to prevent accidents. We landed at the first point we could approach, but having found an open channel close to the shore, we were obliged to ferry the goods across on pieces of ice. The fresh meat being expended, we had to make another inroad on our pounded meat, The evening was very warm, and the musquitoes numerous. A large fire was made to apprise the hunters of our advance. The scenery of Rock-nest Lake is picturesque, its shores are rather low, except at the Rock's-nest, and two or three eminences on the eastern side. The only wood is the pine, which is twenty or thirty feet high, and about one foot in diameter. Our distance to-day was six miles.

July 1.—Our guide directed us to proceed towards a deep bay on the north side of the lake, where he

supposed we should find the river. In consequence of
the bad state of the ice, we employed all the different
modes of traveling we had previously followed in attaining this place ; and, in crossing a point of land,
had the misfortune to lose one of the dogs, which set
off in pursuit of some reindeer. Arriving at the bay,
we only found a stream that fell into it from the
north-east, and looked in vain for the Copper-Mine
River. This circumstance confused the guide, and he
confessed that he was now doubtful of the proper
route ; we, therefore, halted, and despatched him,
with two men, to look for the river from the top of the
high hills near the Nest-rock. During this delay a
slight injury was repaired, which one of the canoes had
received. We were here amused by the interesting
spectacle of a wolf chasing two reindeer on the ice.
The pursuer being alarmed at the sight of our men,
gave up the chase when near to the hindmost, much to
our regret, for we were calculating upon the chance of
sharing in his capture.

At four P.M. our men returned, with the agreeable
information that they had seen the river flowing at the
base of the Rock-nest. The canoes and stores were
immediately placed on the ice, and dragged thither ;
we then embarked, but soon had to cut through a barrier of drift ice that blocked up the way. We afterwards descended two strong rapids, and encamped

near to the discharge of a small stream which flows from an adjoining lake. The Copper-Mine River, at this point, is about two hundred yards wide, and ten feet deep, and flows very rapidly over a rocky bottom. The scenery of its banks is picturesque, the hills shelve to the water-side, and are well covered with wood, and the surface of the rocks is richly ornamented with lichens. The Indians say that the same kind of country prevails as far as Mackenzie's River in this parallel ; but that the land to the eastward is perfectly barren. Akaitcho and one of the Indians killed two deer, which were immediately sent for. Two of the hunters arrived in the night, and we learned that their companions, instead of being in advance, as we supposed, were staying at the place where we first found the river open. They had only seen our fires last evening, and had sent to examine who we were. The circumstance of having passed them was very vexatious, as they had three deer *en cache* at their encampment. However, an Indian was sent to desire those who remained to join us, and bring the meat.

We embarked at nine A. M. on July 2nd, and descended a succession of strong rapids for three miles. We were carried along with extraordinary rapidity, shooting over large stones, upon which a single stroke would have been destructive to the canoes ; and we were also in danger of breaking them, from the want of the long poles which lie along their bottoms and equalize their cargoes, as they plunged very much, and on one occasion the first canoe was almost filled with the waves.   But there was no re-ceding after we had once launched into the stream, and our safety depended on the skill and dexterity of the bowmen and steersmen.   The banks of the river here are rocky, and the scenery beautiful ; con-sisting of gentle elevations and dales wooded to the edge of the stream, and flanked on both sides at the distance of three or four miles by a range of round-backed barren hills, upwards of six hundred feet high. At the foot of the rapids the high lands receded to a greater distance, and the river flowed with a more gentle current, in a wider channel, through a level and open country consisting of alluvial sand.   In one place the passage was blocked up by drift ice, still covered to some depth with snow.   A channel for the canoes was made for some way with the hatchets and poles ; but on reaching the more compact part we were under the necessity of transporting the canoes and cargoes across it ; an operation of much hazard, as the snow concealed the numerous holes which the water had made in the ice.   This expansion of the river being mistaken by the guide for a lake, which he spoke of as the last on our route to the sea, we supposed that we should have no more ice to cross, and therefore encamped after passing through it, for the purpose of fitting the canoes properly for the voyage, and to provide poles, which are not only necessary to strengthen them when placed in the bottom, but essentially requisite for the safe management of them in dangerous rapids. The guide began afterwards to doubt whether the lake he meant was not further on, and he was sent with two men to examine into the fact, who returned in the evening with the information of its being below us, but that there was an open channel through it. This day was very sultry, several plants appeared in flower.

The men were employed in repairing their canoes to a late hour, and commenced very early next morning, as we were desirous of availing ourselves of every part of this favorable weather for their operations. The hunters arrived in the course of the night. It appeared that the dog which escaped from us two days ago came into the vicinity of their encampment, howling piteously; seeing him without his harness, they came to the hasty conclusion that our whole party had perished in a rapid; and throwing away part of their baggage, and leaving the meat behind them, they set off with the utmost haste to join Longlegs. Our messenger met them in their flight, but too far advanced to admit of their returning for the meat.

Akaitcho scolded them heartily for their thoughtlessness in leaving the meat, which we so much wanted.
They expressed their regret, and being ashamed of
their panic, proposed to remedy the evil as much as
possible by going forward, without stopping until they
came to a favorable spot for hunting, which they expected to do about thirty or forty miles below our
present encampment. Akaitcho accompanied them,
but previous to setting off he renewed his charge that
we should be on our guard against the bears, which
was occasioned by the hunters having fired at one this
morning as they were descending a rapid in their
canoe. As their small canoes would only carry five
persons, two of the hunters had to walk in turns along
the banks.

In our rambles round the encampment, we witnessed
with pleasure the progress which the vegetation had
made within the few last warm days ; most of the
trees had put forth their leaves, and several flowers
ornamented the moss-covered ground ; many of the
smaller summer birds were observed in the woods, and
a variety of ducks, gulls, and plovers, were seen on the
banks of the river. The river is about three hundred
yards wide at this part, is deep and flows over a bed
of alluvial sand. We caught some trout of considerable size with our lines, and a few white fish in
the nets, which maintained us, with a little assistance

from the pemmican. The repair of our canoes was completed this evening. Previous to embarking I issued an order that no rapid should in future be descended until the bowmen had examined it, and decided upon its being safe to run. Wherever the least danger was to be apprehended, or the crew had to disembark for the purpose of lightening the canoe, the ammunition, guns and instruments, were always to be put out and carried along the bank ; that we might be provided with the means of subsisting ourselves, in case of any accident befalling the canoes.

At four in the morning of July 4th, we embarked and descended a succession of very agitated rapids, but took the precaution of landing the articles mentioned yesterday, wherever there appeared any hazard ; notwithstanding all our precautions the leading canoe struck with great force against a stone, and the bark was split, but this injury was easily repaired, and we regretted only the loss of time. At eleven we came to an expansion of the river where the current ran with less force, and an accumulation of drift ice had, in consequence, barred the channel ; which the canoes and cargoes were carried over. The ice in many places adhered to the banks, and projected in wide ledges several feet thick over the stream, which had hollowed them out beneath. On one occasion, as the people were embarking from one of these ledges, it suddenly gave way, and three men were precipitated into the water, but were rescued without further damage than a sound ducking, and the canoe fortunately (and narrowly) escaped being crushed. Perceiving one of the Indians sitting on the east bank of the river, we landed, and having learned from him that Akaitcho and the hunters had gone in pursuit of a herd of musk oxen, we encamped, having come twenty-four miles and a half.

In the afternoon they brought us the agreeable intelligence of their having killed eight cows, of which four were full grown. All the party were immediately despatched to bring in this seasonable supply. A young cow, irritated by the firing of the hunters, ran down to the river, and passed close to me when walking at a short distance from the tents. I fired and wounded it, when the animal instantly turned, and ran at me, but I avoided its fury by jumping aside and getting upon an elevated piece of ground. In the mean time some people came from the tents, and it took to flight.

The musk oxen, like the buffalo, herd together in bands, and generally frequent the barren grounds during the summer months, keeping near to the banks of the river, but retire to the woods in winter. They seem to be less watchful than most other wild animals, and when grazing are not difficult to approach, provided the hunters go against the wind ; when two or three men get so near a herd as to fire at them from different points, these animals, instead of separating or running away, huddle closer together, and several are generally killed ; but if the wound is not mortal they become enraged and dart in the most furious manner at the hunters, who must be very dexterous to evade them. They can defend themselves by their powerful horns against the wolves and bears, which, as the Indians say, they not unfrequently kill.

The musk oxen feed on the same substances with the reindeer, and the prints of the feet of these two animals are so much alike that it requires the eye of an experienced hunter to distinguish them. The largest of these animals killed by us did not exceed in weight three hundred pounds. The flesh has a musky, disagreeable flavor, particularly when the animal is lean, which unfortunately for us, was the case with all that were now killed by us.

During this day's march the river varied in breadth from one hundred to two hundred feet, and except in two open spaces, a very strong current marked a deep descent the whole way. It flows over a bed of gravel, of which also its immediate banks are composed. Near to our encampment it is bounded by cliffs of fine sand from one hundred to two hundred feet high. Sandy plains extend on a level with the summit of these cliffs, and at the distance of six or seven miles are terminated by ranges of hills eight hundred or one thousand feet high. The grass on these plains affords excellent pasturage for the musk oxen, and they generally abound here. The hunters added two more to our stock in the course of the night. As we had now more meat than the party could consume fresh, we delayed our voyage next day for the purpose of drying it. The hunters were supplied with more ammunition and sent forward ; but Akaitcho, his brother, and another Indian remained with us.

It may here be proper to mention, that the officers had treated Akaitcho more distantly since our departure from Point Lake, for the purpose of shewing him their opinion of his misconduct. The diligence in hunting, however, which he had evinced at this place, induced us to receive him more familiarly when he came to the tent this evening. During our conversation he endeavored to excite suspicions in our minds against the Hook, by saying, "I am aware that you consider me the worst man of my nation ; but I know the Hook to be a great rogue, and, I think, he will disappoint you."

On the morning of the 6th we embarked, and descended a series of rapids, having twice unloaded the canoes where the water was shallow. After passing the mouth of the Fairy Lake River the rapids ceased.

The main stream was then about three hundred yards wide, and generally deep, though, in one part, the channel was interrupted by several sandy banks, and low alluvial islands covered with willows. It flows between banks of sand thinly wooded, and as we advanced the barren hills approached the water's edge.

At ten we rejoined our hunters, who had killed a deer, and halted to breakfast. We sent them forward; one of them, who was walking along the shore afterwards, fired upon two brown bears, and wounded one of them, which instantly turned and pursued him. His companions in the canoes put ashore to' his assistance, but did not succeed in killing the bears, which fled upon the reinforcement coming up. During the delay thus occasioned we overtook them, and they continued with us during the rest of the day.

CHAPTER VIII.

On the 11th we traveled nine miles to the foot of
the Copper Mountains, the day being hot.   On the
12th passed on our way twelve miles.   In the evening
we had the gratification of meeting Junius, who was
hastening back to inform us that they had found four
Esquimaux tents at the fall which we recognized to be
the one described by Mr. Hearne.   The inmates were
asleep at the time of their arrival, but rose soon afterwards, and then Augustus presented himself, and had
some conversation across the river.   He told them the
white people had arrived, who would make them very
useful presents.   The information of our arrival seemed to alarm them very much, but as the noise of the
rapid prevented them from hearing distinctly, one of
them came nearer to him in his canoe, and received
the rest of the message.   He would not, however,
land on his side of the river, but returned to their
tents without receiving the present.   His language
differed in some respects from Augustus's, but they
understood each other tolerably well.   Augustus

trusting for a supply of provision to the Esquimaux, had neglected to carry any with him, and this was the main cause of Junius's return. We now encamped, having come fourteen miles. After a few hours' rest, Junius set off again to rejoin his companion, being accompanied by Hepburn, who was directed to remain about two miles above the fall, to arrest the canoes on their passage, lest we should too suddenly surprise the Esquimaux. About ten P.M. we were mortified by the appearance of the Indians with Mr. Wentzel, who had in vain endeavored to restrain them from following us. The only reason assigned by Akaitcho for this conduct was, that he wished a re-assurance of my promise to establish peace between his nation and the Esquimaux. I took this occasion of pointing out again the necessity of their remaining behind, until we had obtained the confidence and good will of their enemies. After supper Dr. Richardson ascended a lofty hill about three miles from the encampment, and obtained the first view of the sea ; it appeared to be covered with ice. A large promontory, which I named Cape Hearne, bore N.E., and its lofty mountains proved to be the blue land we had seen in the forenoon, and which had led us to believe the sea was still far distant. He saw the sun set a few minutes before midnight from the same elevated situation. It did not rise during the half hour he remained there, but before he reached the encampment its rays gilded the tops of the hills.

The night was warm and we were much annoyed by the musquitoes.

June 15.—We this morning experienced as much difficulty as before in prevailing upon the Indians to remain behind, and they did not consent to do so until I had assured them that they should lose the reward which had been promised, if they proceeded any farther, until we had prepared the Esquimaux to receive them.   We left a Canadian with them, and proceeded on our journey, not without apprehension that they would follow us, and derange our whole plan by their obstinacy·   Two of the officers and a party of the men walked on the shore, to lighten the canoes.   The river, in this part, flows between high sand-stone cliffs, reddish slate clay rocks, and shelving banks of white clay, and is full of shoals and dangerous rapids.   One of these was termed Escape Rapid, from both the canoes having narrowly escaped foundering in its high waves.   We had entered the rapid before we were aware, and the steepness of the cliffs preventing us from landing, we were indebted to the swiftness of our descent for our preservation.   Two waves made a complete breach over the canoes ; a third would in all probability have filled and overset them, which must have proved fatal to every one in them.   The powder

fortunately escaped the water, which was soon discharged when we reached the bottom of the rapid.
At noon we perceived Hepburn lying on the left bank
of the river, and we landed immediately to receive his
information. As he represented the water to be shoal
the whole way to the rapid, (below which the Esquimaux were,) the shore party were directed to continue
their march to a sandy bay at the head of the fall,
and there await the arrival of the canoes. The land
in the neighborhood of the rapid, is of the most singular form : large irregular sand hills bounding both
banks, apparently so unconnected that they resemble
icebergs ; the country around them consisting of high
round green hills. The river became wide in this part
and full of shoals, but we had no difficulty in finding
a channel through them. On regaining the shore
party, we regretted to find that some of the men had
incautiously appeared on the tops of the hills, just at
the time Augustus was conversing with one of the
Esquimaux, who had approached in his canoe, and
was almost persuaded to land. The unfortunate appearance of so many people at this instant, revived
his fears, and he crossed over to the eastern bank of
the river, and fled with the whole of his party. We
learned from Augustus that this party, consisting of
four men and as many women, had manifested a
friendly disposition. Two of the men were very tall.

The man who first came to speak to him, inquired the number of canoes that we had with us, expressed himself to be not displeased at our arrival, and desired him to caution us not to attempt running the rapid, but to make the portage on the west side of the river. Notwithstanding this appearance of confidence and satisfaction, it seems they did not consider their situation to be free from danger, as they retreated the first night to an island somewhat farther down the river, and in the morning they returned and threw down their lodges, as if to give notice to any of their nation that might arrive, that there was an enemy in the neighborhood. From seeing all their property strewed about, and ten of their dogs left, we entertained the hope that these poor people would return after their first alarm had subsided ; and therefore I determined on remaining until the next day, in the expectation of seeing them, as I considered the opening of an early communication to be a matter of the greatest importance in our state of absolute ignorance respecting the sea coast. The canoes and cargoes were carried across the portage, and we encamped on the north side of it. We sent Augustus and Junius across the river to look for the runaways, but their search was fruitless. They put a few pieces of iron and trinkets in their canoes, which were lying on the beach. We also sent some men to put up the stages of fish, and secure

them as much as possible from the attacks of the dogs.
Under the covering of their tents were observed some
stone kettles and hatchets, a few fish spears made of
copper, two small bits of iron, a quantity of skins,
and some dried salmon, which was covered with maggots, and half putrid. The entrails of the fish were
spread out to dry. A great many skins of small birds
were hung up to a stage, and even two mice were preserved in the same way. Thus it would appear that
the necessities of these poor people induce them to
preserve every article that can be possibly used as food.
Several human skulls, which bore the marks of violence, and many bones were strewed about the ground
near to the encampment, and as the spot exactly answers the description given by Mr. Hearne, of the
place where the Chipewyans who accompanied him
perpetrated the dreadful massacre on the Esquimaux,
we had no doubt of this being the place, notwithstanding the difference in its position as to latitude and
longitude given by him, and ascertained by our observation. We have, therefore, preserved the appellation of Bloody Fall, which he bestowed upon it.
This rapid is a sort of shelving cascade, about three
hundred yards in length, having a descent of from ten
to fifteen feet. It is bounded on each side by high
walls of red sand stone, upon which rests a series of
lofty green hills. On its north side, close to the east

bank, is the low rocky island which the Esquimaux
deserted.   We caught forty excellent fish of the salmon and white fish species in a single net below the
rapid.   We had not seen any trees during this day's
journey; our fuel consisted of small willows and
pieces of dried wood that were picked up near to the
encampment.   The ground is well clothed with grass,
and nourishes most of the shrubs and berry-bearing
plants that we have seen north of Fort Enterprize;
and the country altogether has a richer appearance
than the barren lands of the Copper Indians.   We
had a distinct view of the sea from the summit of a
hill behind the tents; it appeared choked with ice
and full of islands.

On the morning of the 16th three men were sent up
the river to search for dried wood to make floats for
the nets.   Adam, the interpreter, was also despatched
with a Canadian to inform Akaitcho of the flight of
the Esquimaux.   We were preparing to go down to
the sea in one of the canoes, leaving Mr. Back to await
the return of the men who were absent; but just as
the crew were putting the canoe in the water, Adam
arrived in the utmost consternation, and informed us
that a party of Esquimaux were pursuing the men
whom he had sent to collect floats.   The orders for
embarking were instantly countermanded, and we
went with a party of men to their rescue.   We soon

met our people returning at a slow pace, and learned
that they had come unawares upon the Esquimaux
party, which consisted of six men, with their women
and children, who were traveling towards the rapid
with a considerable number of dogs carrying their
baggage. The women hid themselves on the first
alarm, but the men advanced, and stopping at some
distance from our men, began to dance in a circle,
tossing up their hands in the air, and accompanying
their motions with much shouting, to signify, I conceive, their desire of peace. Our men saluted them
by pulling off their hats, and making bows, but
neither party was willing to approach the other; and,
at length, the Esquimaux retired to the hill, from
whence they had descended when first seen. We
proceeded in the hope of gaining an interview with
them, but lest our appearance in a body should alarm
them, we advanced in a long line, at the head of
which was Augustus. We were led to their baggage,
which they had deserted, by the howling of the dogs;
and on the summit of the hill we found, lying behind
a stone, an old man, who was too infirm to effect his
escape with the rest. He was much terrified when
Augustus advanced, and probably expected immediate
death; but that the fatal blow might not be unre-
venged, he seized his spear, and made a thrust with it
at his supposed enemy. Augustus, however, easily

repressed his feeble effort, and soon calmed his fears
by presenting him with some pieces of iron, and
assuring him of his friendly intentions. Dr. Richardson and I then joined them, and, after receiving our
presents, the old man was quite composed, and became communicative. His dialect differed from that
used by Augustus, but they understood each other
tolerably well.

It appeared that his party consisted of eight men
and their families, who were returning from a hunting
excursion with dried meat. After being told who we
were, he said, that he had heard of white people from
different parties of his nation which resided on the sea-
coast to the eastward ; and to our inquiries respecting
the provision and fuel we might expect to get on our
voyage, he informed us that the reindeer frequent the
coast during summer, the fish are plentiful at the
mouths of the rivers, the seals are abundant, but there
are no sea-horses nor whales, although he remembered one of the latter, which had been killed by some
distant tribe, having been driven on shore on his
part of the coast by a gale of wind ; that musk oxen
were to be found a little distance up the rivers, and
that we should find drift wood along the shore. He
had no knowledge of the coast to the eastward beyond
the next river, which he called Nappa-arktok-towock,
or Tree River. The old man, contrary to the Indian

practice, asked each of our names ; and, in reply to a similar question on our part, said his was Terregannœuck, or the White Fox ; and that his tribe denominated themselves Nagge-ook-tor-mœoot, or Deer Horn Esquimaux. They usually frequent the Bloody Fall during this and the following moons, for the purpose of salting salmon, and then retire to a river which flows into the sea, a short way to the westward, (since denominated Richardson's River,) and pass the winter in snow-houses.

After this conversation, Terregannœuck proposed going down to his baggage, and we then perceived he was too infirm to walk without the assistance of sticks. Augustus, therefore, offered him his arm, which he readily accepted, and, on reaching his store, he distributed pieces of dried meat to each person, which, though highly tainted, were immediately eaten ; this being an universal token among the Indians of peaceable intention.

We then informed him of our desire to procure as much meat as we possibly could, and he told us that he had a large quantity concealed in the neighborhood, which he would cause to be carried to us when his people returned.

I now communicated to him that we were accompanied by some Copper Indians, who were very desirous to make peace with his nation, and that they

had requested me to prevail upon the Esquimaux to
receive them in a friendly manner ; to which he replied, he should rejoice to see an end put to the hostility that existed between the nations, and, therefore,
would most gladly welcome our companions.   Having
despatched Adam to inform Akaitcho of this circumstance, we left Terragannœuck, in the hope that his
party would rejoin him ; but as we had doubts whether the young men would venture upon coming to
our tents, on the old man's bare representation, we
sent Augustus and Junius back in the evening, to remain with him until they came, that they might fully
detail to them our intentions.

The countenance of Terregannœuck was oval, with
a sufficiently prominent nose, and had nothing very
different from an European face, except in the small-
ness of his eyes, and, perhaps, in the narrowness of
his forehead.   His complexion was very fresh and red,
and he had a longer beard than I have hitherto seen
on any of the Aboriginal inhabitants of America.   It
was between two and three inches long, and perfectly
white.   His face was not tattoed.   His dress consisted
of a shirt, or jacket with a hood, wide breeches, reaching only to the knee, and tight leggins sewed to the
shoes, all of deers' skins.   The soles of the shoes were
made of seal-skin, and stuffed with feathers instead of
socks.   He was bent with age, but appeared about

five feet ten inches high. His hands and feet were small in proportion to his height. Whenever Terregannœuck received a present, he placed each article first on his right shoulder, then on his left ; and when he wished to express still higher satisfaction, he rubbed it over his head. He held hatchets, and other iron instruments, in the highest esteem. On seeing his countenance in a glass for the first time, he exclaimed, " I shall never kill deer more," and immediately put the mirror down. The tribe to which he belongs repair to the sea in spring, and kill seals ; as the season advances they hunt deer and musk oxen at some distance from the coast. Their weapon is the bow and arrow, and they get sufficiently near to the deer, either by crawling, or leading these animals by ranges of turf towards a spot where the archer can conceal himself. Their bows are formed of three pieces of fir, the centre piece alone bent, the other two lying in the same straight line with the bowstring ; the pieces are neatly tied together with sinew. Their canoes are similar to those we saw in Hudson's Straits, but smaller. They get fish constantly in the rivers, and in the sea as soon as the ice breaks up. This tribe does not make use of nets, but they are tolerably successful with the hook and line. Their cooking utensils are made of pot-stone, and they form very neat dishes of fir, the sides being made of thin deal bent into an oval form, secured at the ends by sewing, and fitted so nicely to the bottom as to be perfectly water tight. They have also large spoons made of the horns of the musk oxen.

Akaitcho and the Indians arrived at our tents in the evening, and we learned that they had seen the Esquimaux the day before, and endeavored, without success, to open a communication with them. They exhibited no hostile intention, but were afraid to come near. Akaitcho keeping out of their sight, followed them at a distance, expecting that ultimately finding themselves enclosed between our party and his, they would be compelled to come to a parley with one of us. Akaitcho had seen Terregannœuck soon after our departure ; he was much terrified at their approach, and thrust his spear at Akaitcho as he had done at Augustus ; but he was soon reconciled after the demonstrations of kindness the Indians made, in cutting off the buttons from their dress to present to him.

July 17.—We waited all this forenoon in momentary expectation of the return of Augustus and Junius, but as they did not appear at two P.M., I sent Mr. Hood, with a party of men, to inquire into the cause of their detention, and to bring the meat which Terregannœuck had promised us. He returned at midnight with the information, that none of the Esquimaux had yet ventured to come near Terregannœuck except his aged wife, who had concealed herself among the rocks at our first interview ; and she told him the rest of the party had gone to a river, a short distance to the westward, where there was another party of Esquimaux fishing. Augustus and Junius had erected the tent, and done every thing in their power to make the old man comfortable in their absence. Terregannœuck being unable to walk to the place where the meat was concealed, readily pointed the spot out to Mr. Hood, who went thither ; but after experiencing much difficulty in getting at the column of rock on which it was deposited, he found the meat too putrid for our use. The features of Terregannœuck's wife were remarkable for roundness and flatness ; her face was much tattoed, her dress differed little from the old man's.

In the afternoon a party of nine Esquimaux appeared on the east bank of the river, about a mile below our encampment, carrying their canoes and baggage on their backs ; but they turned and fled as soon as they perceived our tents. The appearance of so many different bands of Esquimaux terrified the Indians to such a degree, that they determined on leaving us the next day, lest they should be surrounded, and their retreat cut off. I endeavored, by the offer of any remuneration they would choose, to prevail upon one or two of the hunters to proceed, but in vain ; and

I had much difficulty even in obtaining their promise to wait at the Copper Mountains for Mr. Wentzel and the four men, whom I intended to discharge at the sea.

The fears which our interpreters, St. Germain and Adam, entertained respecting the voyage, were now greatly increased, and both of them came this evening to request their discharges, urging that their services could be no longer requisite, as the Indians were going from us. St. Germain even said that he had understood he was only engaged to accompany us as long as the Indians did, and persisted in this falsehood until his agreement to go with us throughout the voyage had been twice read to him. As these were the only two of the party on whose skill in hunting we could rely, I was unable to listen for a moment to their desire of quitting us, and lest they should leave us by stealth, their motions were strictly watched. This was not an unnecessary precaution, as I was informed that they had actually laid a plan for eloping ; but the rest of the men knowing that their own safety would have been compromised had they succeeded, kept a watchful eye over them. We knew that the dread of the Esquimaux would prevent these men from leaving us as soon as the Indians were at a distance, and we trusted to their becoming reconciled to the journey when once the novelty of a sea voyage had worn off.

July 18.—As the Indians persevered in their determination of setting out this morning, I reminded them through Mr. Wentzel and St. Germain, of the necessity of our having the deposit of provision made at Fort Enterprize, and received a renewed assurance of their attending to that point. They were also desired to put as much meat as they could *en cache* on the banks of the Copper-Mine River on their return. We then furnished them with as much ammunition as we could spare, and they took their departure, promising to wait three days for Mr. Wentzel at the Copper Mountains. We afterwards learned that their fears did not permit them to do so, and that Mr. Wentzel did not rejoin them until they were a day's march to the southward of the mountains.

We embarked at five A.M. and proceeded towards the sea, which is about nine mile distant from the Bloody Fall. After passing a few rapids, the river became wider, and more navigable for canoes, flowing between banks of alluvial sand. We encamped at ten on the western bank at its junction with the sea. The river is here about a mile wide, but very shallow, being barred nearly across by sand banks, which run out from the main land on each side to a low alluvial island that lies in the centre, and forms two channels; of these the westermost only is navigable even for canoes, the other being obstructed by a stony bar. The islands to seaward are high and numerous, and fill the horizon in many points of the compass ; the only open space, seen from an eminence near the encampment, being from N.bE. to N.E.bN. Towards the east the land was like a chain of islands, the ice surrounded the islands apparently in a compact body, leaving a channel between its edge and the main of about three miles. The water in this channel was of a clear green color, and decidedly salt. Mr. Hearne could have only tasted it at the mouth of the river, when he pronounced it to be merely brackish. A rise and fall of four inches in the water was observed. The shore is strewed with a considerable quantity of drift timber, which is principally of the wood of the *populus balsamifera,* but none of it of great size. We also picked up some decayed wood far out of the reach of the water. A few stunted willows were growing near the encampment. Some ducks, gulls, and partridges were seen to-day. As I had to make up despatches for England to be sent by Mr. Wentzel, the nets were set in the interim, and we were rejoiced to find that they produced a sufficiency of fish to supply the party. The fish caught were, the Copper-Mine River salmon, white fish, and two species of pleuronectes. We felt a considerable change of temperature on reaching the sea-coast, produced by the winds changing from the southward to the N.W. Our Canadian voyagers complained much of the cold, but they were amused with their first view of the sea, and particularly with the sight of the seals that were swimming about near the entrance of the river, but these sensations gave place to despondency before the evening had elapsed. They were terrified at the idea of a voyage through an icy sea in bark canoes. They speculated on the length of the journey, the roughness of the sea, the uncertainty of provisions, the exposure to cold where we could expect no fuel, and the prospect of having to traverse the barren grounds to get to some establishment. The two interpreters expressed their apprehensions with the least disguise, and again urgently applied to be discharged ; but only one of the Canadians made a similar request. Judging that the constant occupation of their time as soon as we were enabled to commence the voyage, would prevent them from conjuring up so many causes of fear, and that familiarity with the scenes on the coast, would in a short time enable them to give scope to their natural cheerfulness, the officers endeavored to ridicule their fears, and happily succeeded for the present. The manner in which our faithful Hepburn viewed the element that he had been so long accustomed to, contributed not a little to make them ashamed of their fears.

On the morning of the 19th, Dr. Richardson, accom-

panied by Augustus, paid another visit to Terregannœuck, to see if he could obtain any additional information respecting the country to the eastward ; but
he was disappointed at finding that his affrighted family had not yet rejoined him, and the old man could
add nothing to his former communication.   The Doctor remarked that Terregannœuck had a great dislike
to mentioning the name of the Copper-Mine River,
and that he evaded the question with much dexterity
as often as it was put to him ; but that he willingly
told the name of a river to the eastward, and also of
his tribe.   He attempted to persuade Augustus to remain with him, and offered him one of his daughters
for a wife.   These Esquimaux strike fire with two
stones, catching the sparks in the down of the catkins
of a willow.

The despatches being finished were delivered this
evening to Mr. Wentzel, who parted from us at eight
P. M. with Parent, Gagnier, Dumas, and Forcier,
Canadians, whom I had discharged for the purpose of
reducing our expenditure of provisions as much as
possible.   The remainder of the party, including
officers, amounted to twenty persons.   I made Mr.
Wentzel acquainted with the probable course of our
future proceedings, and mentioned to him that if we
were far distant from this river, when the season or
other circumstances rendered it necessary to put a stop

to our advance, we should, in all probability, be unable to return to it, and should have to travel across the barren grounds towards some established post; in which case I told him that we should certainly go first to Fort Enterprize, expecting that he would cause the Indians to place a supply of dried provision there, as soon as possible after their arrival in its vicinity. My instructions to him were, that he should proceed to Point Lake, transport the canoe that was left there to Fort Enterprize, where he was to embark the instruments and books, and carry them to Slave Lake, and to forward the box containing the journals, &c., with the present despatches by the next winter packet to England. But before he quitted Fort Enterprize, he was to be assured of the intention of the Indians to lay up the provision we required, and if they should be in want of ammunition for that purpose, to procure it if possible from Fort Providence, or the other forts in Slave Lake, and send it immediately to them by the hunters who accompanied him thither. I also requested him to ascertain from Akaitcho and the other leading Indians, where their different parties would be hunting in the months of September and October, and to leave this information in a letter at Fort Enterprize, for our guidance in finding them, as we should require their assistance. Mr. Wentzel was furnished with a list of the stores that had been promised to Akaitcho and his party as a remuneration for their services, as well as with an official request to the North-West Company that these goods might be paid to them on their next visit to Fort Providence, which they expected to make in the latter part of November.   I desired him to mention this circumstance to the Indians as an encouragement to their exertion in our behalf, and to promise them an additional reward for the supply of provision they should collect at Fort Enterprize.

If Mr. Wentzel met the Hook, or any of his party, he was instructed to assure them that he was provided with the necessary documents to get them payment for any meat they should put *en cache* for our use ; and to acquaint them, that we fully relied on their fulfilling every part of the agreement they had made with us.   Whenever the Indians, whom he was to join at the Copper Mountains, killed any animals on their way to Fort Enterprize, he was requested to put *en cache* whatever meat could be spared, placing conspicuous marks to guide us to them ; and I particularly begged he would employ them in hunting in our service, immediately after his arrival at the house.

When Mr. Wentzel's party had been supplied with ammunition, our remaining stock consisted of one thousand balls, and a little more than the requisite

proportion of powder. A bag of small shot was missing, and we afterwards discovered that the Canadians
had secreted and distributed it among themselves, in
order that when provision should become scarce, they
might privately procure ducks and geese, and avoid
the necessity of sharing them with the officers.

CHAPTER IX.

^{1821.} _{July 21.} We intended to have embarked early this morning, and to have launched upon an element, which was more congenial with our habits than the fresh-water navigations, and their numerous difficulties and impediments we had hitherto encountered, but which was altogether new to our Canadian voyagers. We were detained, however, by a strong north-east gale, which continued the whole day, with constant thunder showers; the more provoking as our nets procured but few fish, and we had to draw upon our store of dried meat; which, with other provision for the journey, amounted only to fifteen days' consumption. Indeed, we should have preferred going dinnerless to bed rather than encroach on our small stock, had we not been desirous of satisfying the appetites, and cheering the spirits of our Canadian companions at the commencement of our voyage. These thoughtless people would, at any time, incur the hazard of absolute starvation, at a future period, for the present gratification of their appetites; to indulge which they

do not hesitate, as we more than once experienced, helping themselves secretly ; it being, in their opinion, no disgrace to be caught in the act of pilfering food.

Our only luxury now was a little salt, which had long been our substitute both for bread and vegetables. Since our departure from Point Lake we had boiled the Indian tea plant, *ledum palustre,* which produced a beverage in smell much resembling rhubarb ; notwithstanding which we found it refreshing, and were gratified to see this plant flourishing abundantly, though of dwarfish growth, on the sea-shore.

July 21.—The wind, which had blown strong through the night, became moderate in the morning, but a dense fog prevented us from embarking until noon, when we commenced our voyage on the Hyperborean Sea. Soon afterwards we landed on an island where the Esquimaux had erected a stage of drift timber, and stored up many of their fishing implements and winter sledges, together with a great many dressed seal, musk ox, and deer skins. Their spears headed with bone, and many small articles of the same material, were worked with extreme neatness, as well as their wooden dishes, and cooking utensils of stone ; and several articles very elegantly formed of bone, were evidently intended for some game, but Augustus was unacquainted with their use. We took from this deposit four seal-skins to repair our shoes,

and left in exchange a copper-kettle, and some awls
and beads.

We paddled all day along the coast to the eastward, on the inside of a crowded range of islands, and
saw very little ice; the "blink" of it, however, was
visible to the northward, and one small iceberg was
seen at a distance. A tide was distinguishable among
the islands by the foam floating on the water, but we
could not ascertain its direction. In the afternoon
St. Germain killed, on an island, a fat deer, which
was a great acquisition to us; it was the first we had
seen for some months in good condition.

Having encamped on the main shore, after a run of
thirty-seven miles, we set up a pole to ascertain the
rise and fall of the water, which was repeated at every
halting-place, and Hepburn was ordered to attend to
the result. We found the coast well covered with
vegetation, of moderate height, even in its outline,
and easy of approach. The islands are rocky and barren, presenting high cliffs of a columnar structure. I
have named the westernmost group of those we passed "Berens' Isles," in honor of the Governor of the
Hudson's Bay Company; and the easternmost, "Sir
Graham Moore's Islands." At the spot where we
landed, some muscle-shells and a single piece of sea-
weed lay on the beach; this was the only spot on
the coast where we saw shells. We were rejoiced to

find the beach strewed with abundance of small drift-wood, none of it recent.

It may be remarked that the Copper-Mine River does not bring down any drift-wood; nor does any other known stream, except Mackenzie's River; hence, from its appearance on this part of the coast, an easterly current may be inferred. This evening we were all in high glee at the progress we had made; the disappearance of the ice, and the continuance of the land in an eastern direction, and our future prospects formed an enlivening subject of conversation. The thermometer varied during the day between 43° and 45°. The fishing nets were set, but produced nothing.

On the 22d we embarked at four A.M., and having the benefit of a light breeze continued our voyage along the coast, under sail, until eleven, when we halted to breakfast, and to obtain the latitude. The coast up to this point presented the same general appearance as yesterday, namely, a gravelly or sandy beach, skirted by green plains; but as we proceeded, the shore became exceedingly rocky and sterile; and, at last, projecting considerably to the northward, it formed a high and steep promontory. Some ice had drifted down upon this cape, which we feared might check our progress; but, as the evening was fine, we ventured upon pushing the canoes through the small channels formed among it. After pursuing this kind of navigation, with some danger and more anxiety, we landed and encamped on a smooth rocky point; from whence we perceived, with much satisfaction, that the ice consisted only of detached pieces, which would be removed by the first breeze. We sounded in seventeen fathoms, close to the shore, this day. The least depth ascertained by the lead, since our departure from the river, was six fathoms; and it may be remarked, that any ship might pass safely between the islands and the main. The water is of a light green color, but not very clear; and it is much less salt than that of the Atlantic, judging from our recollection of its taste. In the course of the day we saw geese and ducks with their young, and two deer; and experienced very great variations of temperature, from the light breezes blowing alternately from the ice and the land. The name of " Lawford's Islands" was bestowed on a group we passed in the course of the day, as a mark of my respect for Vice-Admiral Lawford, under whose auspices I first entered the naval service.

A fresh breeze blowing through the night had driven the ice from the land, and opened a channel of a mile in width; we therefore embarked at nine A.M. to pursue our journey along the coast, but at the distance of nine miles were obliged to seek shelter in Port Epworth, the wind having become adverse, and too strong to admit of our proceeding. The Tree

River of the Esquimaux, which discharges its waters
into this bay, appears to be narrow, and much interrupted by rapids.   The fishing-nets were set, but they
obtained only one white fish and a few bull-heads.
This part of the coast is the most sterile and inhospitable that can be imagined.   One trap cliff succeeds
another with a tiresome uniformity, and their debris
cover the narrow valleys that intervene, to the exclu-
sion of every kind of herbage.   From the summit of
these cliffs the ice appeared in every direction.

The wind abating, at eight P.M. we re-embarked,
and soon afterwards discovered, on an island, a reindeer, which the interpreters fortunately killed.   Resuming our voyage we were much impeded by the ice,
and, at length, being unable to force a passage through
a close stream that had collected round a cape, we
put ashore at four A.M.   On the 24th, several stone
fox-traps, and other traces of the Esquimaux, were
seen near to the encampment.   The horizontal refrac-
tion varied so much this morning, that the upper
limb of the sun twice appeared at the horizon before
it finally rose.

For the last two days the water rose and fell about
nine inches.   The tides, however, seemed to be very
irregular, and we could not determine the direction of
the ebb or flood.   A current setting to the eastward
was running about two miles an hour during our stay.

The ice having removed a short distance from the shore, by eleven A.M. we embarked, and with some difficulty effected a passage ; then making a traverse across Gray's Bay, we paddled up under the eastern shore against a strong wind. The interpreters landed here, and went in pursuit of a deer, but had no success. This part of the coast is indented by deep bays, which are separated by peninsulas formed like wedges, sloping many miles into the sea, and joined by low land to the main ; so that often mistaking them for islands, we were led by a circuitous route round the bays. Cliffs were numerous on the islands, which were all of the trap formation.

At seven, a thunder-storm coming on, we encamped at the mouth of a river about eighty yards wide, and set four nets. This stream, which has received the name of Wentzel, after our late companion, discharges a considerable body of water. Its banks are sandy and clothed with herbage. The Esquimaux had recently piled up some drift timber here. A few ducks, ravens, and snow birds, were seen to-day. The distance we made was thirty-one miles.

July 25.—We had constant rain with thunder during the night. The nets furnished only three salmon-trout. We attributed the want of greater success to the entrance of some seals into the mouth of the river. Embarking at six A.M., we paddled against a cold breeze, until the spreading of a thick fog caused us to land. The rocks here consisted of a beautiful mixture of red and gray granite, traversed from north to south by veins of red felspar, which were crossed in various directions by smaller veins filled with the same substance.

At noon the wind coming from a favorable quarter tempted us to proceed, although the fog was unabated. We kept as close as we could to the main shore, but having to cross some bays, it became a matter of doubt whether we had not left the main, and were running along an island. Just as we were endeavoring to double a bold cape, the fog partially cleared away, and allowed us an imperfect view of a chain of islands on the outside, and of much heavy ice which was pressing down upon us. The shore near us was so steep and rugged that no landing of the cargoes could be effected, and we were preserved only by some men jumping on the rocks, and thrusting the ice off with poles. There was no alternative but to continue along this dreary shore, seeking a channel between the different masses of ice which had accumulated at the various points. In this operation both the canoes were in imminent danger of being crushed by the ice, which was now tossed about by the waves that the gale had excited. We effected a passage, however, and keeping close to the shore, landed at the entrance

of Detention Harbor at nine P. M., having come
twenty-eight miles.   An old Esquimaux encampment
was traced on this spot ; and an ice chisel, a copper
knife, and a small iron knife were found under the
turf.   I have named this cape after Mr. Barrow of the
Admiralty, to whose exertions are mainly owing the
discoveries that have recently been made in Arctic
geography.   An opening on its eastern side has received the appellation of Inman Harbor, after my
friend the Professor at the Royal Naval College,
Portsmouth ; and to a group of islands to seaward of
it, we gave the name of Jameson, in honor of the distinguished Professor of Mineralogy at Edinburgh.

We had much wind and rain during the night, and
by the morning of the 26th a great deal of ice had
drifted into the inlet.   We embarked at four and attempted to force a passage, when the first canoe got
enclosed, and remained for some time in a very perilous situation ; the pieces of ice, crowded together by
the action of the current and wind, pressing strongly
against its feeble sides.   A partial opening, however,
occurring, we landed without having sustained any
serious injury.   Two men were then sent round the
bay, and it was ascertained that instead of having
entered a narrow passage between an island and the
main, we were at the mouth of a harbor, having an
island at its entrance ; and that it was necessary to

return by the way we came, and get round a point to the northward. This was, however, impracticable, the channel being blocked up by drift ice; and we had no prospect of release except by a change of wind. This detention was extremely vexatious, as we were losing the benefit of a fair wind, and expending our stock of provision. In the afternoon the weather cleared up, and several men went hunting, but they were unsuccessful. During the day the ice floated backwards and forwards in the harbor, moved by currents, not regular enough to deserve the name of tide, and which appeared to be governed by the wind. We perceived great diminution by melting in the pieces near us. That none of this ice survives the summer is evident, from the rapidity of its decay; and because no ice of last year's formation was hanging on the rocks. Whether any body of it exists at a distance from the shore, we cannot determine.

The land around Cape Barrow, and to Detention Harbor, consists of steep craggy mountains of granite rising so abruptly from the water's edge, as to admit of few landing places even for a canoe. The higher parts attain an elevation of one thousand four hundred or one thousand five hundred feet; and the whole is entirely destitute of vegetation.

On the morning of the 27th the ice remained stationary at the entrance; we went to the bottom of the harbor, and carried the canoes and cargoes about a mile and a half across the point of land that forms the east side of it; but the ice was not more favorable there for our advancement than at the place we had left. It consisted of small pieces closely packed together by the wind extending along the shore, but leaving a clear passage beyond the chain of islands with which the whole of this coast is girt. Indeed, when we started we had little hope of finding a passage; and the principal object in moving was, to employ the men, in order to prevent their reflecting upon and discussing the dangers of our situation, which we knew they were too apt to do when leisuré permitted. Our observations place the entrance of Detention Harbor in latitude 67° 53' 45", longitude 110° 41' 20" W., variation 40° 49' 34" E. It is a secure anchorage, being sheltered from the wind in every direction; the bottom is sandy.

July 28.—As the ice continued in the same state, several of the men were sent out to hunt; and one of them fired no less than four times at deer, but unfortunately without success. It was satisfactory, however, to ascertain that the country was not destitute of animals. We had the mortification to discover that two of the bags of pemmican, which was our principal reliance, had become mouldy by wet. Our beef, too, had been so badly cured, as to be scarcely eatable ; this was occasioned by our having been compelled, through haste, to dry it by fire instead of the sun. It was not, however, the quality of our provision that gave us uneasiness, but its diminution, and the utter incapacity to obtain any addition. Seals were the only animals that met our view at this place, and these we could never approach.

Dr. Richardson discovered near the beach a small vein of galena, traversing gneiss rocks, and the people collected a quantity of it in the hope of adding to our stock of balls ; but their endeavors to smelt it, were, as may be supposed, ineffectual. The drift timber on this part of the coast consists of pine and tacca mahac, (*populus balsamifera*) most probably from Macken-zie's, or some other river to the eastward of the Cop-per-Mine. It all appears to have lain long in the water, the bark being completely worn off, and the ends of the pieces rubbed perfectly smooth. There was a sharp frost last night, which formed a pretty thick crust of ice in a kettle of water that stood in the tents ; and for several nights past thin films of ice have been formed on the salt water amongst the cakes of stream ice.* Notwithstanding this state of tem-perature, we were tormented by swarms of musqui-toes ; we had persuaded ourselves that these pests could not sustain the cold in the vicinity of the sea,

* This is termed *bay ice* by the Greenland-men.

but it appears they haunt every part of this country in defiance of climate. Mr. Back made an excursion to a hill at seven or eight miles distance, and from its summit he perceived the ice close to the shore as far as his view extended.

On the morning of the 29th the party attended divine service. About noon the ice appearing less compact, we embarked to change our situation, having consumed all the fuel within our reach. The wind came off the land just as the canoes had started, and we determined on attempting to force a passage along the shore ; in which we fortunately succeeded, after seven hours' labor and much hazard to our frail vessels. The ice lay so close that the crews disembarked on it, and effected a passage by bearing against the pieces with their poles ; but in conducting the canoes through the narrow channels thus formed, the greatest care was requisite, to prevent the sharp projecting points from breaking the bark. They fortunately received no material injury, though they were split in two places.

At the distance of three miles, we came to the entrance of a deep bay, whose bottom was filled by a body of ice so compact as to preclude the idea of a passage through it ; whilst at the same time, the traverse across its mouth was attended with much danger, from the approach of a large field of ice, which was driving down before the wind. The dread of further detention, however, prevented us from hesitating ; and we had the satisfaction of landing in an hour and a half on the opposite shore, where we halted to repair the canoes and to dine. I have named this bay after my friend Mr. Daniel Moore of Lincoln's Inn ; to whose zeal for science, the Expedition was indebted for the use of a most valuable chronometer. Its shores are picturesque ; sloping hills receding from the beach, and clothed with verdure, bound its bottom and western side ; and lofty cliffs of slate clay, with their intervening grassy valleys, skirt its eastern border. Embarking at midnight, we pursued our voyage without interruption, passing between the Stockport and Marcet Islands and the main, until six A.M. on July 30th ; when having rounded Point Kater, we entered Arctic Sound, and were again involved in a stream of ice, but after considerable delay extricated ourselves, and proceeded towards the bottom of the inlet in search of the mouth of a river, which we supposed it to receive, from the change in the color of the water.

About ten A.M. we landed, to breakfast on a small deer which St. Germain had killed : and sent men in pursuit of some others in sight, but with which they did not come up. Re-embarking, we passed the river without perceiving it, and entered a deep arm of the

sound ; which I have named Baillie's Cove, in honor
of a relative of the lamented Mr. Hood.   As it was
too late to return, we encamped, and by walking across
the country, discovered the river, whose mouth being
barred by low sandy islands and banks, was not perceived when we passed it.   Course and distance from
Galena Point to this encampment, were S.E.¾S.—
forty-one miles.

From the accounts of Black-meat and Boileau at
Fort Chipewyan, we considered this river to be the
Anatessy ; and Cape Barrow to be the projection
which they supposed. to be the N.E. termination of
America.   The outline of the coast, indeed, bears
some resemblance to the chart they sketched ; and
the distance of this river from the Copper-Mine, nearly
coincides with what we estimated the Anatessy to be,
from their statements.   In our subsequent journey,
however, across the barren grounds, we ascertained
that this conjecture was wrong, and that the Anatessy,
which is known to come from Rum Lake, must fall
into the sea to the eastward of this place.

Our stock of provision being now reduced to eight
days' consumption, it had become a matter of the first
importance to obtain a supply ; and as we had learned
from Terregannœuck that the Esquimaux frequent
the rivers at this season, I determined on seeking a
communication with them here, with the view of ob-

taining relief for our present wants, or even shelter for the winter, if the season should prevent us from returning either to the Hook's party, or Fort Enterprize ; and I was the more induced to take this step at this time, as several deer had been seen to-day, and the river appeared good for fishing ; which led me to hope we might support the party during our stay, if not add to our stock by our own exertions in hunting and fishing.   Augustus, Junius, and Hepburn, were therefore furnished with the necessary presents, and desired to go along the bank of the river as far as they could, on the following day, in search of the natives, to obtain provision and leather, as well as information respecting the coast.

They started at four A.M., and at the same time our hunters were sent off in search of deer ; and the rest of the party proceeded in the canoes to the first cascade in the river, at the foot of which we encamped, and set four nets.   This cascade, produced by a ridge of rocks crossing the stream, is about three or four feet in height, and about two hundred and fifty yards wide.   Its position by our observations is latitude 67° 19' 23" N., longitude 109° 44' 30" W., variation 41° 43' 22', dip 88° 58' 48".   I have named this river Hood, as a small tribute to the memory of our lamented friend and companion.   It is from three to four hundred yards wide below the cascade, but it is in many

places very shallow. The banks, bottom, and adjacent hills, are formed of a mixture of sand and clay.
The ground was overspread with small willows and the
dwarf birch, both too diminutive for fuel; and the
stream brought down no drift wood. We were mortified to find the nets only procured one salmon and
five white fish, and that we had to make another inroad upon our dried meat.

August 1.—At two this morning the hunters returned with two small deer and a brown bear. Augustus and Junius arrived at the same time, having
traced the river twelve miles further up, without discovering any vestige of inhabitants. We had now
an opportunity of gratifying our curiosity respecting
the bear so much dreaded by the Indians, and of whose
strength and ferocity we had heard such terrible accounts. It proved to be a lean male of a yellowish
brown color, and not longer than a common black
bear. It made a feeble attempt to defend itself, and
was easily despatched. The flesh was brought to the
tent, but our fastidious voyagers supposing, from its
leanness, the animal had been sickly, declined eating
it; the officers, however, being less scrupulous, boiled
the paws, and found them excellent.

We embarked at ten A.M., and proceeding down
the river, took on board another deer that had been
killed by Credit last evening. We then ran along

the eastern shore of Arctic Sound, distinguished by
the name of Bank's Peninsula, in honor of the late
Right Honorable Sir Joseph Banks, President of the
Royal Society; and rounding Point Wollaston at its
eastern extremity, opened another extensive sheet of
water; and the remainder of the afternoon was spent
in endeavoring to ascertain, from the tops of the hills,
whether it was another bay, or merely a passage enclosed by a chain of islands. Appearances rather
favoring the latter opinion, we determined on proceeding through it to the southward. During the delay
four more deer were killed, all young and lean. It
appears that the coast is pretty well frequented by
reindeer at this season; but it is rather singular, that
hitherto we have killed none (excepting the first) but
young ones of last season, which were all too.lean to
have been eaten by any but persons who had no choice.

We paddled along the western shore with the intention of encamping, but were prevented from the want
of drift wood on the beach. This induced us to make
a traverse to an island, where we put up at midnight,
having found a small bay, whose shores furnished us
with a little fire-wood. A heavy gale came on from
the westward, attended with constant rain, and one of
the squalls overthrew our tents. The course and distance made to-day were north-east sixteen miles and
a half. I may here mention, that Arctic Sound ap-

pears to be the most convenient, and perhaps the best, place for ships to anchor that we have seen along the coast; at this season especially, when they might increase their stock of provision, if provided with good marksmen. Deer are numerous in its vicinity, musk-oxen also may be found up Hood's River, and the fine sandy bottom of the bays promise favorably for fishing with the seine. The hills on the western side are even in their outline and slope gradually to the water's edge. The rocks give place to an alluvial sandy soil, towards the bottom of the sound; but on Banks' Peninsula rocky eminences again prevail, which are rugged and uneven, but they are intersected by valleys, now green; along their base is a fine sandy beach. From Point Wollaston to our present encampment the coast is skirted with trap cliffs, which have often a columnar form, and are very difficult of access. These cliffs lie in ranges parallel to the shore, and the deer that we killed were feeding in small marshy grassy plats that lie in the valleys between them.

Being detained by the continuance of the gale, on the 2d of August some men were sent out to hunt, and the officers visited the tops of the highest hills, to ascertain the best channels to be pursued. The wind abating at ten P.M., we embarked and paddled round the southern end of the island, and continued our course to the south-east. Much doubt at this time prevailed as to the land on the right being the main shore, or merely a chain of islands. The latter opinion was strengthened by the broken appearance of the land, and the extensive view we had up Brown's Channel, (named after my friend Mr. Robert Brown,) the mouth of which we passed, and were in some apprehension of being led away from the main shore; and, perhaps, after passing through a group of islands, of coming to a traverse greater than we durst venture upon in canoes. On the other hand, the continuous appearance of the land on the north side of the channel, and its tending to the southward, produced a fear that we were entering a deep inlet.

In this state of doubt we landed often, and endeavored, from the summits of the highest hills adjoining the shore, to ascertain the true nature of the coast, but in vain, and we continued paddling through the channel all night against a fresh breeze, which, at half past four, increased to a violent gale, and compelled us to land. The gale diminished a short time after noon on the 3d, and permitted us to re-embark and continue our voyage until four P.M., when it returned with its former violence, and finally obliged us to encamp, having come twenty-four miles on a south-east three-quarter south course.

From the want of drift wood to make a fire we had fasted all day, and were under the necessity, in the

evening, of serving out pemmican, which was done
with much reluctance, especially as we had some fresh
deers' meat remaining.　The inlet, when viewed from
a high hill adjoining to our encampment, exhibited so
many arms, that the course we ought to pursue was
more uncertain than ever.　It was absolutely necessary,
however, to see the end of it before we could determine that it was not a strait.　Starting at three A.M.,
on the 4th, we paddled the whole day through channels, from two to five or six miles wide, all tending to
the southward.　In the course of the day's voyage we
ascertained, that the land which we had seen on our
right hand since yesterday morning, consisted of several large islands, which have been distinguished by
the names of Goulburn, Elliot, and Young ; but the
land on our left preserved its unbroken appearance,
and when we encamped, we were still uncertain whether it was the eastern side of a deep sound or merely
a large island.　It differed remarkably from the main
shore, being very rugged, rocky, and sterile, whereas
the outline of the main on the opposite side was even,
and its hills covered with a comparatively good sward
of grass, and exhibited little naked rock.　There was
no drift timber, but the shores near the encampment
were strewed with small pieces of willow, which indi-
cated our vicinity to the mouth of a river.　This fuel
enabled us to make a hearty supper off a small deer
killed this evening.

The shallows we passed to-day were covered with shoals of *capelin*, the angmaggœñk of the Esquimaux. It was known to Augustus, who informed us that it frequents the coast of Hudson's Bay, and is delicate eating. The course and distance made was, south by east half east, thirty-three miles.

After paddling twelve miles in the morning of the 5th, we had the mortification to find the inlet terminated by a river ; the size of which we could not ascertain, as the entrance was blocked by shoals. I have named this stream Back, as a mark of my friendship for my associate. We were somewhat consoled for the loss of time in exploring this inlet, by the success of Junius in killing a musk-ox, the first we had seen on the coast ; and afterwards by the acquisition of the flesh of a bear, that was shot as we were returning up the eastern side in the evening. The latter proved to be a female, in very excellent condition ; and our Canadian voyagers, whose appetite for fat meat is insatiable, were delighted.

We encamped on the shores of a sandy bay, and set the nets ; and finding a quantity of dried willows on the beach, we were enabled to cook the bear's flesh, which was superior to any meat we had tasted on the coast. The water fell two feet at this place during the night. Our nets produced a great variety of fish, namely, a salmon-trout, some round fish, tittameg, bleak, star-fish, several herrings, and a flat fish resembling plaice, but covered on the back with horny excrescences.

On the 6th we were detained in the encampment by stormy weather until five P.M., when we embarked and paddled along the northern shore of the inlet; the weather still continuing foggy, but the wind moderate. Observing on the beach a she bear with three young ones, we landed a party to attack them ; but, being approached without due caution, they took the alarm and scaled a precipitous rocky hill, with a rapidity that baffled all pursuit. At eight o'clock, the fog changing into rain, we encamped. Many seals were seen to-day, but as they kept in deep water we did not fire at them.

On August 7th the atmosphere was charged with fog and rain all the day, but as the wind was moderate, we pursued our journey ; our situation, however, was very unpleasant, being quite wet and without room to stretch a limb, much less to obtain warmth by exercise. We passed a cove, which I have named after my friend Mr. W. H. Tinney ; and proceeded along the coast until five P.M., when we put up on a rocky point nearly opposite to our encampment on the 3d, having come twenty-three miles on a north-north-west course.

We were detained on the 8th by a northerly gale,

which blew violently throughout the day, attended by fog and rain. Some of the men went out to hunt, but they saw no other animal than a white wolf, which could not be approached. The fresh meat being expended, a little pemmican was served out this evening.

The gale abated on the morning of the 9th ; and the sea, which it had raised, having greatly subsided, we embarked at seven A.M., and after paddling three or four miles, opened Sir J. A. Gordon's Bay, into which we penetrated thirteen miles, and then discovered from the summit of a hill that it would be vain to procced in this direction, in search of a passage out of the inlet.

Our breakfast diminished our provision to two bags of pemmican, and a single meal of dried meat. The men began to apprehend absolute want of food, and we had to listen to their gloomy forebodings of the deer entirely quitting the coast in a few days. As we were embarking, however, a large bear was discovered on the opposite shore, which we had the good fortune to kill ; and the sight of this fat meat relieved their fears for the present. Dr. Richardson found in the stomach of this animal the remains of a seal, several marmots, a large quantity of the liquorice root of Mackenzie, which is common on these shores, and some berries. - There was also intermixed with these substances a small quantity of grass.

We got again into the main inlet, and paddled along its eastern shore until forty minutes after eight A.M., when we encamped in a small cove. We found a single log of drift wood ; it was pine, and sufficiently large to enable us to cook a portion of the bear, which had a slight fishy taste, but was deemed very palatable.

August 10.—We followed up the east border of the inlet about twenty-four miles, and at length emerged into the open sea ; a body of islands to the westward concealing the channel by which we had entered. Here our progress was arrested by returning bad weather. We killed a bear and its young cub of this year, on the beach near to our encampment. We heartily congratulated ourselves at having arrived at the eastern entrance of this inlet, which had cost us nine invaluable days in exploring. It contains several secure harbors, especially near the mouth of Back's River, where there is a sandy bottom in forty fathoms. There also fish are plentiful, and reindeer and muskoxen may be procured at this season, by spending a little time in hunting.

On the 3d and 4th of August we observed a fall of more than two feet in the water during the night. There are various irregular and partial currents in the inlet, which may be attributed to the wind. I have distinguished it by the name Bathurst's Inlet, in hon-

or of the noble Secretary of State, under whose orders
I had the honor to act. It runs about seventy-six
miles south-east from Cape Everitt, but in coasting
its shores we went about one hundred and seventy-four
geographical miles. It is remarkable that none of the
Indians with whom we had spoken had mentioned this
inlet ; and we subsequently learned, that in their journeys they strike across from the mouth of one river
to the mouth of another, without tracing the intermediate line of coast.

August 11.—Embarking at five A.M., we rounded
Point Everitt, and then encountered a strong breeze
and heavy swell, which by causing the canoes to pitch
very much, greatly impeded our progress. Some deer
being seen grazing in a valley near the beach, we landed, and sent St. Germain and Adam in pursuit of
them, who soon killed three which were very small
and lean.. Their appearance, however, quite revived
the spirits of our men, who had suspected that the
deer had retired to the woods. It would appear, from
our not having seen any in passing along the shores of
Bathurst's Inlet, that at this season they confine themselves to the sea-coast and the islands. The magpie
berries (*arbutus alpina*) were found quite ripe at this
place, and very abundant on the acclivities of the hills.
We also ascended the highest hill, and gained a view
of a distant chain of islands, extending as far as the

eye could reach, and perceived a few patches of ice
still remaining near to some of them ; but in every
other part the sea was quite open.   Resuming our
voyage after noon, we proceeded along the coast, which
is fringed by islands ; and, at five P.M., entered another bay, where we were for some time involved in our
late difficulties by the intricacy of the passages ; but
we cleared them in the afternoon, and encamped near
.the northern entrance of the bay, at a spot which had
recently been visited by a small party of Esquimaux,
as the remains of some eggs, containing young, were
lying beside some half-burnt fire-wood.   There were
also several piles of stones put up by them.   I have
named this bay after my friend, Captain David Buchan, of the Royal Navy.   It appears to be a safe anchorage, being well sheltered from the wind and sea by
islands ; the bottom is sandy.   Its shores are high,
and composed of red sand-stone.   Two deer were seen
on its beach, but could not be approached.   The distance we made to-day was eighteen miles and three-
quarters.

Embarking at four on the morning of the 12th, we
proceeded against a fresh piercing north-east wind,
which raised the waves to a height that quite terrified
our people, accustomed only to the navigation of rivers
and lakes.   We were obliged, however, to persevere in
our advance, feeling, as we did, that the short season

for our operations was hastening away; but after rounding Cape Croker the wind became so strong that we could proceed no further. The distance we had made being only six miles on a north-east by east course. The shore on which we encamped is formed of the debris of red sand-stone, and is destitute of vegetation. The beach furnishes no drift wood, and we dispensed with our usual meal rather than expend our pemmican. Several deer were seen, but the hunters could not approach them; they killed two swans. We observed the latitude 68° 1′ 20″, where we halted to breakfast this morning.

August 13.—Though the wind was not diminished, we were urged, by the want of fire-wood, to venture upon proceeding. We paddled close to the shore for some miles, and then ran before the breeze with reefed sails, scarcely two feet in depth. Both the canoes received much water, and one of them struck twice on sunken rocks. At the end of eighteen miles we halted to breakfast in a bay, which I have named after Vice-Admiral Sir William Johnstone Hope, one of the Lords of the Admiralty.

We found here a considerable quantity of small willows, such as are brought down by the rivers we have hitherto seen; and hence we judged, that a river discharges itself into the bottom of this bay. A paddle was also found, which Augustus, on examination,

declared to be made after the fashion of the White
Goose Esquimaux, a tribe with whom his countrymen
had had some trading communication, as has been
mentioned in a former part of the Narrative.

This morning we passed the embouchure of a pretty
large stream, and saw the vestiges of an Esquimaux
encampment not above a month old.   Having obtained
the latitude 68° 6' 40" N., we recommenced our voyage under sail, taking the precaution to embark all the
pieces of willow we could collect, as we had found the
drift wood become more scarce as we advanced.   Our
course was directed to a distant point, which we supposed to be a cape, and the land stretching to the
westward of it to be islands ; but we soon found ourselves in an extensive bay, from which no outlet could
be perceived but the one by which we had entered.
After examining, however, from the top of a hill, we
found a winding shallow passage running to the north-
west, which we followed for a short time and then encamped, having come twenty-three miles, north by
east half east.

Some articles left by the Esquimaux attracted our
attention ; we found a winter sledge raised upon four
stones, with some snow-shovels, and a small piece of
whalebone.   An ice-chisel, a knife, and some beads,
were left at this pile.   The shores of this bay, which
I have named after Sir George Warrender, are low

and clayey, and the country for many miles is level, and much intersected with water ; but we had not leisure to ascertain whether they were branches of the bay or fresh-water lakes. Some white geese were seen this evening, and some young grey ones were caught on the beach, being unable to fly. We fired at two reindeer, but without success.

On August 14th we paddled the whole day along the northern shores of the sound, returning towards its mouth. The land which we were now tracing is generally so flat, that it could not be described from the canoes at the distance of four miles, and is invisible from the opposite side of the sound, otherwise a short traverse might have saved us some days. The few eminences that are on this side were mistaken for islands when seen from the opposite shore ; they are for the most part cliffs of basalt, and are not above one hundred feet high ; the subjacent strata are of white sand-stone. The rocks are mostly confined to the capes and shores, the soil inland being flat, clayey, and barren. Most of the headlands shewed traces of visits from the Esquimaux, but none of them recent. Many ducks were seen to-day, belonging to a species termed by the voyagers, from their cry, " caccawees." We also saw some grey geese and swans. The only seal we procured during our voyage, was killed this day ; it happened to be blind, and our men imagining it to be in bad health, would not taste the flesh ; we, however, were less nice.

We encamped at the end of twenty-four miles' march, on the north-west side of a bay, to which I have given the name of my friend Captain Parry, now employed in the interesting research for a North-West Passage. Drift wood had become very scarce, and we found none near the encampment ; a fire, however, was not required, as we served out pemmican for supper, and the evening was unusually warm.

On the following morning the breeze was fresh, and the waves rather high. In paddling along the west side of Parry's Bay, we saw several deer, but owing to the openness of the country, the hunters could not approach them. They killed, however, two swans that were moulting, several cranes, and many grey geese. We procured also some caccawees, which were then moulting and assembled in immense flocks. In the evening, having rounded Point Beechy, and passed Hurd's Islands, we were exposed to much inconvenience and danger from a heavy rolling sea ; the canoes receiving many severe blows, and shipping a good deal of water, which induced us to encamp at five P.M. opposite to Cape Croker, which we had passed on the morning of the 12th ; the channel, which lay between our situation and it, being about seven miles wide. We had now reached the northern point of entrance into this sound, which I have named in honor of Lord Viscount Melville, the First Lord of the Admiralty. It is thirty miles wide from east to west, and twenty from north to south ; and in coasting it we had sailed eighty-seven and a quarter geographical miles. Shortly after the tents were pitched, Mr. Back reported from the steersmen that both canoes had sustained material injury during this day's voyage. I found upon examination that fifteen timbers of the first canoe were broken, some of them in two places, and that the second canoe was so loose in the frame that its timbers could not be bound in the usual secure manner, and consequently there was danger of its bark separating from the gunwales if exposed to a heavy sea. Distressing as were these circumstances, they gave me less pain than the discovery that our people, who had hitherto displayed, in following us through dangers and difficulties no less novel than appalling to them, a courage beyond our expectation, now felt serious apprehensions for their safety, which so possessed their minds that they were not restrained even by the presence of their officers from expressing them. Their fears, we imagined, had been principally excited by the interpreters, St. Germain and Adam, who from the outset had foreboded every calamity ; and we now strongly suspected that their recent want of success in their hunting excursions, had proceeded from an intentional relaxation in their efforts to kill deer, in order that the want of provision might compel us to put a period to our voyage.

I must now mention that many concurrent circumstances had caused me, during the few last days, to meditate on the approach of this painful necessity. The strong breezes we had encountered for some days, led me to fear that the season was breaking up, and severe weather would soon ensue, which we could not sustain in a country destitute of fuel. Our stock of provision was now reduced to a quantity of pemmican only sufficient for three days' consumption, and the prospect of increasing it was not encouraging, for though reindeer were seen, they could not be easily approached on the level shores we were now coasting, besides, it was to be apprehended they would soon migrate to the south. It was evident that the time spent in exploring the Arctic and Melville Sounds, and Bathurst's Inlet, had precluded the hope of reaching Repulse Bay, which at the outset of the voyage we had fondly cherished ; and it was equally obvious that as our distance from any of the trading establishments would increase as we proceeded, the hazardous traverse across the barren grounds, which we should have to make, if compelled to abandon the canoes upon any part of the coast, would become greater.

I this evening communicated to the officers my sentiments on these points, as well as respecting our return, and was happy to find that their opinions coincided with my own. We were all convinced of the necessity of putting a speedy termination to our advance, as the hope which we had cherished of meeting the Esquimaux and procuring provision from them, could now scarcely be entertained; but yet we were desirous of proceeding, until the land should be seen trending again to the eastward; that we might be satisfied of its separation from what we had conceived, in passing from Cape Barrow to Bathurst's Inlet, to be a great chain of islands. As it was necessary, however, at all events, to set a limit to our advance, I announced my determination of returning after four days examination, unless, indeed, we should previously meet the Esquimaux, and be enabled to make some arrangement for passing the winter with them. This communication was joyfully received by the men, and we hoped that the industry of our hunters being once more excited, we should be able to add to our stock of provision.

It may here be remarked that we observed the first regular return of the tides in Warrender's and Parry's Bays; but their set could not be ascertained. The rise of the water did not amount to more than two feet. Course to-day south one quarter east—nine miles and a quarter.

August 16.—Some rain fell in the night, but the morning was unusually fine. We set forward at five A. M., and the men paddled cheerfully along the coast for ten miles, when a dense fog caused us to land on Slate-clay Point. Here we found more traces of the Esquimaux, and the skull of a man placed between two rocks. The fog dispersed at noon, and we discerned a group of islands to the northward, which I have named after Vice-Admiral Sir George Cockburn, one of the Lords of the Admiralty. Re-embarking, we rounded the point and entered Walker's Bay, where, as in other instances, the low beach which lay between several high trap cliffs, could not be distinguished until we had coasted down the east side nearly to the bottom of the bay. When the continuity of the land was perceived, we crossed to the western shore, and on landing, discovered a channel leading through a group of islands. Having passed through this channel, we ran under sail by the Porden Islands, across Riley's Bay, and rounding a cape which now bears the name of my lamented friend Captain Flinders, had the pleasure to find the coast trending north-north-east, with the sea in the offing unusually clear of islands ; a circumstance which afforded matter of wonder to our Canadians, who had not previously had an uninterrupted view of the ocean.

Our course was continued along the coast until

eight P.M., when a change in the wind and a threatening thunder squall induced us to encamp ; but the water was so shallow, that we found some difficulty in approaching the shore. Large pieces of drift wood gave us assurance that we had finally escaped from the bays. Our tents were scarcely pitched before we were assailed by a heavy squall and rain, which was succeeded by a violent gale from west-north-west ; which thrice overset the tents in the course of the night. The wind blew with equal violence on the following day, and the sea rolled furiously upon the beach. The Canadians had now an opportunity of witnessing the effect of a storm upon the sea ; and the sight increased their desire of quitting it.

Our hunters were sent out, and saw many deer, but the flatness of the country defeated their attempts to approach them ; they brought, however, a few unfledged geese. As there was no appearance of increasing our stock of provision, the allowance was limited to a handful of pemmican, and a small portion of portable soup to each man per day. The thermometer this afternoon stood at 41°. The following observations were obtained : latitude 68° 18′ 50″ N., longitude 110′ 5′ 15″ W. ; but 109° 25′ 00″ W. was used in the construction of the chart, as the chronometers were found, on our return to Hood's River, to have altered their rates ; variation 44° 15′ 46″ E., and dip of the needle 89° 31′ 12″.

On August 18th the stormy weather and sea continuing, there was no prospect of our being able to embark. Dr. Richardson, Mr. Back, and I, therefore, set out on foot to discover whether the land within a day's march, inclined more to the east. We went from ten to twelve miles along the coast, which continued flat, and kept the same direction as the encampment. The most distant land we saw had the same bearing north-north-east, and appeared like two islands; which we estimated to be six or seven miles off; the shore on their inside seemingly trended more to the east, so that it is probable Point Turnagain, for so this spot was named, forms the pitch of a low flat cape.

Augustus killed a deer in the afternoon, but the men were not able to find it. The hunters found the burrows of a number of white foxes, and Hepburn killed one of these animals, which proved excellent eating, esteemed by us as equal to the young geese, with which it was boiled, and far superior to the lean deer we had upon the coast. Large flocks of geese passed over the tents, flying to the southward. The lowest temperature to-day was 38°.

Though it will appear from the chart, that the position of Point Turnagain is only six degrees and a half to the east of the mouth of the Copper-Mine River, we sailed, in tracing the deeply-indented coast, five hundred and fifty-five geographic miles, which is little less than the direct distance between the Copper-Mine River and Repulse Bay ; supposing the latter to be in the longitude assigned to it by Middleton.

When the many perplexing incidents which occurred during the survey of the coast are considered in connection with the shortness of the period, during which operations of the kind can be carried on, and the distance we had to travel before we could gain a place of shelter for the winter, I trust it will be judged that we prosecuted the enterprize as far as was prudent, and abandoned it only under a well-founded conviction that a further advance would endanger the lives of the whole party, and prevent the knowledge of what had been done from reaching England. The active assistance I received from the officers, in contending with the fears of the men, demands my warmest gratitude.

Our researches as far as they have gone, seem to favor the opinion of those who contend for the practicability of a North-West Passage. The general line of coast probably runs east and west, nearly in the latitude assigned to Mackenzie's River, the Sound into which Kotzebue entered, and Repulse Bay ; and very little doubt can, in my opinion, be entertained of the existence of a continued sea, in or about that line of direction. The existence of whales, too, on this part of the coast, evidenced by the whalebone we found in Esquimaux Cove, may be considered as an argument for an open sea ; and a connection with Hud-

son's Bay is rendered more probable from the same
kind of fish abounding on the coasts we visited, and
on those to the north of Churchill River. I allude
more particularly to the Capelin or Salmo Arcticus,
which we found in large shoals in Bathurst's Inlet,
and which not only abounds, as Augustus told us, in
the bays in his country, but swarms in the Greenland
firths. The portion of the sea over which we passed
is navigable for vessels of any size ; the ice we met,
particularly after quitting Detention Harbor, would
not have arrested a strong boat. The chain of islands
affords shelter from all heavy seas, and there are good
harbors at convenient distances. I entertain indeed,
sanguine hopes that the skill and exertions of my
friend Captain Parry will soon render this question no
longer problematical. His task is doubtless an
arduous one, and, if ultimately successful, may occupy
two and perhaps three seasons ; but confiding as I do,
from personal knowledge, in his perseverance and
talent for surmounting difficulties, the strength of his
ships, and the abundance of provisions with which
they are stored, I have very little apprehension of his
safety. As I understand his object was to keep the
coast of America close on board, he will find in the
spring of the year, before the breaking up of the ice
can permit him to pursue his voyage, herds of deer
flocking in abundance to all parts of the coast, which
may be procured without difficulty ; and, even later

in the season, additions to his stock of provision may be obtained on many parts of the coast, should circumstances give him leisure to send out hunting parties. With the trawl or seine nets also, he may almost every where get abundance of fish even without retarding his progress. Under these circumstances I do not conceive that he runs any hazard of wanting provisions, should his voyage be prolonged even beyond the latest period of time which is calculated upon. Drift timber may be gathered at many places in considerable quantities, and there is a fair prospect of his opening a communication with the Esquimaux, who come down to the coast to kill seals in the spring, previous to the ice breaking up ; and from whom, if he succeeds in conciliating their good will, he may obtain provision, and much useful assistance.

If he makes for Copper-Mine River, as he probably will do, he will not find it in the longitude as laid down on the charts ; but he will probably find what would be more interesting to him, a post which we erected on the 26th August at the mouth of Hood's River, which is nearly, as will appear hereafter, in that longitude, with a flag upon it, and a letter at the foot of it, which may convey to him some useful information. It is possible, however, that he might keep outside of the range of islands which skirt this part of the coast.

CHAPTER. X.

1821.
August 17. MY original intention, whenever the season
should compel us to relinquish the survey, had been
to return by the way of the Copper-Mine River, and,
in pursuance of my arrangement with the Hook to
travel to Slave Lake through the line of woods extending thither by the Great Bear and Marten Lakes, but
our scanty stock of provision and the length of the
voyage rendered it necessary to make for a nearer
place. We had already found that the country, between Cape Barrow and the Copper-Mine River, would
not supply our wants, and this it seemed probable
would now be still more the case ; besides, at this advanced season, we expected the frequent recurrence of
gales, which would cause great detention, if not danger in proceeding along that very rocky part of the
coast.

I determined, therefore, to make at once for Arctic
Sound, where we had found the animals more numerous than at any other place ; and entering Hood's

River, to advance up that stream as far as it was navigable, and then to construct small canoes out of the materials of the larger ones, which could be carried in crossing the barren grounds to Fort Enterprize.

August 19.—We were almost beaten out of our comfortless abodes by rain during the night, and this morning the gale continued without diminution. The thermometer fell to 33°. Two men were sent with Junius to search for the deer which Augustus had killed. Junius returned in the evening bringing part of the meat, but owing to the thickness of the weather, his companions parted from him and did not make their appearance. Divine service was read. On the 20th we were presented with the most chilling prospect, the small pools of water being frozen over, the ground being covered with snow, and the thermometer at the freezing point at mid-day. Flights of geese were passing to the southward. The wind however was more moderate, having changed to the eastward. Considerable anxiety prevailing respecting Belanger and Michel, the two men who strayed from Junius yesterday, the rest were sent out to look for them. The search was successful, and they all returned in the evening. The stragglers were much fatigued, and had suffered severely from the cold, one of them having his thighs frozen, and what under our circumstances was most grievous, they had thrown away all the

meat. The wind during the night returned to the
north-west quarter, blew more violently than ever, and
raised a very turbulent sea. The next day did not
improve our condition, the snow remained on the
ground, and the small pools were frozen. Our hunters were sent out, but they returned after a fatiguing
day's march without having seen any animals. We
made a scanty meal off a handful of pemmican, after
which only half a bag remained.

The wind abated after midnight, and the surf diminished rapidly, which caused us to be on the alert
at a very early hour on the 22d, but we had to wait
until six A.M. for the return of Augustus, who had
continued out all night on an unsuccessful pursuit of
deer. It appears that he walked a few miles farther
along the coast, than the party had done on the 18th,
and from a sketch he drew on the sand, we were confirmed in our former opinion that the shore inclined
more to the eastward beyond Point Turnagain. He
also drew a river of considerable size, that discharges its waters into Walker's Bay ; on the banks
of which stream he saw a piece of wood, such as the
Esquimaux use in producing fire, and other marks so
fresh that he supposed they had recently visited the
spot. We therefore left several iron materials for
them. Our men, cheered by the prospect of returning,
embarked with the utmost alacrity ; and, paddling

with unusual vigor, carried us across Riley's and Walker's Bays, a distance of twenty miles before noon, when we landed on Slate-Clay Point, as the wind had freshened too much to permit us to continue the voyage. The whole party went to hunt, but returned without success in the evening, drenched with the heavy rain which commenced soon after they had set out. Several deer were seen, but could not be approached in this naked country; and as our stock of pemmican did not admit of serving out two meals, we went dinnerless to bed.

Soon after our departure to-day, a sealed tin-case, sufficiently buoyant to float, was thrown overboard, containing a short account of our proceedings, and the position of the most conspicuous points. The wind blew off the land, the water was smooth, and as the sea is in this part more free from islands than in any other, there was every probability of its being driven off the shore into the current; which, as I have before mentioned, we suppose, from the circumstance of Mackenzie's River being the only known stream that brings down the wood we have found along the shores, to set to the eastward.

August 23.—A severe frost caused us to pass a comfortless night. At 2 P.M. we set sail, and the men voluntarily launched out to make a traverse of fifteen miles across Melville Sound, before a strong wind and heavy sea. The privation of food, under which our voyagers were then laboring, absorbed every other terror ; otherwise the most powerful persuasion could not have induced them to attempt such a traverse. It was with the utmost difficulty that the canoes were kept from turning their broadsides to the waves, though we sometimes steered with all the paddles. One of them narrowly escaped being overset by this accident, happening, in mid-channel, where the waves were so high that the mast-head of our canoe was often hid from the other, though it was sailing within hail.

The traverse, however, was made ; we were then near a high rocky lee shore, on which a heavy surf was beating. The wind being on the beam, the canoes drifted fast to leeward ; and, on rounding a point, the recoil of the sea from the rocks was so great that they were with difficulty kept from foundering. We looked in vain for a sheltered bay to land in ; but, at length, being unable to weather another point, we were obliged to put ashore on the open beach, which, fortunately, was sandy at this spot. The debarkation was effected without further injury than the splitting of the head of the second canoe, which was easily repaired.

Our encampment being near to the place where we killed the deer on the 11th, almost the whole party went out to hunt, but they returned in the evening

without having seen any game. The berries, however, were ripe and plentiful, and, with the addition
of some country tea, furnished a supper. There were
some showers in the afternoon, and the weather was
cold, the thermometer being 42°, but the evening and
night were calm and fine. It may be remarked that
the musquitoes disappeared when the late gales commenced.

August 24.—Embarking at three A.M., we stretched across the eastern entrance of Bathurst's Inlet, and
arrived at an island, which I have named after Colo-
nel Barry, of Newton Barry. Some deer being seen
on the beach, the hunters went in pursuit of them,
and succeeded in killing three females, which enabled
us to save our last remaining meal of pemmican.
They saw also some fresh tracks of musk oxen on the
banks of a small stream, which flowed into a lake in
the centre of the island. These animals must have
crossed a channel, at least three miles wide, to reach
the nearest of these islands. Some specimens of variegated pebbles and jasper were found here imbedded
in the amygdaloidal rock.

Re-embarking at two P.M., and continuing through
what was supposed to be a channel between two
islands, we found our passage barred by a gravelly
isthmus of only ten yards in width ; the canoes and
cargoes were carried across it, and we passed into

Bathurst's Inlet through another similar channel, bounded on both sides by steep rocky hills. The wind then changing from S.E. to N.W. brought heavy rain, and we encamped at seven P.M., having advanced eighteen miles.

August 25.—Starting this morning with a fresh breeze in our favor, we soon reached that part of Barry's Island where the canoes were detained on the 2d and 3d of this month, and contrary to what we then experienced, the deer were now plentiful. The hunters killed two, and we were relieved from all apprehension of an immediate want of food. One would suppose the deer were about to retire to the main shore, from their assembling at this time in such numbers on the islands nearest the coast. Those we saw were generally females with their young, and all of them very lean.

The wind continued in the same direction until we had rounded Point Wollaston, and then changed to a quarter which enabled us to steer for Hood's River, which we ascended as high as the first rapid, and encamped. Here terminated our voyage on the Arctic sea, during which we had gone over six hundred and fifty geographical miles. Our Canadian voyagers could not restrain their expressions of joy at having turned their backs on the sea, and they passed the evening talking over their past adventures with much humor and no little exaggeration. The consideration that the most painful, and certainly the most hazardous, part of the journey was yet to come, did not depress their spirits at all. It is due to their character to mention that they displayed much courage in encountering the dangers of the sea, magnified to them by their novelty.

The shores between Cape Barrow and Cape Flinders, including the extensive branches of Arctic and Melville Sounds, and Bathurst's Inlet, may be comprehended in one great gulf, which I have distinguished by the appellation of George IV.'s Coronation Gulf, in honor of His Most Gracious Majesty, the latter name being added to mark the time of its discovery. The Archipelago of islands which fringe the coast from Copper-Mine River to Point Turnagain, I have named in honor of His Royal Highness the Duke of York.

It may be deserving of notice, that the extremes in temperature of the sea water during our voyage were 53° and 35°, but its general temperature was between 43° and 48°. Throughout our return from Point Turnagain we observed that the sea had risen several feet above marks left at our former encampments. This may, perhaps, be attributed to the north-west gales.

August 26.—Previous to our departure this morning, an assortment of iron materials, beads, looking-glasses, and other articles were put up in a conspicuous situation for the Esquimaux, and the English Union was planted on the loftiest sand-hill, where it might be seen by any ships passing in the offing. Here also, was deposited in a tin box, a letter containing an outline of our proceedings, the latitude and longitude of the principal places, and the course we intended to pursue towards Slave Lake.

Embarking at eight A. M. we proceeded up the river, which is full of sandy shoals, but sufficiently deep for canoes in the channels. It is from one hundred to two hundred yards wide, and is bounded by high and steep banks of clay. We encamped at a cascade of eighteen or twenty feet high, which is produced by a ridge of rock crossing the river, and the nets were set. A mile below this cascade Hood's River is joined by a stream half its own size, which I have called James' Branch. Bear and deer tracts had been numerous on the banks of the river when we were here before, but not a single recent one was to be seen at this time. Crédit, however, killed a small deer at some distance inland, which, with the addition of berries, furnished a delightful repast this evening. The weather was remarkably fine, and the temperature so mild, that the musquitoes again made their appearance, but not in any great numbers. Our distance made to-day was not more than six miles.

The next morning the net furnished us with ten white fish and trout. , Having made a further deposit of iron work for the Esquimaux, we pursued our voyage up the river, but the shoals and rapids in this part were so frequent, that we walked along the banks the whole day, and the crews labored hard in carrying the canoes thus lightened over the shoals or dragging them up the rapids, yet our journey in a direct line was only about seven miles. In the evening we encamped at the lower end of a narrow chasm through which the river flows for upwards of a mile. The walls of this chasm are. upwards of two hundred feet high, quite perpendicular, and in some places only a few yards apart. The river precipitates itself into it over a rock, forming two magnificent and picturesque falls close to each other. The upper fall is about sixty feet high, and the lower one at least one hundred, but perhaps considerably more, for the narrowness of the chasm into which it fell prevented us from seeing its bottom, and we could merely discern the top of the spray far beneath our feet. The lower fall is divided into two, by an insulated column of rock which rises about forty feet above it. The whole descent of the river at this place probably exceeds two hundred and fifty feet. The rock is very fine felspathose sandstone. It has a smooth surface and a light red color. I have named these magnificent cascade " Wilberforce Falls," as a

tribute of my respect for that distinguished philan-
thropist and Christian. Messrs. Back and Hood took
beautiful sketches of this majestic scene.

The river being surveyed from the summit of a hill,
above these falls, appeared so rapid and shallow, that
it seemed useless to attempt proceeding any farther in
the large canoes. I therefore determined on con-
structing out of their materials two smaller ones of
sufficient size to contain three persons, for the purpose
of crossing any river that might obstruct our progress.
This operation was accordingly commenced, and by
the 31st both the canoes being finished, we prepared
for our departure on the following day.

The leather which had been preserved for making
shoes was equally divided among the men, two pair of
flannel socks were given to each person, and such articles of warm clothing as remained, were issued to
those who most required them. They were also furnished with one of the officers' tents. This being
done, I communicated to the men my intention of
proceeding in as direct a course as possible to the part
of Point Lake, opposite to our spring encampment,
which was only distant one hundred and forty-nine
miles in a straight line. They received the communication cheerfully, considered the journey to be short,
and left me, in high spirits, to arrange their own
packages. The stores, books, &c., which were not

absolutely necessary to be carried, were then put up in boxes to be left *en cache* here, in order that the men's burdens might be as light as possible.

The next morning was warm, and very fine. Every one was on the alert at an early hour, being anxious to commence the journey. Our luggage consisted of ammunition, nets, hatchets, ice chisels, astronomical instruments, clothing, blankets, three kettles, and the two canoes, which were each carried by one man. The officers carried such a portion of their own things as their strength would permit ; the weight carried by each man was about ninety pounds, and with this we advanced at the rate of about a mile an hour, including rests. In the evening the hunters killed a lean cow, out of a large drove of musk-oxen ; but the men were too much laden to carry more than a small portion of its flesh. The alluvial soil, which towards the mouth of the river spreads into plains, covered with grass and willows, was now giving place to a more barren and hilly country ; so that we could but just collect sufficient brush wood to cook our suppers. The part of the river we skirted to-day was shallow, and flowed over a bed of sand ; its width about one hundred and twenty yards. About midnight our tent was blown down by a squall, and we were completely drenched with rain before it could be re-pitched.

In the morning of the 1st of September a fall of

snow took place ; the canoes became a cause of delay,
by the difficulty of carrying them in a high wind, and
they sustained much damage from the falls of those
who had charge of them. The face of the country
was broken by hills of moderate elevation, but the
ground was plentifully strewed with small stones,
which, to men bearing heavy burdens, and whose feet
were protected only by soft moose skin shoes, occasioned great pain. At the end of eleven miles we encamped, and sent for a musk-ox and a deer, which St. Germain and Augustus had killed. The day was extremely cold, the thermometer varying between 34° and 36°.
In the afternoon a heavy fall of snow took place, on
the wind changing from north-west to south-west.
We found no wood at the encampment, but made a
fire of moss to cook the supper, and crept under our
blankets for warmth. At sun rise the thermometer
was at 31°, and the wind fresh from north-west ; but
the weather became mild in the course of the forenoon,
and the snow disappeared from the gravel. The afternoon was remarkably fine, and the thermometer rose
to 50°. One of the hunters killed a musk-ox. The
hills in this part are lower and more round-backed
than those we passed yesterday, and exhibited but little naked rock ; they were covered with lichens.

Having ascertained from the summit of the highest
hill near the tents, that the river continued to preserve

a west course ; and fearing that by pursuing it further we might loose much time, and unnecessarily walk over a great deal of ground, I determined on quitting its banks the next day, and making as directly as we could for Point Lake. We accordingly followed the river on the 3d, only to the place where the musk-ox had been killed last evening, and after the meat was procured, crossed the river in our two canoes lashed together. We now emerged from the valley of the river, and entered a level, but very barren country, varied only by small lakes and marshes, the ground being covered with small stones. Many old tracks of rein-deer were seen in the clayey soil, and some more recent ones of the musk-ox. We encamped on the borders of Wright's River, which flows to the eastward ; the direct distance walked to-day being ten miles and three-quarters. The next morning was very fine, and as the day advanced, the weather became quite warm. We set out at six A.M., and having forded the river, walked over a perfectly level country, interspersed with small lakes, which communicated with each other, by streams running in various directions. No berry-bearing plants were found in this part, the surface of the earth being thinly covered in the moister places with a few grasses, and on the drier spots with lichens.

Having walked twelve miles and a half, we encamped at seven P.M., and distributed our last piece of pemmican, and a little arrow-root for supper, which afforded but a scanty meal. This evening was warm, but dark clouds overspread the sky. Our men now began to find their burdens very oppressive, and were much fatigued by this day's march, but did not complain. One of them was lame from an inflammation in the knee. Heavy rain commenced at midnight, and continued without intermission until five in the morning, when it was succeeded by snow on the wind changing to north-west, which soon increased to a violent gale. As we had nothing to eat, and were destitute of the means of making a fire, we remained in our beds all the day ; but the covering of our blankets was insufficient to prevent us from feeling the severity of the frost, and suffering inconvenience from the drifting of the snow into our tents. There was no abatement of the storm the next day ; our tents were completely frozen, and the snow had drifted around them to a depth of three feet, and even on the inside there was a covering of several inches on our blankets. Our suffering from cold, in a comfortless canvass tent in such weather, with the temperature at 20°, and without fire, will easily be imagined ; it was, however, less than that which we felt from hunger.

The morning of the 7th cleared up a little, but the wind was still strong, and the weather extremely cold. From the unusual continuance of the storm, we feared

the winter had set in with all its rigor, and that by
longer delay we should only be exposed to an accumulation of difficulties ; we therefore prepared for our
journey, although we were in a very unfit condition
for starting, being weak from fasting, and our garments stiffened by the frost.   We had no means
of making a fire to thaw them, the moss, at all times
difficult to kindle, being now covered with ice and
snow.   A considerable time was consumed in packing
up the frozen tents and bed clothes, the wind blowing
so strong that no one could keep his hands long out of
his mittens.

Just as we were about to commence our march, I
was seized with a fainting fit, in consequence of ex-
haustion and sudden exposure to the wind ; but
after eating a morsel of portable soup, I recovered, so
far as to be able to move on.   I was unwilling at first
to take this morsel of soup, which was diminishing
the small and only remaining meal of the party ; but
several of the men urged me to it, with much kindness.
The ground was covered a foot deep with snow, the
margin of the lakes was incrusted with ice, and the
swamps over which we had to pass were entirely
frozen ; but the ice not being sufficiently strong to
bear us, we frequently plunged knee-deep in water.
Those who carried the canoes were repeatedly blown
down by the violence of the wind, and they often fell,

from making an insecure step on a slippery stone ; on one of these occasions, the largest canoe was so much broken as to be rendered utterly unserviceable. This was felt as a serious disaster, as the remaining canoe having through mistake been made too small, it was doubtful whether it would be sufficient to carry us across a river. Indeed we had found it necessary in crossing Hood's River, to lash the two canoes together. As there was some suspicion that Benoit, who carried the canoe, had broken it intentionally, he having on a former occasion been overheard by some of the men to say, that he would do so when he got it in charge, we closely examined him on the point ; he roundly denied having used the expressions attributed to him, and insisted that it was broken by his falling accidentally ; and as he brought men to attest the latter fact, who saw him tumble, we did not press the matter further. I may here remark, that our people had murmured a good deal at having to carry two canoes, though they were informed of the necessity of taking both, in case it should be deemed advisable to divide the party ; which it had been thought probable we should be obliged to do, if animals proved scarce, in order to give the whole the better chance of procuring sub-sistence, and also for the purpose of sending forward some of the best walkers to search for Indians, and to get them to meet us with supplies of provision. The power of doing this was now at an end. As the accident could not be remedied, we turned it to the best account, by making a fire of the bark and timbers of the broken vessel, and cooked the remainder of our portable soup and arrow-root. This was a scanty meal after three days' fasting, but it served to allay the pangs of hunger, and enabled us to proceed at a quicker pace than before. The depth of the snow caused us to march in Indian file, that is, in each other's steps ; the voyagers taking it in turn to lead the party. A distant object was pointed out to this man in the direction we wished to take, and Mr. Hood followed immediately behind him, to renew the bearings, and keep him from deviating more than could be helped from the mark. It may be here observed, that we proceeded in this manner throughout our route across the barren grounds.

In the afternoon we got into a more hilly country, where the ground was strewed with large stones. The surface of these was covered with lichens of the *genus gyrophora*, which the Canadians term *tripe de roche*. A considerable quantity was gathered, and with half a partridge each, (which were shot in the course of the day,) furnished us with a slender supper, which we cooked with a few willows, dug up from beneath the deep snow. We passed a comfortless night in our damp clothes, but took the precaution of sleeping upon our socks and shoes to prevent them from freezing. This plan was afterwards adopted throughout the journey.

At half-past five in the morning we proceeded ; and after walking about two miles, came to Cracroft's River, flowing to the westward, with a very rapid current over a rocky channel. We had much difficulty in crossing this, the canoe being useless, not only from the bottom of the channel being obstructed by large stones, but also from its requiring gumming, an operation which, owing to the want of wood and the frost, we were unable to perform. However, after following the course of the river some way, we effected a passage by means of a range of large rocks that crossed a rapid. As the current was strong, and many of the rocks were covered with water to the depth of two or three feet, the men were exposed to much danger in carrying their heavy burdens across, and several of them actually slipped into the stream, but were immediately rescued by the others. Junius went farther up the river in search of a better crossing place, and did not rejoin us to-day. As several of the party were drenched from head to foot, and we were all wet to the middle, our clothes became stiff with the frost, and we walked with much pain for the remainder of the day. The march was continued to a late hour, being anxious to rejoin the hunters who had gone before, but we were obliged to encamp at the end of ten miles and a quarter, without seeing them. Our only meal to-day consisted of a partridge each, (which the hunters shot,) mixed with *tripe de roche*. This repast, although scanty for men with appetites such as our daily fatigue created, proved a cheerful one, and was received with thankfulness. Most of the men had to sleep in the open air, in consequence of the absence of Crédit, who carried their tent ; but we fortunately found an unusual quantity of roots to make a fire, which prevented their suffering much from the cold, though the thermometer was at 17°.

We started at six on the 9th, and at the end of two miles regained our hunters, who were halting on the borders of a lake amidst a clump of stunted willows. This lake stretched to the westward as far as we could see, and its waters were discharged by a rapid stream one hundred and fifty yards wide. Being entirely ignorant where we might be led by pursuing the course of the lake, and dreading the idea of going a mile unnecessarily out of the way, we determined on crossing the river if possible ; and the canoe was gummed for the purpose, the willows furnishing us with fire. But we had to await the return of Junius before we could make the traverse. In the mean time we gathered a little *tripe de roche*, and breakfasted upon it and a few partridges that were killed in the morning. St.

Germain and Adam were sent upon some recent tracks
of deer. Junius arrived in the afternoon, and informed us that he had seen a large herd of musk-oxen on
the banks of Cracroft's River, and had wounded one
of them, but it had escaped. He brought about four
pounds of meat, the remains of a deer that had been
devoured by the wolves. The poor fellow was much
fatigued, having walked throughout the night, but as
the weather was particularly favorable for our crossing
the river, we could not allow him to rest. After he
had taken some refreshment we proceeded to the river.
The canoe being put into the water was found extremely ticklish, but it was managed with much dexterity
by St. Germain, Adam, and Peltier, who ferried over
one passenger at a time, causing him to lie flat in its
bottom, by no means a pleasant position, owing to its
leakiness, but there was no alternative. The transport
of the whole party was effected by five o'clock, and we
walked about two miles further, and encamped, having come five miles and three-quarters on a south-west
course. Two young alpine hares were shot by St.
Germain, which, with the small piece of meat brought
in by Junius, furnished the supper of the whole party.
There was no *tripe de roche* here. The country had
now become decidedly hilly, and was covered with
snow. The lake preserved its western direction, as
far as I could see from the summit of the highest

mountain near the encampment. We subsequently learned from the Copper Indians, that the part at which we had crossed the river was the *Congecatha wha chaga* of Hearne, of which I had little idea at the time, not only from the difference of latitude, but also from its being so much farther east of the mouth of the Copper-Mine River, than his track is laid down. He only making one degree aud three-quarters difference of longitude, and we upwards of four. Had I been aware of the fact, several days' harassing march, and a disastrous accident would have been prevented by keeping on the western side of the lake, instead of crossing the river. We were informed also, that this river is the Anatessy, or River of Strangers, and is supposed to fall into Bathurst's Inlet; but although the Indians have visited its mouth, their description was not sufficient to identify it with any of the rivers whose mouths we had seen. It probably falls in that part of the coast which was hid from our view by Goulburn's or Elliot's Islands.

September 10.—We had a cold north wind, and the atmosphere was foggy. The thermometer 18° at five A.M. In the course of our march this morning, we passed many small lakes; and the ground, becoming higher and more hilly as we receded from the river, was covered to a much greater depth with snow. This rendered walking not only extremely laborious, but also hazardous in the highest degree ; for the sides of the hills, as is usual throughout the barren grounds, abounding in accumulations of large angular stones, it often happened that the men fell into the interstices with their loads on their backs, being deceived by the smooth appearance of the drifted snow. If any one had broken a limb here, his fate would have been melancholy indeed ; we could neither have remained with him, nor carried him on. We halted at ten to gather *tripe de roche*, but it was so frozen, that we were quite benumbed with cold before a sufficiency could be collected even for a scanty meal. On proceeding, our men were somewhat cheered, by observing on the sandy summit of a hill, from whence the snow had been blown, the summer track of a man ; and afterwards by seeing several deer tracks on the snow. About noon the weather cleared up a little, and, to our great joy, we saw a herd of musk-oxen grazing in a valley below us. The party instantly halted, and the best hunters were sent out ; they approached the animals with the utmost caution, no less than two hours being consumed before they got within gun-shot. In the meantime we beheld their proceedings with extreme anxiety, and many secret prayers were, doubtless, offered up for their success. At length they opened their fire, and we had the satisfaction of seeing one of the largest cows fall ; another was wounded, but escaped. This success infused spirit into our starving party. To skin and cut up the animal was the work of a few minutes. The contents of its stomach were devoured upon the spot, and the raw intestines, which were next attacked, were pronounced by the most delicate amongst us to be excellent. A few willows, whose tops were seen peeping through the snow in the bottom of the valley, were quickly grubbed, the tents pitched, and supper cooked, and devoured with avidity. This was the sixth day since we had had a good meal. The *tripe de roche*, even where we got enough, only serving to allay the pangs of hunger for a short time. After supper, two of the hunters went in pursuit of the herd, but could not get near them.

We were detained all the next day by a strong southerly wind, and were much incommoded in the tents by the drift snow. The temperature was 20°. The average for the last ten days about 24 5°. We restricted ourselves to one meal to-day as we were at rest, and there was only meat remaining sufficient for the next day.

The gale had not diminished on the 12th, and, as we were fearful of its continuance for some time, we determined on going forward; our only doubt regarded the preservation of the canoe, but the men promised to pay particular attention to it, and the most careful

persons were appointed to take it in charge. The
snow was two feet deep, and the ground much broken,
which rendered the march extremely painful. The
whole party complained more of faintness and weakness than they had ever done before ; their strength
seemed to have been impaired by the recent supply of
animal food.   In the afternoon the wind abated, and
the snow ceased ; cheered with the change, we proceeded forward at a quicker pace, and encamped at
six P.M., having come eleven miles.   Our supper consumed the last of our meat.

We set out on the 13th, in thick hazy weather,
and, after an hour's march, had the extreme mortification to find ourselves on the borders of a large lake,
which we subsequently learned from the Indians was
named Contwoy-to, or Rum Lake ; neither of its extremities could be seen. As the portion which lay to
the east seemed the widest, we coasted along to the
westward portion in search of a crossing-place This
lake being bounded by steep and lofty hills, our march
was very fatiguing.   Those sides which were exposed
to the sun were free from snow, and we found upon
them some excellent berries.   We encamped at six P.
M., having come only six miles and a half.   Crédit
was then missing, and he did not return during the
night. We supped off a single partridge and some
tripe de roche ; this unpalatable weed was now quite

nauseous to the whole party, and in several it produced bowel complaints. Mr. Hood was the greatest sufferer from this cause. This evening we were extremely distressed at discovering that our improvident companions, since we left Hood's River, had thrown away three of the fishing nets, and burnt the floats ; they knew we had brought them to procure subsistence for the party, when the animals should fail, and we could scarcely believe the fact of their having wilfully deprived themselves of this resource, especially when we considered that most of them had passed the greater part of their servitude in situations where the nets alone had supplied them with food. Being thus deprived of our principal resource, that of fishing, and the men evidently getting weaker every day, it became necessary to lighten their burdens of every thing except ammunition, clothing, and the instruments that were required to find our way. I, therefore, issued directions to deposit at this encampment the dipping needle, azimuth compass, magnet, a large thermometer, and a few books we had carried, having torn out of these such parts as we should require to work the observations for latitude and longitude. I also promised, as an excitement to the efforts in hunting, my gun to St. Germain, and an ample compensation to Adam, or any of the other men who should kill any animals. Mr. Hood, on this occasion, lent his gun to Michel, the Iroquois, who was very eager in the chase, and often successful.

September 14.—This morning the officers being assembled round a small fire, Perrault presented each of us with a small piece of meat which he had saved from his allowance. It was received with great thankfulness, and such an act of self-denial and kindness, being totally unexpected in a Canadian voyager, filled our eyes with tears. In directing our course to a river issuing from the lake, we met Crédit, who communicated the joyful intelligence of his having killed two deer in the morning. We instantly halted, and having shared the deer that was nearest to us, prepared breakfast. After which, the other deer was sent for, and we went down to the river, which was about three hundred yards wide, and flowed with great velocity through a broken rocky channel. Having searched for a part where the current was most smooth, the canoe was placed in the water at the head of a rapid, and St. Germain, Solomon, Belanger, and I, embarked in order to cross. We went from the shore very well, but in mid-channel the canoe became difficult to manage under our burden, as the breeze was fresh. The current drove us to the edge of the rapid, when Belanger unfortunately applied his paddle to avert the apparent danger of being forced down it, and lost his balance. The canoe was overset in consequence in the middle of the rapid. We fortunately kept hold of it, until we touched a rock where the water did not reach higher than our waists ; here we kept our footing, notwithstanding the strength of the current, until the water was emptied out of the canoe. Belanger then held the canoe steady whilst St. Germain placed me in it, and afterwards embarked himself in a very dexterous manner. It was impossible, however, to embark Belanger, as the canoe would have been hurried down the rapid, the moment he should have raised his foot from the rock on which he stood. We were, therefore, compelled to leave him in his perilous situation. We had not gone twenty yards before the canoe, striking on a sudden rock, went down. The place being shallow, we were again enabled to empty it, and the third attempt brought us to the shore. In the mean time Belanger was suffering extremely, immersed to his middle in the centre of a rapid, the temperature of which was very little above the freezing point, and the upper part of his body covered with wet clothes, exposed in a temperature not much above zero, to a strong breeze. He called piteously for relief, and St. Germain on his return endeavored to embark him, but in vain. The canoe was hurried down the rapid, and when he landed he was rendered by the cold incapable of further exertion, and Adam attempted to embark Belanger, but found it impossible. An attempt was next made to carry out to him a line, made of the slings of the men's loads. This also failed, the current acting so strongly upon it, as to prevent the canoe from steering, and it was finally broken and carried down the stream. At length, when Belanger's strength seemed almost exhausted, the canoe reached him with a small cord belonging to one of the nets, and he was dragged perfectly sense-less through the rapid. By the direction of Dr. Rich-ardson, he was instantly stripped, and being rolled up in blankets, two men undressed themselves and went to bed with him ; but it was some hours before he recovered his warmth and sensations. As soon as Belanger was placed in his bed, the officers immedia-tely sent over my blankets and a person to make a fire. Augustus brought the canoe over, and in return-ing he was obliged to descend both the rapids, be-fore he could get across the stream ; which hazardous service he performed with the greatest coolness and judgment. It is impossible to describe my sensations as I witnessed the various unsuccessful attempts to relieve Belanger. The distance prevented my seeing distinctly what was going on, and I continued pacing up and down upon the rock on which I landed, regard-less of the coldness of my drenched and stiffening gar-ments. The canoe, in every attempt to reach him, was hurried down the rapid, and was lost to the view amongst the rocky islets, with a rapidity that seemed to threaten certain destruction ; once, indeed, I fancied that I saw it overwhelmed in the waves. Such an event would have been fatal to the whole party. Separated as I was from my companions, without gun, ammunition, hatchet, or the means of making a fire, and in wet clothes, my doom would have been speedily sealed. My companions too, driven to the necessity of coasting the lake, must have sunk under the fatigue of rounding its innumerable arms and bays, which, as we have learned from the Indians, are very extensive. By the goodness of Providence, however, we were spared at that time, and some of us have been permitted to offer up our thanksgivings, in a civilized land, for the signal deliverances we then and afterwards experienced.

By this accident I had the misfortune to loose my port-folio, containing my journal from Fort Enterprize, together with all the astronomical and meteorological observations made during the descent of the Copper-Mine River, and along the sea coast, (except those for the dip and variation.) I was in the habit of carrying it strapped across my shoulders, but had taken it off on entering the canoe, to reduce the upper weight. The results of most of the observations for latitude and longitude had been registered in the sketch books, so that we preserved the requisites for the construction of the chart. The meteorological observations, not having been copied, were lost. My companions, Dr. Richardson, Mr. Back, and Mr. Hood, had been so careful in noting every occurrence in their journals, that the loss of mine could fortunately be well supplied. These friends immediately offered me their documents, and every assistance in drawing up another narrative, of which kindness I availed myself at the earliest opportunity afterwards.

September 15.—The rest of the party were brought across this morning, and we were delighted to find Belanger so much recovered as to be able to proceed, but we could not set out until noon, as the men had to prepare substitutes for the slings which were lost yesterday. Soon after leaving the encampment we discerned a herd of deer, and after a long chase a fine male was killed by Perrault; several others were wounded, but they escaped. After this we passed round the north end of a branch of the lake, and ascended the Willingham Mountains, keeping near the border of the lake. These hills were steep, craggy, and covered with snow. We encamped at seven, and enjoyed a substantial meal. The party were in good spirits this evening at the recollection of having crossed the rapid, and being in possession of provision for the next day. Besides we had taken the precaution of bringing away the skin of the deer to eat when the meat should fail. The temperature at six P.M. was 30°.

We started at seven next morning and marched until ten, when the appearance of a few willows, peeping through the snow, induced us to halt and breakfast. Re-commencing the journey at noon, we passed over a more rugged country, where the hills were separated by deep ravines, whose steep sides were equally difficult to descend and to ascend.

The party was quite fatigued, and we encamped, having come ten miles and three-quarters. We observed many summer deer roads, and some recent tracks. Some marks that had been put up by the Indians were also noticed. We have since learned that this is a regular deer pass, and on that account, annually frequented by the Copper Indians. The lake is called by them Contwoy-to, or Rum Lake, in consequence of Mr. Hearne having here given the Indians who accompanied him some of that liquor. They do not get fish here

We walked next day over a more level country, but it was strewed with large stones. These galled our feet a good deal ; we contrived, however, to wade through the snow at a tolerably quick pace until five P.M., having made twelve miles and a half. We had made to-day our proper course, south by east, which we could not venture upon doing before, for fear of

falling again upon some branch of the Contwoy-to.
Some deer were seen in the morning, but the hunters
failed of killing any, and in the afternoon we fell into
the track of a large herd, which had passed the day
before, but did not overtake them.   In consequence
of this want of success we had no breakfast, and but a
scanty supper ; but we allayed the pangs of hunger,
by eating pieces of singed hide.   A little *tripe de roche*
was also obtained.   These would have satisfied us in
ordinary times, but we were now almost exhausted by
slender fare and travel, and our appetites had become
ravenous.   We looked, however, with humble confidence to the great Author and Giver of all good, for
a continuance of the support which had hitherto been
always supplied to us at our greatest need.   The
thermometer varied to-day between 25° and 28°.
The wind blew fresh from the south.

On the 18th the atmosphere was hazy, but the day
was more pleasant for walking than usual.   The country was level and gravelly, and the snow very deep.
We went for a short time along a deeply beaten road,
made by the reindeer, which turned suddenly off to
the south-west, which was a direction so wide of our
course that we could not venture upon following it.
All the small lakes were frozen, and we marched across
those which lay in our track.   We supped off the
tripe de roche which had been gathered during our

halts in the course of the march. Thermometer at six P.M. 32°.

Showers of snow fell without intermission through the night, but they ceased in the morning, and we set out at the usual hour. The men were very faint from hunger, and marched with difficulty, having to oppose a fresh breeze, and to wade through the snow two feet deep. We gained, however, ten miles by four o'clock, and then encamped. The canoe was unfortunately broken by the fall of the person who had it in charge. No *tripe de roche* was seen to-day, but in clearing the snow to pitch the tents we found a quantity of Iceland moss, which was boiled for supper. This weed, not having been soaked, proved so bitter, that few of the party could eat more than a few spoonfuls of it.

Our blankets did not suffice this evening to keep us in tolerable warmth ; the slightest breeze seeming to pierce through our debilitated frames. The reader will, probably, be desirous to know how we passed our time in such a comfortless situation : the first operation after encamping was to thaw our frozen shoes, if a sufficient fire could be made, and dry ones were put on ; each person then wrote his notes of the daily occurrences, and evening prayers were read ; as soon as supper was prepared it was eaten, generally in the dark, and we went to bed, and kept up a cheerful conversation until our blankets were thawed by the heat of our bodies, and we had gathered sufficient warmth to enable us to fall asleep. · On many nights we had not even the luxury of going to bed in dry clothes, for when the fire was insufficient to dry our shoes, we durst not venture to pull them off, lest they should freeze so hard as to be unfit to put on in the morning, and, therefore, inconvenient to carry.

On the 20th we got into a hilly country, and the marching became much more laborious; even the stoutest experienced great difficulty in climbing the craggy eminences. Mr. Hood was particularly weak, and was obliged to relinquish his station of second in the line, which Dr. Richardson now took, to direct the leading man in keeping the appointed course. I was also unable to keep pace with the men, who put forth their utmost speed, encouraged by the hope, which our reckoning had led us to form, of seeing Point Lake in the evening, but we were obliged to encamp without gaining a view of it. We had not seen either deer or their tracks through the day, and this circumstance, joined to the disappointment of not discovering the lake, rendered our voyagers very desponding, and the meagre supper of *tripe de roche* was little calculated to elevate their spirits. They now threatened to throw away their bundles, and quit us, which rash act they would probably have done, if they had known what track to pursue.

Sept. 21.—We set out at seven this morning in dark foggy weather, and changed our course two points to the westward. The party were very feeble, and the men much dispirited ; we made slow progress, having to march over a hilly and very rugged country.

Just before noon the sun beamed through the haze for the first time for six days, and we obtained an observation in latitude 65° 7' 06" N., which was six miles to the southward of that part of Point Lake to which our course was directed. By this observation we discovered that we had kept to the eastward of the proper course, which may be attributed partly to the difficulty of preserving a straight line through an unknown country, unassisted by celestial observations, and in such thick weather, that our view was often limited to a few hundred yards ; but chiefly to our total ignorance of the amount of the variation of the compass.

We altered the course immediately to west-south-west, and fired guns to apprize the hunters who were out of our view, and ignorant of our having done so. After walking about two miles we put up to collect the stragglers. Two partridges were killed, and these with some *tripe de roche,* furnished our supper. Notwithstanding a full explanation was given to the men of the reasons for altering the course, and they were

12*

assured that the observation had enabled us to discover our exact distance from Fort Enterprize, they
could not divest themselves of the idea of our having
lost our way, and a gloom was spread over every countenance. At this encampment Dr. Richardson was
obliged to deposit his specimens of plants and minerals,
collected on the sea-coast, being unable to carry them
any further. The way made to-day was five miles
and a quarter.

Sept. 22.—After walking about two miles this morning, we came upon the borders of a large lake, whose
extremities could not be discerned in consequence of
the density of the atmosphere ; but as its shores seemed to approach nearer to each other to the southward
than to the northward, we determined on tracing it
in that direction. We were grieved at finding the
lake expand very much beyond the contracted part we
had first seen, and incline now to the eastward of
south. As it was considered more than probable, from
the direction and size of the body of water we were
now tracing, that it was a branch of Point Lake ; and
as, in any case, we knew that by passing round its
south end, we must shortly come to the Copper-Mine
River, our course was continued in that direction.
The appearance of some dwarf pines and willows, larger than usual, induced us to suppose the river was
near. We encamped early, having come eight miles.

Our supper consisted of *tripe de roche* and half a partridge each.

Our progress next day was extremely slow, from the difficulty of managing the canoe in passing over the hills, as the breeze was fresh. Peltier, who had it in charge, having received several severe falls, became impatient, and insisted on leaving his burden, as it had already been much injured by the accidents of this day ; and no arguments we could use were sufficient to prevail on him to continue carrying it. Vaillant was, therefore, directed to take it, and we proceeded forward. Having found he got on very well, and was walking even faster than Mr. Hood could, in his present debilitated state, I pushed forward to stop the rest of the party, who had got out of our sight during the delay which the discussion about the canoe had occasioned. I accidentally passed the body of the men, and followed the tracks of two persons, who had separated from the rest, until two P.M., when, not seeing any person, I retraced my steps, and on my way met Dr. Richardson, who had also missed the party whilst he was employed gathering *tripe de roche*, and we went back together in search of them. We found they had halted among some willows, where they had picked up some pieces of skin, and a few bones of deer that had been devoured by the wolves last spring. They had rendered the bones friable by burning, and

eaten them, as weÏl as the skin ; and several of them
had added their old shoes to the repast.   Peltier and
Vaillant were with them, having left the canoe, which,
they said, was so completely broken by another fall,
as to be rendered incapable of repair, and entirely useless.   The anguish this intelligence occasioned may be
conceived, but it is beyond my power to describe it.
Impressed, however, with the necessity of taking it
forward, even in the state these men represented it to
be, we urgently desired them to fetch it ; but they declined going, and the strength of the officers was inadequate to the task.   To their infatuated obstinacy on
this occasion, a great portion of the melancholy circumstances which attended our subsequent progress may,
perhaps, be attributed.   The men now seemed to have
lost all hope of being preserved ; and all the arguments we could use failed in stimulating them to the
least exertion.   After consuming the remains of the
bones and horns of the deer we resumed our march,
and, in the evening, reached a contracted part of the
lake, which perceiving to be shallow, we forded and
encamped on the opposite side.   Heavy rain began
soon afterwards, and continued all the night.   On the
following morning the rain had so wasted the snow,
that the tracks of Mr. Back and his companions, who
had gone before with the hunters, were traced with
difficulty ; and the frequent showers during the day

almost obliterated them. The men became furious at
the apprehension of being deserted by.the hunters, and
some of the strongest throwing down their bundles,
prepared to set out after them, intending to leave the
more weak to follow as they could. The entreaties
and threats of the officers, however, prevented their
executing this mad scheme ; but not before Solomon
Belanger was despatched with orders for Mr. Back to
halt until we should join him. Soon afterwards a thick
fog came on, but we continued our march and overtook
Mr. Back, who had been detained in consequence of
his companions having followed some recent tracks of
deer. After halting an hour, during which we refreshed ourselves with eating our old shoes and a few scraps
of leather, we set forward in the hope of ascertaining
whether an adjoining piece of water was the Copper-
Mine River or not, but were soon compelled to return
and encamp, for fear of a separation of the party, as
we could not see each other at ten yards' distance.
The fog diminishing towards the evening, Augustus
was sent to examine the water, but having lost his
way he did not reach the tents before midnight, when
he brought the information of its being a lake. We
supped upon *tripe de roche*, and enjoyed a comfortable fire, having found some pines, seven or eight feet
high, in a valley near the encampment.

The bounty of Providence was most seasonably
manifested to us next morning. in our killing five

small deer out of a herd, which came in sight as we were on the point of starting. This unexpected supply reanimated the drooping spirits of our men, and filled every heart with gratitude.

The voyagers instantly petitioned for a day's rest, which we were most reluctant to grant, being aware .of the importance of every moment at this critical period of our journey. But they so earnestly and strongly pleaded their recent sufferings, and their conviction, that the quiet enjoyment of two substantial meals, after eight days' famine, would enable them to proceed next day more vigorously, that we could not resist their entreaties. The flesh, the skins, and even the contents of the stomachs of the deer were equally distributed among the party by Mr. Hood, who had volunteered, on the departure of Mr. Wentzel, to perform the duty of issuing the provision. This invidious task he had all along performed with great impartiality, but seldom without producing some grumbling amongst the Canadians ; and on the present occasion, the hunters were displeased that the heads, and some other parts, had not been added to their portions. It is proper to remark, that Mr. Hood always took the smallest portion for his own mess, but this weighed little with these men, as long as their own appetites remained unsatisfied. We all suffered much inconvenience from eating animal food after our long abstinence, but particularly those men who indulged themselves beyond moderation. We learned, in the evening, that the Canadians, with their usual thoughtlessness, had consumed above a third of their portions of meat.

We set out early on the 26th, and, after walking about three miles along the lake, came to the river, which we at once recognized, from its size, to be the Copper-Mine. It flowed to the northward, and after winding about five miles, terminated in Point Lake. Its current was swift, and there were two rapids in this part of its course, but in a canoe we could have crossed with ease and safety. These rapids, as well as every other part of the river, were carefully examined in search of a ford ; but finding none, the expedients occurred, of attempting to cross on a raft made of the willows which were growing there, or in a vessel framed with willows, and covered with the canvass of the tents ; but both these schemes were abandoned, through the obstinacy of the interpreters and the most experienced voyagers, who declared that they would prove inadequate to the conveyance of the party, and that much time would be lost in the attempt. The men, in fact, did not believe that this was the Copper-Mine River, and so little confidence had they in our reckoning, and so much had they bewildered themselves on the march, that some of them asserted it was Hood's River, and others that it was the Bethe-tessy, (a river which rises from a lake to the

northward of Rum Lake, and holds a course to the
sea parallel to the Copper-Mine.) In short, their
despondency had returned, and they all despaired of
seeing Fort Enterprize again. However, the steady
assurances of the officers, that we were actually on the
banks of the Copper-Mine River, and that the distance to Fort Enterprize did not exceed forty miles,
made some impression upon them, which was increased upon our finding some bear-berry plants, which is
reported by the Indians not to grow to the eastward
of that river. Then they deplored their folly and impatience in breaking the canoe, being all of opinion,
that had it not been so completely demolished on the
23d, it might have been repaired sufficiently to take
the party over. We again closely interrogated Peltier and Vaillant as to its state, with the intention of
sending for it ; but they persisted in the declaration,
that it was in a totally unserviceable condition.
St. Germain being again called upon, to endeavor to
construct a canoe frame from willows, stated that he
was unable to make one sufficiently large. It became
necessary, therefore, to search for pines of sufficient
size to form a raft ; and being aware that such trees
grow on the borders of Point Lake, we considered it
best to trace its shores in search of them ; we, therefore, resumed our march, carefully looking, but in
vain, for a fordable part, and encamped at the east
end of Point Lake.

CHAPTER XI.

As there was little danger of our losing the path of our hunters whilst we coasted the shores of this lake, I determined on again sending Mr. Back forward, with the interpreters, to hunt. I had in view, in this arrangement, the further object of enabling Mr. Back to get across the lake with two of these men, to convey the earliest possible account of our situation to the Indians. Accordingly I instructed him to halt at the first pines he should come to, and then prepare a raft ; and if his hunters had killed animals, so that the party could be supported whilst we were making our raft, he was to cross immediately with St. Germain and Beauparlant, and send the Indians to us as quickly as possible with supplies of meat.

We had this evening the pain of discovering that two of our men had stolen part of the officers' provision, which had been allotted to us with strict impartiality. This conduct was the more reprehensible, as it was plain that we were suffering, even in a greater degree than themselves, from the effects of famine, owing to our being of a less robust habit, and less accustomed to privations.   We had no means of punishing this crime, but by the threat that they should forfeit their wages, which had now ceased to operate.

Mr. Back and his companions set out at six in the morning, and we started at seven.   As the snow had entirely disappeared, and there were no means of distinguishing the footsteps of stragglers, I gave strict orders, previously to our setting out, for all the party to keep together: and especially I desired the two Esquimaux not to leave us, they having often strayed in search of the remains of animals.   Our people, however, through despondency, had become careless and disobedient, and had ceased to dread. punishment, or hope for reward.   Much time was lost in halting and firing guns to collect them, but the labor of walking was so much lightened by the disappearance of the snow, that we advanced seven or eight miles along the lake before noon, exclusive of the loss of distance in rounding its numerous bays.   At length we came to an arm, running away to the north-east, and apparently connected with the lake which we had coasted on the 22d, 23d, and 24th of the month.

The idea of again rounding such an extensive piece of water and of traveling over so barren a country was dreadful, and we feared that other arms, equally large, might obstruct our path, and that the strength of the party would entirely fail, long before we could reach the only part where we were certain of finding wood, distant in a direct line twenty-five miles. While we halted to consider of this subject, and to collect the party, the carcass of a deer was discovered in the cleft of a rock into which it had fallen in the spring. It was putrid, but it was little less acceptable to us on that account, in our present circumstances ; and a fire being kindled, a large portion of it was devoured on the spot, affording us an unexpected breakfast, for in order to husband our small remaining portion of meat, we had agreed to make only one scanty meal a day. The men, cheered by this unlooked-for supply, became sanguine in the hope of being able to cross the stream on a raft of willows, although they had before declared such a project impracticable, and they un-animously entreated us to return back to the rapid, a request which accorded with our own opinion, and was therefore acceded to. Crédit and Junius, how-ever, were missing, and it was also necessary to send notice of our intention to Mr. Back and his party. Augustus being promised a reward, undertook the task, and we agreed to wait for him at the rapid. It was supposed he could not fail meeting with the two stragglers on his way to or from Mr. Back, as it was likely they would keep on the borders of the lake. He

accordingly set out after Mr. Back, whilst we returned
about a mile towards the rapid, and encamped in a
deep valley amongst some large willows. We supped
on the remains of the putrid deer, and the men having
gone to the spot where it was found, scraped together
the contents of its intestines which were scattered on
the rock, and added them to their meal. We also
enjoyed the luxury to-day of eating a large quantity
of excellent blueberries and cranberries, (*vaccinium
uliginosum* and *v. vitus idœa*,) which were laid bare
by the melting of the snow, but nothing could allay
our inordinate appetites.

In the night we heard the report of Crédit's gun in
answer to our signal muskets, and he rejoined us in
the morning, but we got no intelligence of Junius.
We set out about an hour after daybreak, and encamped at two P.M. between the rapids, where the
river was about one hundred and thirty yards wide,
being its narrowest part.

Eight deer were seen by Michel and Crédit, who
loitered behind the rest of the party, but they could
not approach them. A great many shots were fired
by those in the rear at partridges, but they missed, or
at least did not choose to add what they killed to the
common stock. We subsequently learned that the
hunters often secreted the partridges they shot, and
eat them unknown to the officers. Some *tripe de*

roche was collected, which we boiled for supper, with the moiety of the remainder of our deer's meat. The men commenced cutting the willows for the construction of the raft. As an excitement to exertion, I promised a reward of three hundred livres to the first person who should convey a line across the river, by which the raft could be managed in transporting the party.

September 29.—Strong south-east winds with fog in the morning, more moderate in the evening. Temperature of the rapid 38°. The men began at an early hour to bind the willows in fagots for the construction of the raft, and it was finished by seven ; but as the willows were green, it proved to be very little buoyant, and was unable to support more than one man at a time. Even on this, however, we hoped the whole party might be transported, by hauling it from one side to the other, provided a line could be carried to the other bank. Several attempts were made by Belanger and Benoit, the strongest men of the party, to convey the raft across the stream, but they failed for want of oars. A pole constructed by tying the tent poles together, was too short to reach the bottom at a short distance from the shore ; and a paddle which had been carried from the sea coast by Dr. Richardson, did not possess sufficient power to move the raft in opposition to a strong breeze, which blew from the

opposite shore.   All the men suffered extremely from
the coldness of the water, in which they were necessarily immersed up to the waists, in their endeavors to
aid Belanger and Benoit ; and having witnessed repeated failures, they began to consider the scheme as
hopeless.   At this time Dr. Richardson, prompted by
a desire of relieving his suffering companions, proposed
to swim across the stream with a line, and to haul the
raft over.   He launched into the stream with the line
round his middle, but when he had got a short distance from the bank, his arms became benumbed with
cold, and he lost the power of moving them ; still he
persevered, and turning on his back, had nearly gained
the opposite bank, when his legs also became power-
less, and to our infinite alarm we beheld him sink.
We instantly hauled upon the line and he came again
on the surface, and was gradually drawn ashore in an
almost lifeless state.   Being rolled up in blankets, he
was placed before a good fire of willows, and fortunately was just able to speak sufficiently to give some
slight directions respecting the manner of treating
him.   He recovered strength gradually, and by the
blessing of God was enabled in the course of a few
hours to converse, and by the evening was sufficiently
recovered to remove into the tent.   We then regretted
to learn, that the skin of his whole left side was
deprived of feeling in consequence of exposure to too

great heat.   He did not perfectly recover the sensation of that side until the following summer.   I cannot describe what every one felt at beholding the
skeleton which the Doctor's debilitated frame exhibited.   When he stripped, the Canadians simultaneously exclaimed, " Ah que nous sommes maigres."   I
shall best explain his state and that of the party, by
the following extract from his journal : " It may be
worthy of remark, that I would have had little hesitation in any former period of my life, of plunging into
water even below 38° Fahrenheit ; but at this time
I was reduced almost to skin and bone, and like the
rest of the party, suffered from degrees of cold that
would have been disregarded whilst in health and
vigor.   During the whole of our march we experienced
that no quantity of clothing could keep us warm
whilst we fasted, but on those occasions on which we
were enabled to go to bed with full stomachs, we
passed the night in a warm and comfortable manner."

In following the detail of our friend's narrow escape,
I have omitted to mention, that when he was about to
step into the water, he put his foot on a dagger, which
cut him to the bone ; but this misfortune could not
stop him from attempting the execution of his gene-
ous undertaking.

In the evening Augustus came in.   He had walked
a day and a half beyond the place from whence we

turned back, but had neither seen Junius nor Mr. Back.   Of the former he had seen no traces, but he had followed the tracks of Mr. Back's party for a considerable distance, until the hardness of the ground rendered them imperceptible.   Junius was well equipped with ammunition, blankets, knives, a kettle, and other necessaries ; and it was the opinion of Augustus, that when he found he could not rejoin the party, he would endeavor to gain the woods on the west end of Point Lake, and follow the river until he fell in with the Esquimaux, who frequent its mouth. The Indians too, with whom we have since conversed upon this subject, are confident that he would be able to subsist himself during the winter.   Crédit, on his hunting excursion to-day, found a cap, which our people recognized to belong to one of the hunters who had left us in the spring.   This circumstance produced the conviction of our being on the banks of the Copper-Mine River, which all the assertions of the officers had hitherto failed to do with some of the party ; and it had the happy effect of reviving their spirits considerably.   We consumed the last of our deer's meat this evening at supper.

Next morning the men went out in search of dry willows, and collected eight large fagots, with which they formed a more buoyant raft than the former, but the wind being still adverse and strong, they delayed attempting to cross until a more favorable opportunity. Pleased, however, with the appearance of this raft, they collected some *tripe de roche,* and made a cheerful supper. Dr. Richardson was gaining strength, but his leg was much swelled and very painful. An observation for latitude placed the encampment in ·65° 00' 00'' N., the longitude being 112° 20' 00'' W., deduced from the last observation.

On the morning of the 1st of October, the wind was strong, and the weather as unfavorable as before for crossing on the raft. We were rejoiced to see Mr. Back and his party in the afternoon. They had traced the lake about fifteen miles farther than we did, and found it undoubtedly connected, as we had supposed, with the lake we fell upon on the 22d of September, and dreading, as we had done, the idea of coasting its barren shores, they returned to make an attempt at crossing here. St. Germain now proposed to make a canoe of the fragments of painted canvass, in which we wrapped up our bedding. This scheme appearing practicable, a party was sent to our encampment of the 24th and 25th last, to collect pitch amongst the small pines that grew there, to pay over the seams of the canoe.

In the afternoon we had a heavy fall of snow, which continued all the night. A small quantity of *tripe de roche* was gathered ; and Crédit, who had been hunt-

ing, brought in the antlers and back bone of a deer
which had been killed in the summer. The wolves
and birds of prey had picked them clean, but there
still remained a quantity of the spinal marrow which
they had not been able to extract. This, although
putrid, was esteemed a valuable prize, and the spine
being divided into portions, was distributed equally.
After eating the marrow, which was so aerid as to ex-
cruciate the lips, we rendered the bones friable by burning, and ate them also.

On the following morning the ground was covered
with snow to the depth of a foot and a half, and the
weather was very stormy. These circumstances rendered the men again extremely despondent ; a settled
gloom hung over their countenances, and they refused
to pick *tripe de roche*, choosing rather to go entirely
without eating, than to make any exertion. The
party which went for gum returned early in the morning without having found any ; but St. Germain said
he could still make the canoe with the willows covered with the canvass, and removed with Adam to a
clump of willows for that purpose. Mr. Back accompanied them to stimulate his exertion, as we feared
the lowness of his spirits would cause him to be slow
in his operations. Augustus went to fish at the rapid,
but a large trout having carried away his bait, we had
nothing to replace it.

The snow storm continued all the night, and during the forenoon of the 3d. Having persuaded the people to gather some *tripe de roche,* I partook of a meal with them ; and afterwards set out with the intention of going to St. Germain to hasten his operations, but though he was only three-quarters of a mile distant, I spent three hours in a vain attempt to reach him, my strength being unequal to the labor of wading through the deep snow ; and I returned quite exhausted, and much shaken by the numerous falls I had got. My associates were all in the same debilitated state, and poor Hood was reduced to a perfect shadow, from the severe bowel complaints which the *tripe de roche* never failed to give him. Back was so feeble as to require the support of a stick in walking ; and Dr. Richardson had lameness superadded to weakness. The voyagers were somewhat stronger than ourselves, but more indisposed to exertion, on account of their despondency. The sensation of hunger was no longer felt by any of us, yet we were scarcely able to converse upon any other subject than the pleasures of eating. We were much indebted to Hepburn at this crisis. The officers were unable from weakness to gather *tripe de roche* themselves, and Samandrè, who had acted as our cook on the journey from the coast, sharing in the despair of the rest of the Canadians, refused to make the slightest exertions. Hepburn, on the contrary, animated by a firm reliance on the beneficence of the Supreme Being, tempered with resignation to his will, was indefatigable in his exertions to serve us, and daily collected all the *tripe de roche* that was used in the officers' mess. Mr. Hood could not partake of this miserable fare, and a partridge which had been reserved for him was, I lament to say, this day stolen by one of the men.

Oct. 4.—The canoe being finished, it was brought to the encampment, and the whole party being assembled in anxious expectation on the beach, St. Germain embarked, and amidst our prayers for his success, succeeded in reachiug the opposite shore. The canoe was then drawn back again, and another person transported, and in this manner, by drawing it backwards and forwards, they were all conveyed over without any serious accident. By these frequent traverses the canoe was materially injured ; and latterly it filled each time with water before reaching the shore, so that all our garments and bedding were wet, and there was not a sufficiency of willows upon the side on which we now were, to make a fire to dry them.

That no time might be lost in procuring relief, I immediately despatched Mr. Back with St. Germain, Solomon Belanger, and Beauparlant, to search for the Indians, directing him to go to Fort Enterprize, where we expected they would be, or where, at least, a note from Mr. Wentzel would be found to direct us in our search for them. If St. Germain should kill any animals on his way, a portion of the meat was to be put up securely for us, and conspicuous marks placed over it.

It is impossible to imagine a more gratifying change than was produced in our voyagers after we were all safely landed on the southern banks of the river. Their spirits immediately revived, each of them shook the officers cordially by the hand, and declared they now considered the worst of their difficulties over, as they did not doubt of reaching Fort Enterprize in a few days, even in their feeble condition. We had indeed every reason to be grateful, and our joy would have been complete were it not mingled with sincere regret at the separation of our poor Esquimaux, the faithful Junius.

The want of *tripe de roche* caused us to go supperless to bed. Showers of snow fell frequently during the night. The breeze was light next morning, the weather cold and clear. We were all on foot by daybreak, but from the frozen state of our tents and bed clothes, it was long before the bundles could be made, and as usual the men lingered over a small fire they had kindled, so that it was eight o'clock before we started. Our advance from the depth of the snow was slow, and about noon coming to a spot where there was some *tripe de roche,* we stopped to collect it, and breakfasted.   Mr. Hood, who was now very feeble, and Dr. Richardson, who attached himself to him, walked together at a gentle pace in the rear of the party.   I kept with the foremost men, to cause them to halt occasionally, until the stragglers came up.   Resuming our march after breakfast, we followed the track of Mr. Back's party, and encamped early, as all of us were much fatigued, particularly Crédit, who having to-day carried the men's tent, it being his turn to do so, was so exhausted, that when he reached the encampment he was unable to stand.   The *tripe de roche* disagreed with this man and with Vaillant, in consequence of which they were the first whose strength totally failed.   We had a small quantity of this weed in the evening, and the rest of our supper was made up of scraps of roasted leather.   The distance walked to-day was six miles.   As Crédit was very weak in the morning, his load was reduced to little more than his personal luggage, consisting of his blanket, shoes, and gun.   Previous to setting out, the whole party ate the remains of their old shoes, and whatever scraps of leather they had, to strengthen their stomachs for the fatigue of the day's journey.   We left the encampment at nine, and pursued our route over a range of bleak hills.   The wind having increased to a strong gale in the course of the morning, became piercingly cold, and the drift rendered it difficult for those in the rear to follow the track over the heights, whilst in the valleys, where it was sufficiently marked, from the depth of the snow, the labor of walking was proportionably great. Those in advance made as usual frequent halts, yet being unable from the severity of the weather to remain long still, they were obliged to move on before the rear could come up, and the party, of course, straggled very much.

About noon Samandrè coming up, informed us that Crédit and Vaillant could advance no further. Some willows being discovered in a valley near to us, I proposed to halt the party there whilst Dr. Richardson went back to visit them. I hoped too, that when the sufferers received the information of a fire being kindled at so short a distance, they would be cheered, and use their utmost efforts to reach it, but this proved a vain hope. The Doctor found Valliant about a mile and a half in the rear, much exhausted with cold and fatigue. Having encouraged him to advance to the fire, after repeated solicitations he made the attempt, but fell down amongst the deep snow at every step. Leaving him in this situation, the Doctor went about half a mile farther back, to the spot where Crédit was said to have halted, and the track being nearly obliterated by the snow drift, it became unsafe for him to go further. Returning he passed Vaillant, who having moved only a few yards in his absence, had fallen down, was unable to rise, and could scarcely answer his questions. Being unable to afford him any effectual assistance, he hastened on to inform us of his situation. When J. B. Belanger had heard the melancholy account, he went immediately to aid Vaillant, and bring up his burden. Respecting Crédit, we were informed by Samandrè, that he had stopped a short distance behind Vaillant, but that his intention was to return to the encampment of the preceding evening.

When Belanger came back with Vaillant's load, he informed us that he had found him lying on his back, benumbed with cold, and incapable of being roused. The stoutest men of the party were now earnestly entreated to bring him to the fire, but they declared themselves unequal to the task ; and, on the contrary, urged me to allow them to throw down their loads, and proceed to Fort Enterprize with the utmost speed. A compliance with their desire would have caused the loss of the whole party, for the men were totally ignorant of the course to be taken, and none of the officers, who could have directed the march, were sufficiently strong to keep up at the pace they would then walk ; besides, even supposing them to have found their way, the strongest men would certainly have deserted the weak. Something, however, was absolutely necessary to be done, to relieve them as much as possible from their burdens, and the officers consulted on the subject. Mr. Hood and Dr. Richardson proposed to remain behind, with a single attendant, at the first place where sufficient wood and *tripe de roche* should be found for ten days' consumption ; and that I should proceed as expeditiously as possible with the men to the house, and thence send them immediate relief. They strongly urged that this arrangement would contribute to the safety of the rest of the party, by relieving them from the burden of a tent, and several other articles ; and that they might afford aid to Crédit, if he should unexpectedly come up. I was distressed beyond description at the thought of leaving them in such a dangerous situation, and for a long time combated their proposal ; but they strenuously urged, that this step afforded the only chance of safety for the party, and I reluctantly acceded to it. The ammunition, of which we had a small barrel, was also to be left with them, and it was hoped that this deposit would be a strong inducement for the Indians to venture across the barren grounds to their aid. We communicated this resolution to the men, who were cheered at the slightest prospect of alleviation of their present miseries, and they promised with great appearance of earnestness to return to those officers, upon the first supply of food.

The party then moved on ; Vaillant's blanket and
other necessaries were left in the track, at the request
of the Canadians, without any hope, however, of his
being able to reach them. After marching until dusk
without seeing a favorable place for encamping, night
compelled us to take shelter under the lee of a hill,
amongst some willows, with which, after many attempts, we at length made a fire. It was not sufficient, however, to warm the whole party, much less to
thaw our shoes ; and the weather not permitting the
gathering of *tripe de roche,* we had nothing to cook.

The painful retrospection of the melancholy events
of the day banished sleep, and we shuddered as we contemplated the dreadful effects of this bitterly cold night
on our two companions, if still living. Some faint
hopes were entertained of Crédit's surviving the storm,
as he was provided with a good blanket, and had
leather to eat.

The weather was mild next morning. We left the
encampment at nine, and a little before noon came to
a pretty extensive thicket of small willows, near which
there appeared a supply of *tripe de roche* on the face
of the rocks. At this place Dr. Richardson and Mr.
Hood determined to remain, with John Hepburn, who
volunteered to stop with them. The tent was securely
pitched, a few willows collected, and the ammunition
and all other articles were deposited, except each man's

clothing, one tent, a sufficiency of ammunition for the journey, and the officer's journals. I had only one blanket, which was carried for me, and two pair of shoes. The offer was now made for any of the men, who felt themselves too weak to proceed, to remain with the officers, but none of them accepted it. Michel alone felt some inclination to do so. After we had united in thanksgiving and prayers to Almighty God, I separated from my companions, deeply afflicted that a train of melancholy circumstances should have demanded of me the severe trial of parting from friends in such a condition, who had become endeared to me by their constant kindness, and co-operation, and a participation of numerous sufferings. This trial I could not have been induced to undergo, but for the reasons they had so strongly urged the day before, to which my own judgment assented, and for the sanguine hope I felt of either finding a supply of provision at Fort Enterprize, or meeting the Indians in the immediate vicinity of that place, according to my arrangements with Mr. Wentzel and Akaitcho. Previously to our starting, Peltier and Benoit repeated their promises, to return to them with provision, if any should be found at the house, or to guide the Indians to them, if any were met.

Greatly as Mr. Hood was exhausted, and, indeed, incapable as he must have proved, of encountering the fatigue of our next day's journey, so that I felt his resolution to be prudent, I was sensible that his determination to remain, was mainly prompted by the disinterested and generous wish to remove impediments to the progress of the rest of the party. Dr. Richardson and Hepburn, who were both in a state of strength to keep pace with the men, beside this motive which they shared with him, were influenced in their resolution to remain ; the former by the desire which had distinguished his character, throughout the expedition, of devoting himself to the succor of the weak, and the latter by the zealous attachment he had ever shewn towards his officers.

We set out without waiting to take any of the *tripe de roche,* and walked at a tolerable pace, and in an hour arrived at a fine group of pines, about a mile and a quarter from the tent. We sincerely regretted not having seen these before we had separated from our companions, as they would have been better supplied with fuel here, and there appeared to be more *tripe de roche* than where we had left them.

Descending afterwards into a more level country, we found the snow very deep, and the labor of wading through it so fatigued the whole party, that we were compelled to encamp, after a march of four miles and a half. Belanger and Michel were left far behind, and when they arrived at the encampment appeared quite exhausted. The former, bursting into tears, declared his inability to proceed with the party, and begged me to let him go back next morning to the tent, and shortly afterwards Michel made the same request. I was in hopes they might recover a little strength by the night's rest, and therefore deferred giving any permission until the morning. The sudden failure in the strength of these men cast a gloom over the rest, which I tried in vain to remove, by repeated assurances that the distance to Fort Enterprize was short, and that we should, in all probability, reach it in four days. Not being able to find any *tripe de roche*, we drank an infusion of the Labrador tea plant, (*ledum palustre*,) and ate a few morsels of burnt leather for supper. We were unable to raise the tent, and found its weight too great to carry it on; we, therefore, cut it up, and took a part of the canvass for a cover. The night was bitterly cold, and though we lay as close to each other as possible, having no shelter, we could not keep ourselves sufficiently warm to sleep. A strong gale came on after midnight, which increased the severity of the weather. In the morning Belanger and Michel renewed their request to be permitted to go back to the tent, assuring me they were still weaker than on the preceding evening, and less capable of going forward; and they urged, that the stopping at a place where there was a supply of *tripe*

de roche was their only chance of preserving life ; under these circumstances, I could not do otherwise than
yield to their desire.   I wrote a note to Dr. Richardson and Mr. Hood, informing them of the pines we
had passed, and recommending their removing thither.
Having found that Michel was carrying a considerable
quantity of ammunition, I desired him to divide it
among my party, leaving him only ten balls and a little shot, to kill any animals he might meet on his
way to the tent.   This man was very particular in his
inquiries respecting the direction of the house, and
the course we meant to pursue ; he also said, that if
he should be able, he would go and search for Vaillant and Crédit ; and he requested my permission to
take Vaillant's blanket, if he should find it, to which
I agreed, and mentioned it in my notes to the officers.

Scarcely were these arrangements finished, before
Perrault and Fontano were seized with a fit of dizziness, and betrayed other symptoms of extreme debility.
Some tea was quickly prepared for them, and after
drinking it, and eating a few morsels of burnt leather,
they recovered, and expressed their desire to go forward ; but the other men, alarmed at what they had
just witnessed, became doubtful of their own strength,
and, giving way to absolute dejection, declared their
own inability to move.   I now earnestly pressed upon
them the necessity of continuing our journey, as the

only means of saving their own lives, as well as those of our friends at the tent ; and, after much entreaty, got them to set out at ten A.M. : Belanger and Michel were left at the encampment, and proposed to start shortly afterwards. By the time we had gone about two hundred yards, Perrault became again dizzy, and desired us to halt, which we did, until he, recovering, proposed to march on. Ten minutes more had hardly elapsed before he again desired us to stop, and, bursting into tears, declared he was totally exhausted, and unable to accompany us further. As the encampment was not more than a quarter of a mile distant, we proposed that he should return to it, and rejoin Belanger and Michel, whom we knew to be still there, from perceiving the smoke of a fresh fire ; and because they had not made any preparation for starting when we left them. He readily acquiesced in the proposition, and having taken a friendly leave of each of us, and enjoined us to make all the haste we could in sending relief, he turned back, keeping his gun and ammunition. We watched him until he was near to the fire, and then proceeded. During these detentions, Augustus becoming impatient of the delay, had walked on, and we lost sight of him. The labor we experienced in wading through the deep snow induced us to cross a moderate sized lake, which lay in our track, but we found this operation far more harassing. As the sur-

face of the ice was perfectly smooth, we slipt at almost
every step, and were frequently blown down by the
wind with such force as to shake our whole frames.

Poor Fontano was completely exhausted by the labor of making this traverse, and we made a halt until
his strength was recruited, by which time the party
was benumbed with cold. Proceeding again, he got
on tolerably well for a little time, but being again
seized with faintness and dizziness, he fell often, and
at length exclaimed that he could go no further. We
immediately stopped, and endeavored to encourage
him to persevere, until we should find some willows,
to encamp ; he insisted, however, that he could not
march any longer through this deep snow ; and said,
that if he should even reach our encampment this
evening, he must be left there, provided *tripe de roche*
could not be procured to recruit his strength. The
poor man was overwhelmed with grief, and seemed desirous to remain at that spot. We were about two
miles from the place where the other men had been
left, and as the track to it was beaten, we proposed to
him to return thither, as we thought it probable he
would find the men still there : at any rate he would
be able to get fuel to keep him warm during the night ;
and, on the next day, he could follow their track to
the officers' tent ; and, should the path be covered by
the snow, the pines we had passed yesterday would
guide him, as they were yet in view.

I cannot describe my anguish on the occasion of separating from another companion under circumstances so distressing. There was, however, no alternative. The extreme debility of the rest of the party, put the carrying him quite out of the question, as he himself admitted ; and it was evident that the frequent delays he must occasion if he accompanied us, and did not gain strength, must have endangered the lives of the whole. By returning he had the prospect of getting to the tent where *tripe de roche* could be obtained, which agreed with him better than with any other of the party, and which he was always very assiduous in gathering. After some hesitation he determined on returning, and set out, having bid each of us farewell in the tenderest manner. We watched him with inexpressible anxiety for some time, and were rejoiced to find, though he had got on slowly, that he kept on his legs better than before. Antonio Fontano was an Italian, and had served many years in De Meuron's regiment. He had spoken to me that very morning, and after his first attack of dizziness, about his father ; and had begged, that should he survive, I would take him with me to England, and put him in the way of reaching home.

The party was now reduced to five persons, Adam, Peltier, Benoit, Samandrè, and myself. Continuing the journey, we came, after an hour's walk, to some

willows, and encamped under the shelter of a rock,
having walked in the whole four miles and a half.
We made an attempt to gather some *tripe de roche,*
but could not, owing to the severity of the weather.
Our supper, therefore, consisted of tea and a few morsels of leather.

Augustus did not make his appearance, but we felt
no alarm at his absence, supposing he would go to the
tent if he missed our track.   Having fire, we procured
a little sleep.   Next morning the breeze was light and
the weather mild, which enabled us to collect some
tripe de roche, and to enjoy the only meal we had for
four days.   We derived great benefit from it, and
walked with considerably more ease than yesterday.
Without the strength it supplied, we should certainly
have been unable to oppose the strong breeze we had
in the afternoon.   After walking about five miles, we
came upon the borders of Marten Lake, and were rejoiced to find it frozen, so that we could continue our
course straight for Fort Enterprize.   We encamped at
the first rapid in Winter River amidst willows and al-
ders ; but these were so frozen, and the snow fell so thick,
that the men had great difficulty in making a fire.
This proving insufficient to warm us, or even thaw
our shoes, and having no food to prepare, we crept
under our blankets.   The arrival in a well known part
raised the spirits of the men to a high pitch, and we

kept up a cheerful conversation until sleep overpowered us. The night was very stormy, and the morning scarcely less so ; but, being desirous to reach the house to-day, we commenced our journey very early. We were gratified by the sight of a large herd of reindeer on the side of the hill near the track, but our only hunter, Adam, was too feeble to pursue them. Our shoes and garments were stiffened by the frost, and we walked in great pain until we arrived at some stunted pines, at which we halted, made a good fire, and procured the refreshment of tea. The weather becoming fine in the afternoon, we continued our journey, passed the Dog-rib Rock, and encamped among a clump of pines of considerable growth, about a mile further on. Here we enjoyed the comfort of a large fire for the first time since our departure from the sea coast ; but this gratification was purchased at the expense of many severe falls that we had in crossing a stony valley, to get to these pines. There was no *tripe de roche,* and we drank tea and ate some of our shoes for supper. Next morning, after taking the usual repast of tea, we proceeded to the house. Musing on what we were likely to find there, our minds were agitated between hope and fear, and, contrary to the custom we had kept up, of supporting our spirits by conversation, we went silently forward.

At length we reached Fort Enterprize, and to our

infinite disappointment and grief found it a perfectly desolate habitation. There was no deposit of provision, no, trace of the Indians, no letter from Mr. Wentzel to point out where the Indians might be found. It would be impossible for me to describe our sensations after entering this miserable abode, and discovering how we had been neglected ; the whole party shed tears, not so much for our own fate, as for that of our friends in the rear, whose lives depended entirely on our sending immediate relief from this place.

I found a note, however, from Mr. Back, stating that he had reached the house two days ago, and was going in search of the Indians, at a part where St. Germain deemed it probable they might be found. If he was unsuccessful, he purposed walking to Fort Providence, and sending succor from thence. But he doubted whether he or his party could perform the journey to that place in their present debilitated state. It was evident that any supply that could be sent from Fort Providence would be long in reaching us, and could not be sufficient to enable us to afford any assistance to our companions behind, and that the only relief for them must be procured from the Indians. I resolved, therefore, on going also in search of them ; but my companions were absolutely incapable of proceeding, and I thought, by halting two or three days, they might gather a little strength, whilst the delay would afford us the chance of learning whether Mr. Back had seen the Indians.

We now looked round for the means of subsistence, and were gratified to find several deer skins, which had been thrown away during our former residence. The bones were gathered from the heap of ashes, these with the skins, and the addition of *tripe de roche*, we considered would support us tolerably well for a time. As to the house, the parchment being torn from the windows, the apartment we selected for our abode was exposed to all the rigor of the season. We endeavored to exclude the wind as much as possible, by placing loose boards against the apertures. The temperature was now between 15° and 20° below zero. We procured fuel by pulling up the flooring of the other rooms, and water for the purpose of cooking by melting the snow. Whilst we were seated round the fire, singing the deer skin for supper, we were rejoiced by the unexpected entrance of Augustus. He had followed quite a different course from ours, and the circumstance of his having found his way through a part of the country he had never been in before, must be considered a remarkable proof of sagacity. The unusual earliness of this winter became manifest to us from the state of things at this spot. Last year at the same season, and still later, there had been very little snow on the ground, and we were surrounded by vast herds of reindeer. Now there were but few recent tracks of these animals, and the snow was upwards of two feet deep. Winter River was then open, now it was frozen two feet thick.

When I arose the following morning, my body and limbs were so swollen that I was unable to walk more than a few yards.˙ Adam was in a still worse condition, being absolutely incapable of rising without assistance. My other companions fortunately experienced this inconvenience in a less degree, and went to collect bones, and some *tripe de roche*, which supplied us with two meals. The bones were quite acrid, and the soup extracted from them excoriated the mouth if taken alone, but it was somewhat milder when boiled with *tripe de roche*, and we even thought the mixture palatable, with the addition of salt, of which a cask had been fortunately left here in the spring. Augustus to-day set two fishing-lines below the rapid. On his way thither he saw two deer, but had not strength to follow them.

On the 13th the wind blew violently from southeast, and the snow drifted so much, that the party was confined to the house. In the afternoon of the following day Belanger arrived with a note from Mr. Back, stating that he had seen no trace of the Indians, and desiring further instructions as to the course he

should pursue. Belanger's situation, however, required our first care, as he came in almost speechless,
and covered with ice, having fallen into a rapid, and
for the third time since we left the coast, narrowly escaped drowning. He did not recover sufficiently to
answer our questions, until we had rubbed him for
some time, changed his dress, and given him some
warm soup. My companions nursed him with the
greatest kindness, and the desire of restoring him to
health seemed to absorb all regard for their own situation. I witnessed with peculiar pleasure this conduct, so different from that which they had recently
pursued, when every tender feeling was suspended by
the desire of self-preservation. They now no longer
betrayed impatience or despondency, but were composed and cheerful, and had entirely given up the
practice of swearing, to which the Canadian voyagers
are so lamentably addicted. Our conversation naturally turned upon the prospect of getting relief, and
upon the means which were best adapted for obtaining it. The absence of all traces of Indians on Winter River, convinced me that they were at this time
on the way to Fort Providence, and that by proceeding towards that post we should overtake them, as
they move slowly when they have their families with
them. This route also offered us the prospect of killing deer, in the vicinity of Reindeer Lake, in which

neighborhood, our men in their journeys to and fro last winter, had always found them abundant. Upon these grounds I determined on taking the route to Fort Providence as soon as possible, and wrote to Mr. Back desiring him to join me at Reindeer Lake, and detailing the occurrences since we had parted, that our friends might receive relief in case of any accident happening to me.

Belanger did not recover sufficient strength to leave us before the 18th. His answers as to the exact part of Round-Rock Lake in which he had left Mr. Back, were very unsatisfactory ; and we could only collect that it was a considerable distance, and he was still going on with the intention of halting at the place where Akaitcho was encamped last summer, about thirty miles off. This distance appeared so great, that I told Belanger it was very unsafe for him to attempt it alone, and that he would be several days in accomplishing it. He stated, however, that as the track was beaten, he should experience little fatigue, and seemed so confident, that I suffered him to depart with a supply of singed hide. Next day I received information which explained why he was so unwilling to acquaint us with the situation of Mr. Back's party. He dreaded that I should resolve upon joining it, when our numbers should be so great as to consume at once everything St. Germain might kill, if by acci-

dent he should be successful in hunting. He even
endeavored to entice away our other hunter Adam,
and proposed to him to carry off the only kettle we
had, and without which we could not have subsisted
two days. Adam's inability to move, however, pre
cluded him from agreeing to the proposal, but he
could assign no reason for not acquainting me with it,
previous to Belanger's departure. I was at first inclined to consider the whole matter as a fiction of
Adam's, but he persisted in his story without waver-
ing ; and Belanger, when we met again, confessed
that every part of it was true. It is painful to have
to record a fact so derogatory to human nature, but I
have deemed it proper to mention it, to shew the difficulties we had to contend with, and the effect which
distress had in warping the feelings and understanding
of the most diligent and obedient of our party ; for
such Belanger had been always esteemed up to this
time.

In making arrangements for our departure, Adam
disclosed to me, for the first time, that he was affected with œdematous swellings in some parts of the
body, to such a degree as to preclude the slightest attempt at marching ; and upon my expressing my surprise at his having hitherto concealed from me the extent of his malady, among other explanations the details of the preceding story came out. It now became

necessary to abandon the original intention of proceeding with the whole party towards Fort Providence, and Peltier and Samandrè having volunteered to remain with Adam, I determined on setting out with Benoit and Augustus, intending to send them relief by the first party of Indians we should meet. My clothes were so much torn, as to be quite inadequate to screen me from the wind, and Peltier and Samandrè fearing that I might suffer on the journey in conse-quence, kindly exchanged with me parts of their dress, desiring me to send them skins in return by the Indians. Having patched up three pair of snow-shoes, and singed a considerable quantity of skin for the journey, we started on the morning of the 20th. Previous to my departure, I packed up the journals of the officers, the charts, and some other documents, together with a letter addressed to the Under Secretary of State, detailing the occurrences of the Expedition up to this period, which package was given in charge to Peltier and Samandrè, with direction that it should be brought away by the Indians who might come to them. I also instructed them to forward succor immediately on its arrival to our companions in the rear, which they solemnly promised to do, and I left a letter for my friends, Richardson and Hood, to be sent at the same time. I thought it necessary to admonish Peltier, Samandrè, and Adam, to eat two meals every day,

in order to keep up their strength, which they promised me they would do. No language that I can
use could adequately describe the parting scene. I
shall only say there was far more calmness and resignation to the Divine will evinced by every one than
could have been expected. We were all cheered by
the hope that the Indians would be found by the one
party, and relief sent to the other. Those who remained entreated us to make all the haste we could,
and expressed their hope of seeing the Indians in ten
or twelve days.

At first starting we were so feeble as scarcely to be
able to move forwards, and the descent of the bank
of the river through the deep snow was a severe labor.
When we came upon the ice, where the snow was less
deep, we got on better, but after walking six hours
we had only gained four miles, and were then compelled by fatigue to encamp on the borders of Round-
Rock Lake. Augustus tried for fish here, but without
success, so that our fare was skin and tea. Compo-
sing ourselves to rest, we lay close to each other for
warmth. We found the night bitterly cold, and the
wind pierced through our famished frames.

The next morning was mild and pleasant for traveling, and we set out after breakfast. We had not,
however, gone many yards before I had the misfortune
to break my snow-shoes, by falling between two rocks

This accident prevented me from keeping pace with Benoit and Augustus, and in the attempt I became quite exhausted. Being convinced that their being delayed on my account might prove of fatal consequence to the rest, I resolved on returning to the house, and letting them proceed alone in search of the Indians. I therefore halted them only whilst I wrote a note to Mr. Back, stating the reason of my return, and requesting he would send meat from Reindeer Lake by these men, if St. Germain should kill any animals there. If Benoit should miss Mr. Back, I directed him to proceed to Fort Providence, and furnished him with a letter to the gentleman in charge of it, requesting immediate supplies might be sent to us.

On my arrival at the house, I found Samandrè very dispirited, and too weak, as he said, to render any assistance to Peltier; upon whom the whole labor of getting wood and collecting the means of subsistence would have devolved. Conscious, too, that his strength would have been unequal to these tasks, they had determined upon taking only one meal each day; under these circumstances I considered my return as particularly fortunate, as I hoped to stimulate Samandrè to exertion, and at any rate I could contribute some help to Peltier. I undertook the office of cooking, and insisted that they should eat twice a day whenever food could be procured, but as I was too weak to pound the bones, Peltier agreed to do that in addition to his more fatiguing task of getting wood. We had a violent snow storm all the next day, and this gloomy weather contributed to the depression of spirits under which Adam and Samandrè were laboring. Neither of them would quit their beds, and they scarcely ceased from shedding tears all day; in vain did Peltier and myself endeavor to cheer them. We had even to use much entreaty before we prevailed upon them to take the meals we had prepared. Our situation was indeed distressing, but in comparison with that of our friends in the rear, we considered it happy. Their condition gave us unceasing solicitude, and was the principal subject of our conversation.

Though the weather was stormy on the 26th, Samandrè assisted me to gather *tripe de roche*. Adam, who was very ill, and could not now be prevailed upon eat this weed, subsisted principally on bones, though he also partook of the soup. The *tripe de roche* had hitherto afforded us our chief support, and we naturally felt great uneasiness at the prospect of being deprived of it, by its being so frozen as to render it impossible for us to gather it.

We perceived our strength decline every day, and every exertion began to be irksome; when we were once seated the greatest effort was necessary in order to rise, and we had frequently to lift each other from our seats ; but even in this pitiable condition we conversed cheerfully, being sanguine as to the speedy arrival of the Indians. We calculated indeed that if they should be near the situation where they had remained last winter, our men would have reached them by this day. Having expended all the wood which we could procure from our present dwelling, without endangering its falling, Peltier began this day to pull down the partitions of the adjoining houses. Though these were only distant about twenty yards, yet the increase of labor in carrying the wood fatigued him so much, that by the evening he was exhausted. On the next day his weakness was such, especially in the arms, of which he chiefly complained, that he with difficulty lifted the hatchet ; still he persevered, Samandré and I assisting him in bringing in the wood, but our united strength could only collect sufficient to replenish the fire four times in the course of the day. As the insides of our mouths had become sore from eating the bone soup, we relinquished the use of it, and now boiled our skin, which mode of dressing we found more palatable than frying it, as we had hitherto done.

On the 29th, Peltier felt his pains more severe, and could only cut a few pieces of wood. Samandré, who was still almost as weak, relieved him a little time, and I assisted them in carrying in the wood. We

endeavored to pick some *tripe de roche*, but in vain,
as it was entirely frozen. In turning up the snow, in
searching for bones, I found several pieces of bark,
which proved a valuable acquisition, as we were almost
destitute of dry wood proper for kindling the fire. We
saw a herd of reindeer sporting on the river, about
half a mile from the house ; they remained there a
considerable time, but none of the party felt themselves sufficiently strong to go after them, nor was
there one of us who could have fired a gun without
resting it.

Whilst we were seated round the fire this evening,
discoursing about the anticipated relief, the conversation was suddenly interrupted by Peltier's exclaiming
with joy, "*Ah! le monde!*" imagining that he heard
the Indians in the other room ; immediately afterwards, to his bitter disappointment, Dr. Richardson
and Hepburn entered, each carrying his bundle. Peltier, however, soon recovered himself enough to express
his joy at their safe arrival, and his regret that their
companions were not with them. When I saw them
alone my own mind was instantly filled with apprehensions respecting my friend Hood, and our other companions, which were immediately confirmed by the
Doctor's melancholy communication, that Mr. Hood
and Michel were dead. Perrault and Fontano had
neither reached the tent. nor been heard of by them.

This intelligence produced a melancholy despondency in the minds of my party, and on that account the particulars were deferred until another opportunity. We were all shocked at beholding the emaciated countenances of the Doctor and Hepburn, as they strongly evidenced their extremely debilitated state. The alteration in our appearance was equally distressing to them, for since the swellings had subsided, we were little more than skin and bone. The Doctor particularly remarked the sepulchral tone of our voices, which he requested us to make more cheerful if possible, unconscious that his own partook of the same key.

Hepburn having shot a partridge, which was brought to the house, the Doctor tore out the feathers, and having held it to the fire a few minutes, divided it into seven portions. Each piece was ravenously devoured by my companions, as it was the first morsel of flesh any of us had tasted for thirty-one days, unless indeed the small gristly particles which we found occasionally adhering to the pounded bones may be termed flesh. Our spirits were revived by this small supply, and the Doctor endeavored to raise them still higher by the prospect of Hepburn's being able to kill a deer next day, as they had seen, and even fired at, several near the house. He endeavored, too, to rouse us to some attention to the comfort of our apartment, and particularly to roll up, in the day, our blankets which (expressly for the convenience of Adam and Samandrè,) we had been in the habit of leaving by the fire where we lay on them. The Doctor having brought his prayer-book and Testament, some prayers and psalms, and portions of scripture, appropriate to our situation, were read, and we retired to bed.

Next morning the Doctor and Hepburn went out early in search of deer ; but, though they saw several herds and fired some shots, they were not so fortunate as to kill any, being too weak to hold their guns steadily. The cold compelled the former to return soon, but Hepburn persisted until late in the evening.

My occupation was to search for skins under the snow, it being now our object immediately to get all that we could, but I had not strength to drag in more than two of those which were within twenty yards of the house until the Doctor came and assisted me. We made up our stock to twenty-six, but several of them were putrid, and scarcely eatable, even by men suffering the extremity of famine. Peltier and Samandrè continued very weak and dispirited, and they were unable to cut fire-wood. Hepburn had in consequence that laborious task to perform after he came back. The Doctor having scarified the swelled parts of Adam's body, a large quantity of water flowed out, and he obtained some ease, but still kept his bed.

After our usual supper of singed skin and bone soup, Dr. Richardson acquainted me with the afflicting circumstances attending the death of Mr. Hood and Michel, and detailed the occurrences subsequent to my departure from them, which I shall give from his journal, in his own words ; but I must here be permitted to express the heart-felt sorrow with which I was overwhelmed at the loss of so many companions ; especially for that of my friend Mr. Hood, to whose zealous and able co-operation I had been indebted for so much valuable assistance during the Expedition, whilst the excellent qualities of his heart engaged my warmest regard. His scientific observations, together with his maps and drawings, evince a variety of talent, which, had his life been spared, must have rendered him a distinguished ornament to his profession, and which will cause his death to be felt as a loss to the service.

CHAPTER XII.

Dr. RICHARDSON'S NARRATIVE.

AFTER Captain Franklin had bidden us farewell, we remained seated by the fire-side as long as the willows, the men had cut for us before they departed, lasted. We had no *tripe de roche* that day, but drank an infusion of the country tea-plant, which was grateful from its warmth, although it afforded no sustenance. We then retired to bed, where we remained all the next day, as the weather was stormy, and the snowdrift so heavy, as to destroy every prospect of success in our endeavors to light a fire with the green and frozen willows, which were our only fuel. Through the extreme kindness and forethought of a lady, the party, previous to leaving London, had been furnished with a small collection of religious books, of which we still retained two or three of the most portable, and they proved of incalculable benefit to us. We read portions of them to each other as we lay in bed, in ad-

dition to the morning and evening service, and found
that they inspired us on each perusal with so strong a
sense of the omnipresence of a beneficent God, that
our situation, even in these wilds, appeared no longer
destitute ; and we conversed, not only with calmness,
but with cheerfulness, detailing with unrestrained
confidence the past events of our lives, and dwelling
with hope on our future prospects. Had my poor
friend been spared to revisit his native land, I should
look back to this period with unalloyed delight.

On the morning of the 29th, the weather, although
still cold, was clear, and I went out in quest of *tripe
de roche*, leaving Hepburn to cut willows for a fire,
and Mr. Hood in bed. I had no success, as yesterday's snow drift was so frozen on the surface of the
rocks that I could not collect any of the weed ; but,
on my return to the tent, I found that Michel, the
Iroquois, had come with a note from Mr. Franklin,
which stated, that this man, and Jean Baptist Belanger being unable to proceed, were about to return to
us, and that a mile beyond our present encampment
there was a clump of pine trees, to which he recommended us to remove the tent. Michel informed us
that he quitted Mr. Franklin's party yesterday morning, but, that having missed his way, he had passed
the night on the snow a mile or two to the northward
of us. Belanger, he said, being impatient, had left

the fire about two hours' earlier, and as he had not arrived, he supposed he had gone astray. It will be seen in the sequel, that we had more than sufficient reason to doubt the truth of this story.

Michel now produced a hare and a partridge which he had killed in the morning. This unexpected supply of provision was received by us with a deep sense of gratitude to the Almighty for his goodness, and we looked upon Michel as the instrument he had chosen to preserve all our lives. He complained of cold, and Mr. Hood offered to share his buffalo robe with him at night : I gave him one of two shirts which I wore, whilst Hepburn, in the warmth of his heart, exclaimed, " How I shall love this man if I find that he does not tell lies like the others." Our meals being finished, we arranged that the greatest part of the things should be carried to the pines the next day ; and after reading the evening service, retired to bed full of hope.

Early in the morning Hepburn, Michel, and myself, carried the ammunition, and most of the other heavy articles to the pines. Michel was our guide, and it did not occur to us at the time that his conducting us perfectly straight was incompatible with his story of having gone astray on his way to us. He now informed us that he had, on his way to the tent, left on the hill above the pines a gun and forty-eight balls, which Perrault had given him when with the rest of Mr. Franklin's party, he took leave of him. It will be seen, on a reference to Mr. Franklin's journal, that Perrault carried his gun and ammunition with him when they parted from Michel and Belanger. After we had made a fire, and drank a little of the country tea, Hepburn and I returned to the tent, where we arrived in the evening, much exhausted with our journey. Michel preferred sleeping where he was, and requested us to leave him the hatchet, which we did, after he had promised to come early in the morning to assist us in carrying the tent and bedding. Mr. Hood remained in bed all day. Seeing nothing of Belanger to-day, we gave him up for lost.

On the 11th, after waiting until late in the morning for Michel, who did not come, Hepburn and I loaded ourselves with the bedding, and accompanied by Mr. Hood, set out for the pines. Mr. Hood was much affected with dimness of sight, giddiness, and other symptoms of extreme debility, which caused us to move very slow, and to make frequent halts. On arriving at the pines, we were much alarmed to find that Michel was absent. We feared that he had lost his way in coming to us in the morning, although it was not easy to conjecture how that could have happened, as our footsteps of yesterday were very distinct. Hepburn went back for the tent, and returned with it after dusk, completely worn out with the fatigue of the day. Michel, too, arrived at the same time, and relieved our anxiety on his account. He reported that he had been in chase of some deer which passed near his sleeping-place in the morning, and although he did not come up with them, yet that he found a wolf which had been killed by the stroke of a deer's horn, and had brought a part of it. We implicitly believed this story then, but afterwards became convinced from circumstances, the detail of which may be spared, that it must have been a portion of the body of Belanger or Perrault. A question of moment here presents itself ; namely, whether he actually murdered these men, or either of them, or whether he found the bodies on the snow. Captain Franklin, who is the best able to judge of this matter, from knowing their situation when he parted from them, suggested the former idea, and that both Belanger and Perrault had been sacrificed. When Perrault turned back, Captain Franklin watched him until he reached a small group of willows, which was immediately adjoining to the fire, and concealed it from view, and at this time the smoke of fresh fuel was distinctly visible. Captain Franklin conjectures, that Michel having already destroyed Belanger, completed his crime by Perrault't death, in order to screen himself from detection. Although this opinion is founded only on circumstances, and is

unsupported by direct evidence, it has been judged
proper to mention it, especially as the subsequent
conduct of the man shewed that he was capable of
committing such a deed. The circumstances are very
strong. It is not easy to assign any other adequate
motive for his concealing from us that Perrault had
turned back, and his request overnight that we should
leave him the hatchet ; and his cumbering himself
with it when he went out in the morning, unlike a
hunter who makes use only of his knife when he kills
a deer, seem to indicate that he took it for the purpose
of cutting up something that he knew to be frozen.
These opinions, however, are the result of subsequent
consideration. We passed this night in the open air.

On the following morning the tent was pitched, and
Michel went out early, refused my offer to accompany
him, and remained out the whole day. He would not
sleep in the tent at night, but chose to lie at the fire-
side.

On the 13th there was a heavy gale of wind, and
we passed the day by the fire. Next day, about two
P.M., the gale abating, Michel set out as he said to
hunt, but returned unexpectedly in a very short time.
This conduct surprised us, and his contradictory and
evasory answers to our questions excited some suspicions, but they did not turn towards the truth.

October 15th.—In the course of this day Michel

expressed much regret that he had stayed behind Mr. Franklin's party, and declared that he would set out for the house at once if he knew the way. We endeavored to soothe him, and to raise his hopes of the Indians speedily coming to our relief, but without success. He refused to assist us in cutting wood, but about noon, after much solicitation, he set out to hunt. Hepburn gathered a kettle of *tripe de roche*, but froze his fingers. Both Hepburn and I fatigued ourselves much to-day in pursuing a flock of partridges from one part to another of the group of willows, in which the hut was situated, but we were too weak to be able to approach them with sufficient caution. In the evening Michel returned, having met with no success.

Next day he refused either to hunt or cut wood, spoke in a very surly manner, and threatened to leave us. Under these circumstances, Mr. Hood and I deemed it better to promise if he would hunt diligently for four days, that then we would give Hepburn a letter for Mr. Franklin, a compass, inform him what course to pursue, and let them proceed together to the fort. The non-arrival of the Indians to our relief, now led us to fear that some accident had happened to Mr. Franklin, and we placed no confidence in the exertions of the Canadians that accompanied him, but we had the fullest confidence in Hepburn's returning the moment he could obtain assistance.

On the 17th I went to conduct Michel to where Vaillant's blanket was left, and after walking about three miles, pointed out the hills to him at a distance, and returned to the hut, having gathered a bagful of *tripe de roche* on the way. It was easier to gather this weed on a march than at the tent, for the exercise of walking produced a glow of heat, which enabled us to withstand for a time the cold to which we were exposed in scraping the frozen surface of the rocks. On the contrary, when we left the fire, to collect it in the neighborhood of the hut, we became chilled at once, and were obliged to return very quickly.

Michel proposed to remain out all night, and to hunt next day on his way back. He returned in the afternoon of the 18th, having found the blanket, together with a bag containing two pistols, and some other things which had been left beside it. We had some *tripe de roche*, in the evening, but Mr. Hood, from the constant griping it produced, was unable to eat more than one or two spoonfuls. He was now so weak as to be scarcely able to sit up at the fire-side, and complained that the least breeze of wind seemed to blow through his frame. He also suffered much from cold during the night. We lay close to each other, but the heat of the body was no longer sufficient to thaw the frozen rime formed by our breaths on the blankets that covered him.

At this period we avoided as much as possible conversing upon the hopelessness of our situation, and generally endeavored to lead the conversation towards our future prospects in life. The fact is, that with the decay of our strength, our minds decayed, and we were no longer able to bear the contemplation of the horrors that surrounded us. Each of us, if I may be allowed to judge from my own case, excused himself from so doing by a desire of not shocking the feelings of the others, for we were sensible of one another's weakness of intellect, though blind to our own. Yet we were calm and resigned to our fate, not a murmur escaped us, and we were punctual and fervent in our addresses to the Supreme Being.

On the 19th Michel refused to hunt, or even to assist in carrying a log of wood to the fire, which was too heavy for Hepburn's strength and mine. Mr. Hood endeavored to point out to him the necessity and duty of exertion, and the cruelty of his quitting us without leaving something for our support ; but the discourse, far from producing any beneficial effect, seemed only to excite his anger, and amongst other expressions he made use of the following remarkable one : " It is no use hunting, there are no animals, you had better kill and eat me." At length, however, he went out, but returned very soon, with a report that he had seen three deer, which he was unable to follow from having wet his foot in a small stream of water thinly covered with ice, and being consequently obliged to come to the fire. The day was rather mild, and Hepburn and I gathered a large kettleful of *tripe de roche ;* Michel slept in the tent this night.

Sunday, October 20.—In the morning we again urged Michel to go a hunting, that he might if possible leave us some provision, to-morrow being the day appointed for his quitting us ; but he shewed great unwillingness to go out, and lingered about the fire, under the pretense of cleaning his gun. After we had read the morning service, I went about noon to gather some *tripe de roche,* leaving Mr. Hood sitting before the tent at the fire-side, arguing with Michel ; Hepburn was employed cutting down a tree at a short distance from the tent, being desirous of accumulating a quantity of fire-wood before he left us. A short time after I went out I heard the report of a gun, and about ten minutes afterwards Hepburn called to me in a voice of great alarm, to come directly. When I arrived, I found poor Hood lying lifeless at the fire-side, a ball having apparently entered his forehead. I was at first horror-struck with the idea, that in a fit of despondency he had hurried himself into the presence of his almighty Judge, by an act of his own hand ; but the conduct of Michel soon gave rise to other thoughts, and excited suspicions which were confirmed, when

upon examining the body, I discovered that the shot
had entered the back part of the head, and passed out
at the forehead, and that the muzzle of the gun had
been applied so close as to set fire to the night-cap behind. The gun, which was of the longest kind supplied
to the Indians, could not have been placed in a position to inflict such a wound, except by a second person.
Upon inquiring of Michel how it happened, he replied,
that Mr. Hood had sent him into the tent for the short
gun, and that during his absence the long gun had
gone off, he did not know whether by accident or not.
He held the short gun in his hand at the time he was
speaking to me. Hepburn afterwards informed me,
that previous to the report of the gun, Mr. Hood and
Michel were speaking to each other in an elevated,
angry tone ; that Mr. Hood being seated at the fire-
side, was hid from him by intervening willows, but
that on hearing the report he looked up, and saw
Michel rising up from before the tent door, or just behind where Mr. Hood was seated, and then going into
the tent. Thinking that the gun had been discharged
for the purpose of cleaning it, he did not go to the fire
at first ; and when Michel called to him that Mr. Hood
was dead, a considerable time had elapsed. Although
I dared not openly to evince any suspicion that I
thought Michel guilty of the deed, yet he repeatedly
protested that he was incapable of committing such

an act, kept constantly on his guard, and carefully
avoided leaving Hepburn and me together. He was
evidently afraid of permitting us to converse in private,
and whenever Hepburn spoke, he inquired if he accused him of the murder. It is to be remarked, that he
understood English very imperfectly, yet·sufficient to
render it unsafe for us to speak on the subject in his
presence. We removed the body into a clump of
willows behind the tent, and, returning to the fire,
read the funeral service in addition to the evening
prayers. The loss of a young officer, of such distinguished and varied talents and application, may be
felt and duly appreciated by the eminent characters
under whose command he had served ; but the calmness with which he contemplated the probable termination of a life of uncommon promise ; and the patience
and fortitude with which he sustained, I may venture
to say, unparalleled bodily sufferings, can only be
known to the companions of his distresses. Owing to
the effect that the *tripe de roche* invariably had, when
he ventured to taste it, he undoubtedly suffered more
than any of the survivors of the party. *Bickersteth's
Scripture Help* was lying open beside the body, as if
it had fallen from his hand, and it is probable that he
was reading it at the instant of his death. We passed the night in the tent together without rest, every
one being on his guard. Next day, having determined

on going to the Fort, we began to patch and prepare
our clothes for the journey. We singed the hair off
a part of the buffalo robe that belonged to Mr. Hood,
and boiled and ate it. Michel tried to persuade me
to go to the woods on the Copper-Mine River, and
hunt for deer, instead of going to the Fort. In the
afternoon a flock of partridges coming near the tent,
he killed several, which he shared with us.

Thick snowy weather and a head wind prevented
us from starting the following day, but on the morning
of the 23d we set out, carrying with us the remainder
of the singed robe. Hepburn and Michel had each a
gun, and I carried a small pistol, which Hepburn had
loaded for me. In the course of the march Michel
alarmed us much by his gestures and conduct, was
constantly muttering to himself, expressed an unwillingness to go to the Fort, and tried to persuade me
to go to the southward to the woods, where he said he
could maintain himself all the winter by killing deer.
In consequence of this behavior, and the expression of
his countenance, I requested him to leave us and to go
to the southward by himself. This proposal increased
his ill-nature, he threw out some obscure hints of
freeing himself from all restraint on the morrow ; and
I overheard him muttering threats against Hepburn,
whom he openly accused of having told stories against
him. He also for the first time, assumed such a tone

of superiority in addressing me, as evinced that he considered us to be completely in his power, and he gave vent to several expressions of hatred towards the white people, or as he termed us in the idiom of the voyagers, the French, some of whom, he said, had killed and eaten his uncle and two of his relations. In short, taking every circumstance of his conduct into consideration, I came to the conclusion, that he would attempt to destroy us on the first opportunity that offered, and that he had hitherto abstained from doing so from his ignorance of the way to the Fort, but that he would never suffer us to go thither in company with him. In the course of the day he had several times remarked that we were pursuing the same course that Mr. Franklin was doing when we left him, and that by keeping towards the setting sun he could find his way himself. Hepburn and I were not in a condition to resist even an open attack, nor could we by any device escape from him. Our united strength was far inferior to his, and, beside his gun, he was armed with two pistols, an Indian bayonet, and a knife. In the afternoon, coming to a rock on which there was some *tripe de roche*, he halted, and said he would gather it whilst we went on, and that he would soon overtake us. Hepburn and I were now left together for the first time since Mr. Hood's death, and he acquainted me with several material circumstances, which he had observed of Michel's behavior, and which confirmed me in the opinion that there was no safety for us except in his death, and he offered to be the instrument of it. I determined, however, as I was thoroughly convinced of the necessity of such a dreadful act, to take the whole responsibility upon myself; and immediately upon Michel's coming up, I put an end to his life by shooting him through the head with a pistol. Had my own life alone been threatened, I would not have purchased it by such a measure ; but I considered myself as intrusted also with the protection of Hepburn's, a man, who, by his humane attentions and devotedness, had so endeared himself to me, that I felt more anxiety for his safety than for my own. Michel had gathered no *tripe de roche*, and it was evident to us that he had halted for the purpose of putting his gun in order, with the intention of attacking us, perhaps, whilst we were in the act of encamping.

I have dwelt in the preceding part of the narrative upon many circumstances of Michel's conduct, not for the purpose of aggravating his crime, but to put the reader in possession of the reasons that influenced me in depriving a fellow creature of life. Up to the period of his return to the tent, his conduct had been good and respectful to the officers, and in a conversation between Captain Franklin, Mr. Hood, and myself, at

Obstruction Rapid, it had been proposed to give him a reward upon our arrival at a post. His principles, however, unsupported by a belief in the divine truths of Christianity, were unable to withstand the pressure of severe distress. His countrymen, the Iroquois, are generally Christians, but he was totally uninstructed and ignorant of the duties inculcated by Christianity; and from his long residence in the Indian country, seems to have imbibed, or retained, the rules of conduct which the southern Indians prescribe to themselves.

On the two following days we had mild but thick snowy weather, and as the view was too limited to enable us to preserve a straight course, we remained encamped amongst a few willows and dwarf pines, about five miles from the tent. We found a species of *cornicularia*, a kind of lichen, that was good to eat when moistened and toasted over the fire; and we had a good many pieces of singed buffalo hide remaining.

On the 26th, the weather being clear and extremely cold, we resumed our march, which was very painful from the depth of the snow, particularly on the margins of the small lakes that lay in our route. We frequently sunk under the load of our blankets, and were obliged to assist each other in getting up. After walking about three miles and a half, however, we were cheered by the sight of a large herd of reindeer, and Hepburn went in pursuit of them ; but his hand being unsteady through weakness he missed.   He was so exhausted by this fruitless attempt, that we were obliged to encamp upon the spot, although it was a very unfavorable one.

Next day we had fine and clear, but cold weather. We set out early, and, in crossing a hill, found a considerable quantity of *tripe de roche*.   About noon we fell upon Little Marten Lake, having walked about two miles.   The sight of a place that we knew inspired us with fresh vigor, and there being comparatively little snow on the ice, we advanced at a pace to which we had lately been unaccustomed.   In the afternoon we crossed a recent track of a wolverene, which, from a parallel mark in the snow, appeared to have been dragging something.   Hepburn traced it, and upon the borders of the lake found the spine of a deer, that it had dropped.   It was clean picked, and at least one season old ; but we extracted the spinal marrow from it, which, even in its frozen state, was so acrid as to excoriate the lips.   We encamped within sight of the Dog-rib Rock, and from the coldness of the night and the want of fuel, rested very ill.

On the 28th we rose at day-break, but from the want of the small fire, that we usually made in the mornings to warm our fingers, a very long time was

spent in making up our bundles. This task fell to
Hepburn's share, as I suffered so much from the cold
as to be unable to take my hands out of my mittens.
We kept a straight course for the Dog-rib Rock,
but owing to the depth of the snow in the valleys we
had to cross, did not reach it until late in the afternoon. We would have encamped, but did not like to
pass a second night without fire ; and though scarcely
able to drag our limbs after us, we pushed on to a
clump of pines, about a mile to the southward of the
rock, and arrived at them in the dusk of the evening.
During the last few hundred yards of our march, our
track lay over some large stones, amongst which I fell
down upwards of twenty times, and became at length
so exhausted that I was unable to stand. If Hepburn had not exerted himself far beyond his strength,
and speedily made the encampment and kindled a
fire, I must have perished on the spot. This night
we had plenty of dry wood.

On the 29th we had clear and fine weather. We
set out at sunrise, and hurried on in our anxiety to
reach the house, but our progress was much impeded
by the great depth of the snow in the valleys. Although every spot of ground over which we traveled
to-day, had been repeatedly trodden by us, yet we got
bewildered in a small lake. We took it for Marten
Lake, which was three times its size, and fancied that

we saw the rapid and the grounds about the fort, although they were still far distant. Our disappointment when this illusion was dispelled, by our reaching the end of the lake, so operated on our feeble minds as to exhaust our strength, and we decided upon encamping; but upon ascending a small eminence to look for a clump of wood, we caught a glimpse of the Big-Stone, a well known rock upon the summit of a hill opposite to the Fort, and determined upon proceeding. In the evening we saw several large herds of reindeer, but Hepburn, who used to be considered a good marksman, was now unable to hold the gun straight, and although he got near them, all his efforts proved fruitless. In passing through a small clump of pines we saw a flock of partridges, and he succeeded in killing one after firing several shots. We came in sight of the fort at dusk, and it is impossible to describe our sensations, when on attaining the eminence that overlooks it, we beheld the smoke issuing from one of the chimneys. From not having met with any footsteps in the snow, as we drew nigh our once cheerful residence, we had been agitated by many melancholy forebodings. Upon entering the now desolate building, we had the satisfaction of embracing Captain Franklin, but no words can convey an idea of the filth and wretchedness that met our eyes on looking around. Our own misery had stolen

upon us by degrees, and we were accustomed to the
contemplation of each other's emaciated figures, but
the ghastly countenances, dilated eye-balls, and
sepulchral voices of Mr. Franklin and those with him,
were more than we could at first bear.

Conclusion of Dr. Richardson's Narrative.

THE morning of the 31st was very cold, the wind
being strong from the north. Hepburn went again in
quest of deer, and the Doctor endeavored to kill some
partridges : both were unsuccessful. A large herd of
deer passed close to the house, the Doctor fired once
at them, but was unable to pursue them. Adam was
easier this day, and left his bed. Peltier and Samandrè
were much weaker, and could not assist in the
labors of the day. Both complained of soreness in
the throat, and Samandrè suffered much from cramps
in his fingers. The Doctor and Hepburn began this
day to cut the wood, and also brought it to the house.
Being too weak to aid in these laborious tasks, I was
employed in searching for bones, and cooking, and attending
to our more weakly companions.

In the evening, Peltier, complaining much of cold, requested of me a portion of a blanket to repair his shirt and drawers. The mending of these articles occupied him and Samandrè until past one A.M., and their spirits were so much revived by the employment, that they conversed even cheerfully the whole time. Adam sat up with them. The Doctor, Hepburn, and myself, went to bed. We were afterwards agreeably surprised to see Peltier and Samandré carry three or four logs of wood across the room to replenish the fire, which induced us to hope they still possessed more strength than we had supposed.

November 1.—This day was fine and mild. Hepburn went hunting, but was as usual unsuccessful. As his strength was rapidly declining, we advised him to desist from the pursuit of deer ; and only to go out for a short time and endeavor to kill a few partridges for Peltier and Samandré. The Doctor obtained a little *tripe de roche*, but Peltier could not eat any of it, and Samandré only a few spoonfuls, owing to the soreness of their throats. In the afternoon Peltier was so much exhausted, that he sat up with difficulty, and looked piteously ; at length he slided from his stool upon his bed, as we supposed to sleep, and in this composed state he remained upwards of two hours, without our apprehending any danger. We were then alarmed by hearing a rattling in his throat, and on the Doctor's examining him he was found to be speechless. He died in the course of the night. Samandré sat up the greater part of the day, and even assisted in pounding some bones; but on witnessing the melancholy state of Peltier, he became very low, and began to complain of cold and stiffness of the joints. Being unable to keep up a sufficient fire to warm him, we laid him down and covered him with several blankets. He did not, however, appear to get better, and I deeply lament to add, he also died before daylight. We removed the bodies of the deceased into the opposite part of the house, but our united strength was inadequate to the task of interring them, or even carrying them down to the river.

It may be worthy of remark that poor Peltier, from the time of Benoit's departure, had fixed on the first of November as the time when he should cease to expect any relief from the Indians, and had repeatedly said that if they did not arrive by that day, he should not survive.

Peltier had endeared himself to each of us by his cheerfulness, his unceasing activity, and affectionate care and attentions, ever since our arrival at this place. He had nursed Adam with the tenderest solicitude the whole time. Poor Samandré was willing to have taken his share in the labors of the party, had he not been wholly incapacitated by his weakness and low spirits. The severe shock occasioned by the sudden dissolution of our two companions rendered us very melancholy. Adam became low and despondent, a change which we lamented the more, as we had perceived he had been gaining strength and spirits for the two preceding days. I was particularly distressed by the thought that the labor of collecting wood must now devolve upon Dr. Richardson and Hepburn, and that my debility would disable me from affording them any material assistance ; indeed both of them most kindly urged me not to make the attempt. They were occupied the whole of the next day in tearing down the logs of which the store-house was built, but the mud plastered between them was so hard frozen that the labor of separation exceeded their strength, and they were completely exhausted by bringing in wood sufficient for less than twelve hours' consumption.

I found it necessary in their absence, to remain constantly near Adam, and to converse with him, in order to prevent his reflecting on our condition, and to keep up his spirits as far as possible. I also lay by his side at night.

On the 3d the weather was very cold, though the atmosphere was cloudy: This morning Hepburn was affected with swelling in his limbs, his strength, as well as that of the Doctor, was rapidly declining ;

15*

they continued, however, to be full of hope. Their utmost exertions could only supply wood to renew the fire thrice, and on making it up the last time we went to bed. Adam was rather in better spirits, but he could not bear to be left alone. Our stock of bones was exhausted by a small quantity of soup we made this evening. The toil of separating the hair from the skins, which in fact were our chief support, had now become so wearisome as to prevent us from eating as much as we should otherwise have done.

November 4.—Calm and comparatively mild weather. The Doctor and Hepburn, exclusive of their usual occupation, gathered some *tripe de roche.* I went a few yards from the house in search of bones, and returned quite fatigued, having found but three. The Doctor again made incisions in Adam's legs, which discharged a considerable quantity of water, and gave him great relief. We read prayers and a portion of the New Testament in the morning and evening, as had been our practice since Dr. Richardson's arrival; and I may remark that the performance of these duties always afforded us the greatest consolation, serving to reanimate our hope in the mercy of the Omnipotent, who alone could save and deliver us.

On the 5th the breezes were light, with dark cloudy weather, and some snow. The Doctor and Hepburn were getting much weaker, and the limbs of the latter were now greatly swelled. They came into the house frequently in the course of the day to rest themselves, and when once seated, were unable to rise without the help of one another, or of a stick. Adam was for the most part in the same low state as yesterday, but sometimes he surprised us by getting up and walking with an appearance of increased strength. His looks were now wild and ghastly, and his conversation was often incoherent.

The next day was fine, but very cold. The swellings in Adam's limbs having subsided, he was free from pain, and arose this morning in much better spirits, and spoke of cleaning his gun ready for shooting partridges, or any animals that might appear near the house, but his tone entirely changed before the day was half over ; he became again dejected, and could scarcely be prevailed upon to eat. The Doctor and Hepburn were almost exhausted. The cutting of one log of wood occupied the latter half an hour ; and the other took as much time to drag it into the house, though the distance did not exceed thirty yards. I endeavored to help the Doctor, but my assistance was very trifling. Yet it was evident that, in a day or two, if their strength should continue to decline at the same rate, I should be the strongest of the party.

I may here remark, that owing to our loss of flesh, the hardness of the floor, from which we were only protected by a blanket, produced soreness over the body, and especially those parts on which the weight rested in lying, yet to turn ourselves for relief was a matter of toil and difficulty. However, during this period, and indeed all along after the acute pains of hunger, which lasted but three or four days, had subsided, we generally enjoyed the comfort of a few hours' sleep. The dreams which for the most part, but not always accompanied it, were usually (though not invariably,) of a pleasant character, being very often about the enjoyments of feasting. In the day-time we fell into the practice of conversing on common and light subjects, although we sometimes discussed with seriousness and earnestness topics connected with religion. We generally avoided speaking directly of our present sufferings, or even of the prospect of relief. I observed, that in proportion as our strength decayed, our minds exhibited symptoms of weakness, evinced by a kind of unreasonable pettishness with each other. Each of us thought the other weaker in intellect than himself, and more in need of advice and assistance. So trifling a circumstance as a change of place recommended by one as being warmer and more comfortable, and refused by the other from a dread of motion, frequently called forth fretful expressions which were no sooner uttered than atoned for, to be repeated perhaps in the course of a few minutes. The same thing often occurred when we endeavored to assist each other in carrying wood to the fire ; none of us were willing to receive assistance, although the task was disproportionate to our strength. On one of these occasions Hepburn was so convinced of this waywardness that he exclaimed, " Dear me, if we are spared to return to England, I wonder if we shall recover our understandings."

November 7.—Adam had passed a restless night, being disquieted by gloomy apprehensions of approaching death, which we tried in vain to dispel. He was so low in the morning as to be scarcely able to speak. I remained in bed by his side to cheer him as much as possible. The Doctor and Hepburn went to cut wood. They had hardly begun their labor, when they were amazed at hearing the report of a musket. They could scarcely believe that there was really any one near, until they heard a shout, and immediately espied three Indians close to the house. Adam and I heard the latter noise, and I was fearful that a part of the house had fallen upon one of my companions, a disaster which had in fact been thought not unlikely. My alarm was only momentary, Dr. Richardson came in to communicate the joyful intelligence that relief had arrived. He and myself immediately addressed thanksgiving to the throne of mercy for this deliverance, but poor Adam was in so low a state that he could scarcely comprehend the information. When the Indians entered, he attempted to rise but sank down again. But for this seasonable interposition of Providence, his existence must have terminated in a few hours, and that of the rest probably in not many days.

The Indians had left Akaitcho's encampment on the 5th November, having been sent by Mr. Back with all possible expedition, after he had arrived at their tents. They brought but a small supply of provisions, that they might travel quickly. It consisted of dried deer's meat, some fat, and a few tongues. Dr. Richardson, Hepburn, and I, eagerly devoured the food, which they imprudently presented to us, in too great abundance, and in consequence we suffered dreadfully from indigestion, and had no rest the whole night. Adam being unable to feed himself, was more judiciously treated by them, and suffered less ; his spirits revived hourly. The circumstance of our eating more food than was proper in our present condition, was another striking proof of the debility of our minds. We were perfectly aware of the danger, and Dr. Richardson repeatedly cautioned us to be moderate ; but he was himself unable to practise the caution he so judiciously recommended.

Boudel-kell, the youngest of the Indians, after resting about an hour, returned to Akaitcho with the intelligence of our situation, and he conveyed a note from me to Mr. Back, requesting another supply of meat as soon as possible. The two others, " Crooked-Foot and the Rat," remained to take care of us, until we should be able to move forward.

The note I received by the Indians from Mr. Back, communicated a tale of distress with regard to himself and his party, as painful as that which we had suffered ; as will be seen hereafter, by his own narrative.

November 8.—The Indians this morning requested us to remove to an encampment on the banks of the river, as they were unwilling to remain in the house in which the bodies of our deceased companions were lying exposed to view. We agreed to remove but the day proved too stormy, and Dr. Richardson and Hepburn having dragged the bodies to a short distance, and covered them with snow, the objections of the Indians to remain in the house were removed, and they began to clear our room of the accumulation of dirt and fragments of pounded bones. The improved state of our apartment, and the large and cheerful fires they kept up, produced in us a sensation of comfort to which we had long been strangers. In the evening they brought in a pile of dried wood, which was lying on the river side, and on which we had often cast a wishful eye, being unable to drag it up the bank. The Indians set about every thing with an activity that amazed us.

Indeed, contrasted with our emaciated figures and extreme debility, their frames appeared to us gigantic, and their strength supernatural. These kind creatures next turned their attention to our personal appearance, and prevailed upon us to shave and wash ourselves. The beards of the Doctor and Hepburn had been untouched since they left the sea coast, and were become of a hideous length, and peculiarly offensive to the Indians.* The Doctor and I suffered extremely from distention, and therefore ate sparingly. Hepburn was getting better, and Adam recovered his strength with amazing rapidity.

November 9.—This morning was pleasantly fine. Crooked-Foot caught four large trout in Winter Lake, which were very much prized, especially by the Doctor and myself, who had taken a dislike to meat, in consequence of our sufferings from repletion, which rendered us almost incapable of moving. Adam and Hepburn in a great measure escaped this. Though the night was stormy, and our apartment freely admitted the wind, we felt no inconvenience, the Indians were so very careful in covering us up, and in keeping a

* The first alvine discharges after we received food, were, as Hearne remarks on a similar occasion, attended with excessive pain. Previous to the arrival of the Indians, the urinary secretion was extremely abundant, and we were obliged to rise from bed in consequence upwards of ten times in a night. This was an extreme annoyance in our reduced state. It may, perhaps, be attributed to the quantity of the country tea that we drank.

good fire ; and our plentiful cheer gave such power of resisting the cold, that we could scarcely believe otherwise than that the season had become milder.

On the 13th, the weather was stormy, with constant snow. The Indians became desponding at the nonarrival of the supply, and would neither go to hunt nor fish. They frequently expressed their fears of some misfortune having befallen Boudel-kell ; and, in the evening, went off suddenly, without apprizing us of their intention, having first given to each of us a handful of pounded meat, which they had reserved. Their departure, at first, gave rise to a suspicion of their having deserted us, not meaning to return, especially as the explanations of Adam, who appeared to be in their secret, were very unsatisfactory. At length, by interrogations, we got from him the information, that they designed to march night and day, until they should reach Akaitcho's encampment, whence they would send us aid. As we had combated their fears about Boudel-kell, they, perhaps, apprehended that we should oppose their determination, and therefore concealed it. We were now left a second time without food, and with appetites recovered, and strongly excited by recent indulgence.

On the following day the Doctor and Hepburn resumed their former occupation of collecting wood, and I was able to assist a little in bringing it into the house. Adam, whose expectation of the arrival of the Indians had been raised by the fineness of the weather, became, towards night, very desponding, and refused to eat the singed skin. The night was stormy, and there was a heavy fall of snow. The next day he became still more dejected. About eleven Hepburn, who had gone out for wood, came in with the intelligence that a party appeared upon the river. The room was instantly swept, and, in compliance with the prejudices of the Indians, every scrap of skin was carefully removed out of sight ; for these simple people imagine, that burning deer-skin renders them unsuccessful in hunting. The party proved to be Crooked-Foot, Thooee-yorre, and the Fop, with the wives of the two latter dragging provisions. They were accompanied by Benoit, one of our own men.

We were rejoiced to learn, by a note from Mr. Back, dated November 11, that he and his companions had so recruited their strength that they were preparing to proceed to Fort Providence. Adam recovered his spirits on the arrival of the Indians, and even walked about the room with an appearance of strength and activity that surprised us all. As it was of consequence to get amongst the reindeer before our present supply should fail, we made preparations for quitting Fort Enterprize the next day ; and, accordingly, at an early hour on the 16th, having united in thanksgiving and prayer, the whole party left the house after breakfast. Our feelings on quitting the Fort, where we had formerly enjoyed much comfort, if not happiness, and, latterly, experienced a degree of misery scarcely to be paralelled, may be more easily conceived than described. The Indians treated us with the utmost tenderness, gave us their snow-shoes and walked without themselves, keeping by our sides, that they might lift us when we fell. We descended Winter River, and, about noon, crossed the head of Round-Rock Lake, distant about three miles from the house, where we were obliged to halt, as Dr. Richardson was unable to proceed. The swellings in his limbs rendered him by much the weakest of the party. The Indians prepared our encampment, cooked for us, and fed us as if we had been children ; evincing humanity that would have done honor to the most civilized people. The night was mild, and fatigue made us sleep soundly.

From this period to the 26th of November we gradually continued to improve, under the kindness and attention of our Indians. On this day we arrived in safety at the abode of our chief and companion, Akaitcho. We were received by the party assembled in the leader's tent, with looks of compassion, and profound silence, which lasted about a quarter of an hour, and by which they meant to express their condolence for our sufferings. The conversation did not be-

gin until we had tasted food. The Chief, Akaitcho,
shewed us the most friendly hospitality, and all sorts
of personal attention, even to cooking for us with his
own hands, an office which he never performs for himself. Annœthaiyazzeh and Humpy, the Chief's two
brothers, and several of our hunters, with their families, were encamped here, together with a number of
old men and women. In the course of the day we
were visited by every person of the band, not merely
from curiosity, I conceive, but rather from a desire to
evince their tender sympathy in our late distress. We
learned that Mr. Back, with St. Germain and Belanger, had gone to Fort Providence ; and that, previous
to his departure, he had left a letter in a *cache* of
pounded meat, which he had missed two days ago.
As we supposed that this letter might acquaint us
with his intentions more fully than we could gather
from the Indians, through our imperfect knowledge
of their language, Augustus, the Esquimaux, whom
we found here in perfect health, and an Indian lad,
were dispatched to bring it.

We found several of the Indian families in great
affliction, for the loss of three of their relatives, who
had been drowned in the August preceding, by the
upsetting of a canoe near to Fort Enterprize. They
bewailed the melancholy accident every morning and
evening, by repeating the names of the persons in a

loud singing tone, which was frequently interrupted by bursts of tears. One woman was so affected by the loss of her only son, that she seemed deprived of reason, and wandered about the tents the whole day, crying and singing out his name.

On the 1st of December we removed with the Indians to the southward.

On the 4th, we again set off after the Indians about noon, and soon overtook them, as they had halted to drag from the water, and cut up and share, a moose-deer, that had been drowned in a rapid part of the river, partially covered with ice. These operations detained us a long time, which was the more disagreeable, as the weather was extremely unpleasant from cold low fogs. We were all much fatigued at the hour of encampment, which was after dark, though the day's journey did not exceed four miles. At every halt the elderly men of the tribe used to make holes in the ice and put in their lines. One of them shared the produce of his fishery with us this evening.

In the afternoon of the 6th, Belanger, and another Canadian, arrived from Fort Providence, sent by Mr. Weeks, with two trains of dogs, some spirits and tobacco for the Indians, a change of dress for ourselves, and a little tea and sugar. They also brought letters for us from England, and from Mr. Back and Mr. Wentzel. By the former we received the gratifying

intelligence of the successful termination of Captain
Parry's voyage ; and were informed of the promotion
of myself and Mr. Back, and of poor Hood, our grief
for whose loss was renewed by this intelligence.   The
gratification which it would otherwise have afforded,
was materially damped by our sincere regret that he
had not lived to receive this just reward of his merit
and services.   The letter from Mr. Back stated, that
the rival Companies in the fur trade had united ; but
that, owing to some cause which had not been explained to him, the goods intended as rewards to
Akaitcho and his band, which we had demanded in the
spring from the North-West Company, were not sent.
There were, however, some stores lying for us at Moose-
deer Island, which had been ordered for the equipment
of our voyagers ; and Mr. Back had gone across to that
establishment, to make a selection of the articles we
could spare for a temporary present to the Indians.
The disappointment at the non-arrival of the goods
was seriously felt by us, as we had looked forward with
pleasure to the time when we should be enabled to
recompense our kind Indian friends, for their tender
sympathy in our distresses, and the assistance they
had so cheerfully and promptly rendered.   I now regretted to find, that Mr. Wentzel and his party, in
their return from the sea, had suffered severely on
their march along the Copper-Mine River, having on

one occasion, as he mentioned, had no food but *tripe de roche* for eleven days.

All the Indians flocked to our encampment to learn the news, and to receive the articles brought for them. Having got some spirits and tobacco, they withdrew to the tent of the Chief, and passed the greater part of the night in singing. We had now the indescribable gratification of changing our linen, which we had worn ever since our departure from the sea-coast.

December 8.—After a long conference with Akaitcho, we took leave of him and his kind companions, and set out with two sledges, heavily laden with provision and bedding, drawn by the dogs, and conducted by Belanger and the Canadian sent by Mr. Weeks. Hepburn and Augustus jointly dragged a smaller sledge, laden principally with their own bedding. Adam and Benoit were left to follow with the Indians. We encamped on the Grassy-Lake Portage, having walked about nine miles, principally on the Yellow-Knife River. It was open at the rapids, and in these places we had to ascend its banks, and walk through the woods for some distance, which was very fatiguing, especially to Dr. Richardson, whose feet were severely galled in consequence of some defect in his snowshoes.

On the 11th, however, we arrived at the Fort; it was still under the charge of Mr. Weeks. He welcomed us in the most kind manner, immediately gave us changes of dress, and did every thing in his power to make us comfortable.

Our sensations, on being once more in a comfortable dwelling, after the series of hardships and miseries we had experienced, will be much better imagined than any language of mine can describe them. Our first act was again to return our grateful praises to the Almighty for the manifold instances of his mercy towards us. Having found here some articles, which Mr. Back had sent across from Moose-deer Island, I determined on awaiting the arrival of Akaitcho and his party, in order to present these to them, and to assure them of the promised reward, as soon as it could possibly be procured.

In the afternoon of the 14th, Akaitcho, with his whole band, came to the Fort. He smoked his customary pipe, and made an address to Mr. Weeks in the hall, previous to his coming into the room in which Dr. Richardson and I were. We discovered at the commencement of his speech to us, that he had been informed that our expected supplies had not come. He spoke of this circumstance as a disappointment, indeed, sufficiently severe to himself, to whom his band looked up for the protection of their interests, but without attaching any blame to us. "The world goes badly," he said, "all are poor, you are poor, the traders appear to be poor, I and my party are poor likewise ; and since the goods have not come in, we cannot have them.   I do not regret having supplied you with provisions, for a Copper Indian can never permit white men to suffer from want of food on his lands, without flying to their aid.   I trust, however, that we shall, as you say, receive what is due next autumn ; and at all events," he added, in a tone of good humor, " it is the first time that the white people have been indebted to the Copper Indians." We assured him the supplies should certainly be sent to him by the autumn, if not before.   He then cheerfully received the small present we made to himself ; and, although we could give a few things only to those who had been most active in our service, the others who, perhaps, thought themselves equally deserving, did not murmur at being left out in the distribution. Akaitcho afterwards expressed a strong desire, that we should represent the character of his nation in a favorable light to our countrymen. " I know," he said, " you write down every occurrence in your books ; but probably you have only noticed the bad things we have said and done, and have omitted to mention the good."   In the course of the desultory conversation which ensued, he said, that he had been always told by us,— to consider the traders in the same light as ourselves ; and that for his part, he looked upon both

16

as equally respectable. This assurance, made in the
presence of Mr. Weeks, was particularly gratifying to
us, as it completely disproved the defence that had
been set up, respecting the injurious reports that had
been circulated against us, amongst the Indians in
the spring ; namely, that they were in retaliation for
our endeavors to lower the traders in the eyes of the
Indians. I take this opportunity of stating my
opinion, that Mr. Weeks, in spreading these reports,
was actuated by a mistaken idea that he was serving
the interest of his employers. On the present occasion,
we felt indebted to him for the sympathy he displayed
for our distresses, and the kindness with which he administered to our personal wants. After this conference, such Indians as were indebted to the Company were paid for the provision they had given us,
by deducting a corresponding sum from their debts ;
in the same way we gave a reward of sixteen skins of
beaver to each of the persons who had come to our relief at Fort Enterprize. As the debts of Akaitcho
and his hunters had been effaced at the time of his
engagement with us, we placed a sum, equal to the
amount of provision they had recently supplied, to
their credit on the Company's books. These things
being, through the moderation of the Indians, adjust-
ed with an unexpected facility, we gave them a keg
of mixed liquors, (five parts water,) and distributed

among them several fathoms of tobacco, and they retired to their tents to spend the night in merriment.

Adam, our interpreter, being desirous of uniting
himself with the Copper Indians, applied to me for
his discharge, which I granted, and gave him a bill
on the Hudson's Bay Company for the amount of his
wages. These arrangements being completed, we prepared to cross the lake.

Mr. Weeks provided Dr. Richardson and me with a
cariole each, and we set out at eleven A.M., on the
15th, for Moose-deer Island. Our party consisted of
Belanger who had charge of a sledge, laden with the
bedding, and drawn by two dogs, our two cariole men
Benoit, and Augustus. Previous to our departure,
we had another conference with Akaitcho, who, as
well as the rest of his party, bade us farewell, with a
warmth of manner rare among the Indians.

The badness of Belanger's dogs and the roughness
of the ice, impeded our progress very much, and obliged us to encamp early. We had a good fire made of
the drift wood, which lines the shores of this lake in
great quantities. The next day was very cold. We
began the journey at nine A.M., and encamped at the
Big Cape, having made another short march, in consequence of the roughness of the ice.

On the 17th, we encamped on the most southerly
of the Reindeer Islands. This night was very stormy,

but the wind abating in the morning, we proceeded, and by sunset reached the fishing huts of the Company at Stony Point.   Here we found Mr. Andrews, a clerk of the Hudson's Bay Company, who regaled us with a supper of excellent white fish, for which this part of Slave Lake is particularly celebrated.   Two men with sledges arrived soon afterwards, sent by Mr. M'Vicar, who expected us about this time.   We set off in the morning before day-break, with several companions, and arrived at Moose-deer Island about one P. M.   Here we were received with the utmost hospitality by Mr. M'Vicar, the chief trader of the Hudson's Bay Company in this district, as well as by his assistant, Mr. M'Auley.   We had also the happiness of joining our friend Mr. Back ; our feelings on this occasion can be well imagined ; we were deeply impressed with gratitude to him for his exertions in sending the supply of food to Fort Enterprize, to which, under Divine Providence, we felt the preservation of our lives to be owing.   He gave us an affecting detail of the proceedings of his party since our separation ; the substance of which I shall convey to the reader, by the following extracts from his Journal.

CHAPTER XIII

Mr. BACK'S NARRATIVE.

^{1821.}
October 4.	Mr. FRANKLIN having directed me to proceed with St. Germain, Belanger, and Beauparlant, to Fort Enterprize, in the hope of obtaining relief for the party, I took leave of my companions, and set out on my journey, through a very swampy country, which, with the cloudy state of the weather, and a keen north-east wind, accompanied by frequent snow showers, retarded us so much that we scarcely got more than four miles, when we halted for the night, and made a meal of *tripe de roche* and some old leather.

On the 5th, we set out early, amidst extremely deep snow, sinking frequently in it up to the thighs, a labor in our enfeebled and almost worn-out state, that nothing but the cheering hopes of reaching the house, and affording relief to our friends, could have enabled us to support. As we advanced, we found to our mortification that the *tripe de roche*, hitherto our sole dependence, began to be scarce, so that we could only collect sufficient to make half a kettleful, which, with the addition of a partridge each, that St. Germain had killed, made us a tolerable meal ; during this day I felt very weak and sore in the joints, particularly between the shoulders. At night we encamped among a small clump of willows.

On the 6th we set out at an early hour, pursuing our route over a range of hills, at the foot of one of which we saw several large pines, and a great quantity of willows ; a sight that encouraged us to quicken our pace, as we were now certain we could not be far from the woods. Indeed we were making considerable progress, when Belanger unfortunately broke through the ice, and sunk up to the hips. The weather being cold, he was in danger of freezing, but some brushwood on the borders of the lake enabled us to make a fire to dry him. At the same time we took the opportunity of refreshing ourselves with a kettle of swamp tea.

My increasing debility had for some time obliged me to use a stick for the purpose of extending my arms ; the pain in my shoulders being so acute, that I could not bear them to remain in the usual position for two minutes together. We halted at five among some small brushwood, and made a sorry meal of an old pair of leather trowsers, and some swamp tea.

The night was cold with a hard frost, and though two persons slept together, yet we could not by any means keep ourselves warm, but remained trembling the whole time. The following morning we crossed several lakes, occasionally seeing the recent tracks of deer, and at noon we fell upon Marten Lake ; and it happened to be the exact spot where we had been the last year with the canoes, and though I immediately recognized the place, the men would not believe it to be the same ; at length, by pointing out several marks, and relating circumstances connected with them, they recovered their memory, and a simultaneous expression of " Mon Dieu, nous sommes sauvés," broke out from the whole. Contrary to our expectations, the lake was frozen sufficiently to bear us, so that we were excused from making the tours of the different bays. This circumstance seemed to add fresh vigor to us, we walked as fast as the extreme smoothness of the ice would permit, intending to reach the Slave Rock that night ; but an unforeseen and almost fatal accident prevented the prosecution of our plan : Belanger (who seemed the victim of misfortune) again broke through the ice, in a deep part near the head of the rapid, but was timely saved, by fastening our worsted belts together, and pulling him out. By urging him forwards as quick as his icy garments would admit of, to prevent his freezing, we reached a few pines, and kindled a fire ; but it was late before he even felt warm, though he was so near the flame as to burn his hair twice ; and to add to our distress, three wolves crossed the lake close to us.

The night of the 7th was extremely stormy, and about ten the following morning, on attempting to go on, we found it totally impossible, being too feeble to oppose the wind and drift, which frequently blew us over, and on attempting to cross a small lake that lay in our way, drove us faster backwards than under all advantages we could get forwards ; therefore we encamped under the shelter of a small clump of pines, secure from the south-west storm that was raging around us. In the evening, from there being no *tripe de roche*, we were compelled to satisfy, or rather allay, the cravings of hunger, by eating a gun cover and a pair of old shoes ; at this time I had hardly strength to get on my legs.

The wind did not in the least abate during the night, but in the morning of the 9th it changed to north-east, and became moderate. We took advantage of this circumstance, and rising with great difficulty, set out, though had it not been for the hope of reaching the house, I am certain, from the excessive faintness which almost overpowered me, that I must have remained where I was. We passed the Slave Rock, and making frequent halts, arrived within a short dis-

tance of Fort Enterprize ; but as we perceived neither
any marks of Indians, nor even of animals, the men
began absolutely to despair : on a nearer approach,
however, the tracks of large herds of deer, which had
only passed a few hours, tended a little to revive their
spirits, and shortly after we crossed the ruinous thres-
hold of the long-sought-for spot ; but what was our
surprise, what our sensations, at beholding every thing
in the most desolate and neglected state ; the doors
and windows of that room in which we expected to
find provision, had been thrown down, and carelessly
left so ; and the wild animals of the woods had resorted there, as to a place of shelter and retreat. Mr.
Wentzel had taken away the trunks and papers, but
had left no note to guide us to the Indians. This was
to us the most grievous disappointment : without the
assistance of the Indians, bereft of every resource, we
felt ourselves reduced to the most miserable state,
which was rendered still worse, from the recollection
that our friends in the rear were as miserable as ourselves. For the moment, however, hunger prevailed,
and each began to gnaw the scraps of putrid and frozen meat that were laying about, without waiting to
prepare them. A fire, however, was made, and the
neck and bones of a deer, found lying in the house,
were boiled and devoured.

I determined to remain a day here to repose ourselves, and then to go in search of the Indians, and in the event of missing them, to proceed to the first trading establishment, which was distant about one hundred and thirty miles, and from thence send succor to my companions. This indeed I should have done immediately, as the most certain manner of executing my purpose, had there been any probability of the river and lakes being frozen to the southward, or had we possessed sufficient strength to have clambered over the rocks and mountains which impeded the direct way ; but as we were aware of our inability to do so, I listened to St. Germain's proposal, which was, to follow the deer into the woods, (so long as they did not lead us out of our route to the Indians,) and if possible to collect sufficient food to carry us to Fort Providence.   We now set about making mittens and snow-shoes, whilst Belanger searched under the snow, and collected a mass of old bones, which when burned and used with a little salt, we found palatable enough, and made a tolerable meal.   At night St. Germain returned, having seen plenty of tracks, but no animals ; the day was cloudy, with fresh breezes, and the river was frozen at the borders.

On the 11th we prepared for our journey, having first collected a few old skins of deer, to serve us as food, and written a note to be left for our commander, to apprize him of our intentions.   We pursued the course of the river to the lower lake, when St. Germain fell in, which obliged us to encamp directly to prevent his being frozen ; indeed we were all glad of stopping, for in our meagre and reduced state it was impossible to resist the weather, which at any other time would have been thought fine ; my toes were frozen, and although wrapped in a blanket I could not keep my hands warm.

The 12th was excessively cold with fresh breezes. Our meal at night consisted of scraps of old deer skins and swamp tea, and the men complained greatly of their increasing debility. The following morning I sent St. Germain to hunt, intending to go some distance down the lake, but the weather becoming exceedingly thick with snow storms, we were prevented from moving. He returned without success, not having seen any animals. We had nothing to eat.

In the morning of the 14th the part of the lake before us was quite frozen. There was so much uncertainty in St. Germain's answers as to the chance of any Indians being in the direction we were then going, (although he had previously said that the leader had told him he should be there,) and he gave me so much dissatisfaction in his hunting excursions, that I was induced to send a note to the Commander, whom I supposed to be by this time at Fort Enterprize, to inform him of our situation ; not that I imagined for a mo-

ment he could better it, but that by all returning to
the Fort we might, perhaps, have better success in
hunting ; with this view I despatched Belanger, much
against his inclination, and told him to return as
quick as possible to a place about four miles further on, where we intended to fish, and to await his
arrival. The men were so weak this day that I could
get neither of them to move from the encampment ;
and it was only necessity that compelled them to cut
wood for fuel, in performing which operation Beauparlant's face became so dreadfully swelled that he
could scarcely see ; I myself lost my temper on the
most trivial circumstances, and was become very peev-
ish ; the day was fine but cold, with a freezing north-
east wind. We had nothing to eat.

October 15.—The night was calm and clear, but
it was not before two in the afternoon that we set out ;
and the one was so weak, and the other so full of complaints, that we did not get more than three-quarters
of a mile from our last encampment, before we were
obliged to put up ; but in this distance we were fortunate enough to kill a partridge, the bones of which
were eaten, and the remainder reserved for baits to
fish with. We were fortunate, however, in collecting
sufficient *tripe de roche* to make a meal ; and I now
anxiously awaited Belanger's return, to know what
course to take. I was now so much reduced, that my

shoulders were as if they would fall from my body, my legs seemed unable to support me, and in the disposition which I then found myself, had it not been for the remembrance of my friends behind, who relied on me for relief, as well as the persons of whom I had charge, I certainly should have preferred remaining where I was, to the miserable pain of attempting to move.

October 16.—We waited until two in the afternoon for Belanger; but not seeing any thing of him on the lake, we set out, purposing to encamp at the Narrows, the place which was said to be so good for fishing, and where, according to St. Germain's account, the Indians never failed to catch plenty ; its distance at most could not be more than two miles. We had not proceeded far before Beauparlant began to complain of increasing weakness. This was so usual with us that no particular notice was taken of it, for in fact there was little difference, all being alike feeble ; among other things he said whilst we were resting, that he should never get beyond the next encampment, for his strength had quite failed him. I endeavored to encourage him by explaining the mercy of the Supreme Being, who ever beholds with an eye of pity those that seek his aid. This passed as common discourse, when he enquired where we were to put up ; St. Germain pointed to a small clump of pines near us, the only

place indeed that offered for fuel. " Well," replied
the poor man, " take your axe, Mr. Back, and I will
follow at my leisure, I shall join you by the time the
encampment is made." This is a usual practice of the
country, and St. Germain and myself went on towards
the spot ; it was five o'clock and not very cold, but
rather milder than we had experienced it for some
time, when, on leaving the ice, we saw a number of
crows perched upon the top of some high pines near
us. St. Germain immediately said that there must
be some dead animals thereabouts, and proceeded to
search, when we saw several heads of deer, half buried
in the snow and ice, without eyes or tongues ; the
previous severity of the weather only having obliged
the wolves and other animals to abandon them. An
expression of " Oh merciful God ! we are saved,"
broke from us both ; and with feelings more easily imagined than described, we shook hands, not knowing
what to say for joy. It was twilight, and a fog was
rapidly darkening the surface of the lake, when St.
Germain commenced making the encampment ; the
task was too laborious for me to render him any assistance, and had we not thus providentially found provision, I feel convinced that the next twenty-four
hours would have terminated my existence. But this
good fortune, in some measure, renovated me for the
moment, and putting out my whole strength, I contriv-

ed to collect a few heads, and with incredible difficulty carried them singly about thirty paces to the fire.

Darkness stole on us apace, and I became extremely anxious about Beauparlant; several guns were fired, to each of which he answered. We then called out, and again heard his responses, though faintly, when I told St. Germain to go and look for him, as I had not strength myself, being quite exhausted. He said, that he had already placed a pine branch on the ice, and he could then hardly find his way back, but if he went now he should certainly be lost. In this situation I could only hope that as Beauparlant had my blanket, and every thing requisite to light a fire, he might have encamped at a little distance from us.

October 17.—The night was cold and clear, but we could not sleep at all, from the pains of having eaten. We suffered the most excruciating torments, though I in particular did not eat a quarter of what would have satisfied me; it might have been from using a quantity of raw or frozen sinews of the legs of deer, which neither of us could avoid doing, so great was our hunger. In the morning, being much agitated for the safety of Beauparlant, I desired St. Germain to go in search of him, and to return with him as quick as possible, when I would have something prepared for them to eat.

It was, however, late when he arrived, with a small

bundle which Beauparlant was accustomed to carry,
and with tears in his eyes, told me that he fcund our
poor companion dead.   Dead !   I could not believe
him.   "It is so, Sir," said St. Germain, "after hal-
looing and calling his name to no purpose, I went towards our last encampment, about three-quarters of a
mile, and found him stretched upon his back on a sand
bank frozen to death, his limbs all extended and
swelled enormously, and as hard as the ice that was
near him ; his bundle was behind him, as if it had
rolled away when he fell, and the blanket which he
wore around his neck and shoulders thrown on one
side.   Seeing that there was no longer life in him, I
threw your covering over him, and placed his snow-
shoes on the top of it."

I had not even thought of so serious an occurrence
in our little party, and for a short time was obliged to
give vent to my grief.   Left with one person and both
of us weak, no appearance of Belanger, a likelihood
that great calamity had taken place amongst our
other companions, and upwards of seventeen days'
march from the nearest Establishment, and myself
unable to carry a burden, all these things pressed
heavy on me ; and how to get to the Indians or to
the Fort I did not know ; but that I might not depress
St. Germain's spirits, I suppressed the feelings which
these thoughts gave rise to, and made some arrange-

ments for the journey to Fort Providence. We continued very weak.

October 18.—While we were this day occupied in scraping together the remains of some deers' meat, we observed Belanger coming round a point apparently scarcely moving. I went to meet him, and made immediate inquiries about my friends. Five, with the Captain, he said, were at the house, the rest were left near the river, unable to proceed; but he was too weak to relate the whole. He was conducted to the encampment, and paid every attention to, and by degrees we heard the remainder of his tragic tale, at which the interpreter could not avoid crying. He then gave me a letter from my friend the Commander, which indeed was truly afflicting. The simple story of Belanger I could hear, but when I read it in another language, mingled with the pious resignation of a good man, I could not sustain it any longer. The poor man was much affected at the death of our lamented companion, but his appetite prevailed over every other feeling; and had I permitted it, he would have done himself an injury; for after two hours' eating, principally skin and sinews, he complained of hunger. The day was cloudy, with snow and fresh breezes from the north-east by east.

The last evening, as well as this morning, the 19th, I mentioned my wishes to the men, that we should

proceed towards Reindeer Lake, but this proposal met
with a direct refusal.   Belanger stated his inability to
move, and St. Germain used similar language ; adding, for the first time, that he did not know the route,
and that it was of no use to go in the direction I mentioned, which was the one agreed upon between the
Commander and myself.   I then insisted that we
should go by the known route, and join the Commander, but they would not hear of it ; they would
remain where they were until they had regained their
strength ; they said I wanted to expose them again to
death (*faire perir*).   In vain did I use every argument to the contrary, for they were equally heedless to
all.   Thus situated, I was compelled to remain, and
from this time to the 25th, we employed ourselves in
looking about for the remnants of the deer and pieces
of skin, which even the wolves had left ; and by
pounding the bones, we were enabled to make a sort of
soup, which strengthened us greatly, though each still
complained of weakness.   It was not without the
greatest difficulty that I could restrain the men from
eating every scrap they found, though they were well
aware of the necessity there was of being economical
in our present situation, and to save whatever they
could for our journey ; yet they could not resist the
temptation, and directly my back was turned they
seldom failed to snatch at the nearest piece to

them, whether cooked or raw it made no difference. We had set fishing-lines, but without any success ; and we often saw large herds of deer crossing the lake at full speed, and wolves pursuing them.

The night of the 25th was cold, with hard frost. Early the next morning I sent the men to cover the body of our departed companion, Beauparlant, with the trunks and branches of trees, which they did ; and shortly after their return I opened his bundle, and found it contained two papers of vermilion, several strings of beads, some fire-steels, flints, awls, fish-hooks, rings, linen, and the glass of an artificial horizon. My two men began to recover a little as well as myself, though I was by far the weakest of the three ; the soles of my feet were cracked all over, and the other parts were as hard as a horn, from constant walking. I again urged the necessity of advancing to join the Commander's party, but they said they were not yet sufficiently strong.

On the 27th we discovered the remains of a deer, on which we feasted. The night was unusually cold, and ice formed in a pint-pot within two feet of a fire. The corruscations of the Aurora were beautifully brilliant ; they served to shew us eight wolves, which we had some trouble to frighten away from our collection of deers' bones ; and, with their howling, and the constant cracking of the ice, we did not get much rest.

Having collected with great care, and by self-denial,
two small packets of dried meat or sinews, sufficient
(for men who knew what it was to fast) to last for
eight days, at the rate of one indifferent meal per day,
we prepared to set out on the 30th.   I calculated that
we should be about fourteen days in reaching Fort
Providence ; and, allowing that we neither killed deer
nor found Indians, we could but be unprovided with
food six days, and this we heeded not whilst the prospect of obtaining full relief was before us.   Accordingly we set out against a keen north-east wind, in order
to gain the known route to Fort Providence.   We
saw a number of wolves and some crows on the middle
of the lake, and supposing such an assembly was not
met idly, we made for them, and came in for a share
of a deer, which they had killed a short time before,
and thus added a couple of meals to our stock.   By
four P.M. we gained the head of the lake, or the direct road to Fort Providence, and some dry wood being
at hand, we encamped ; by accident it was the same
place where the Commander's party had slept on the
19th, the day on which I suppose they had left Fort
Enterprize ; but the encampment was so small, that
we feared great mortality had taken place among them ;
and I am sorry to say the stubborn resolution of my
men, not to go to the house, prevented me from deter-
mining this most anxious point, so that I now almost

dreaded passing their encampments, lest I should see some of our unfortunate friends dead at each spot. Our fire was hardly kindled, when a fine herd of deer passed close to us. St. Germain pursued them a short distance, but with his usual want of success, so that we made a meal off the muscles and sinews we had dried, though they were so tough that we could scarcely cut them. My hands were benumbed throughout the march, and we were all stiff and fatigued. The marching of two days weakened us all very much, and the more so on account of our exertion to follow the tracks of our Commander's party ; but we lost them, and concluded that they were not before us. Though the weather was not cold, I was frozen in the face, and was so reduced and affected by these constant calamities, as well in mind as in body, that I found much difficulty in proceeding even with the advantages I had enjoyed.

November 3.—We set out before day, though, in fact, we were all better adapted to remain, from the excessive pain which we suffered in our joints, and proceeded till one P.M., without halting, when Belanger, who was before, stopped, and cried out, "Footsteps of Indians." It is needless to mention the joy that brightened the countenances of each at this unlooked-for sight ; we knew relief must be at hand, and considered our sufferings at an end. St. Germain inspected the tracks, and said that three persons had passed the day before ; and that he knew the remainder must be advancing to the southward, as it was customary with Indians, when they sent to the trading establishment on the first ice. On this information we encamped, and, being too weak to walk myself, I sent St. Germain to follow the tracks, with instructions to the Chief of the Indians to provide immediate assistance for such of our friends who might be at Fort Enterprize, as well as for ourselves, and to lose no time in returning to me. I was now so exhausted, that had we not seen the tracks this day, I had determined on remaining at the next encampment, until the men could have sent aid from Fort Providence. We had finished our small portion of sinews, and were preparing for rest, when an Indian boy made his appearance with meat. St. Germain had arrived before sunset at the tents of Akaitcho, whom he found at the spot where he had wintered last year; but imagine my surprise, when he gave me a note from the Commander, and said, that Benoit and Augustus, two of the men, had just joined them. The note was so confused, by the pencil marks being partly rubbed out, that I could not decipher it clearly ; but it informed me, that he had attempted to come with the two men, but finding his strength inadequate to the task, he relinquished nis design, and returned to Fort Enterprize, to await relief with the others. There was another note for the gentleman in charge of Fort Providence, desiring him to send meat, blankets, shoes, and tobacco. Akaitcho wished me to join him on the ensuing day, at a place which the boy knew, where they were going to fish ; and I was the more anxious to do so, on account of my two companions : but particularly to hear a full relation of what had happened, and of the Commander's true situation, which I suspected to be much worse than he had described.

In the afternoon I joined the Indians, and repeated to Akaitcho what St. Germain had told him ; he seemed much affected, and said, he would have sent relief directly, though I had not been there ; indeed, his conduct was generous and humane. The next morning, at an early hour, three Indians, with loaded sledges of meat, skins, shoes, and a blanket, set out for Fort Enterprize ; one of them was to return directly with an answer from Captain Franklin, to whom I wrote ; but in the event of his death, he was to bring away all the papers he could find ; and he promised to travel with such haste, as to be able to return to us on the fourth day. I was now somewhat more easy, having done all in my power to succor my unfortunate companions ; but was very anxious for the return of the messenger. The Indians brought me meat in small quantities, though sufficient for our daily consumption ; and, as we had a little ammunition, many were paid on the spot for what they gave.

On the 9th I had the satisfaction of seeing the Indian arrive from Fort Enterprize. At first he said they were all dead, but shortly after he gave me a note, which was from the Commander, and then I learned all the fatal particulars which had befallen them. I now proposed that the Chief should immediately send three sledges, loaded with meat, to Fort Enterprize, to make a *cache* of provision at our present encampment, and also, that he should here await the arrival of the Commander. By noon, two large trains, laden with meat, were sent off for Fort Enterprize. The next day we proceeded on our journey, and arrived at Fort Providence on the 21st of November.

Conclusion of Mr. Back's Narrative.

I HAVE little now to add to the melancholy detail into which I felt it proper to enter ; but I cannot omit to state, that the unremitting care and attentions of our kind friends, Mr. M'Vicar and Mr. M'Auley, together with the improvement of our diet, materially contributed to the restoration of our health ; so that, by the end of February, the swellings of our limbs, which had returned upon us, had entirely subsided, and we were able to walk to any part of the island. Our appetites gradually moderated, and we nearly regained our ordinary state of body before the spring. Hepburn alone suffered from a severe attack of rheumatism, which confined him to his bed for some weeks. The usual symptoms of spring having appeared, on the 25th of May we prepared to embark for Fort Chipewyan. Fortunately, on the following morning, a canoe arrived from that place with the whole of the stores which we required for the payment of Akaitcho and the hunters. It was extremely gratifying to us to be thus enabled, previous to our departure, to make arrangements respecting the payment of our late Indian companions ; and the more so, as we had recently discovered that Akaitcho, and the whole of the tribe, in consequence of the death of the leader's mother, and the wife of our old guide Keskarrah, had broken and destroyed every useful article belonging to them, and that they were in the greatest distress. It was an additional pleasure to find our stock of ammunition was more than sufficient to pay them what was due, and that we could make a considerable present of this most essential article to every individual that had been attached to the Expedition.

We quitted Moose-deer Island at five P.M., on the
26th, accompanied by Mr. M'Vicar and Mr. M'Auley,
and nearly all the voyagers at the establishment, having resided there about five months, not a day of which
had passed without our having cause of gratitude, for
the kind and unvaried attentions of Mr. M'Vicar and
Mr. M'Auley.   These gentlemen accompanied us as
far as Fort Chipewyan, where we arrived on the 2d of
June ; here we met Mr. Wentzel, and the four men,
who had been sent with him from the mouth of the
Copper-Mine River; and I think it due to that gentleman, to give his own explanation of the unfortunate
circumstances which prevented him from fulfilling my
last instructions, respecting the provisions to have
been left for us at Fort Enterprize.*

* " After you sent me back from the mouth of the Copper-Mine
River, and I had overtaken the Leader, Guides, and Hunters on the
fifth day leaving the sea-coast, as well as on our journey up the River,
they always expressed the same desire of fulfilling their promises,
although somewhat dissatisfied at being exposed to privation while on
our return, from a scarcity of animals ; for as I have already stated in
my first communication from Moose-Deer Island, we had been eleven
days with no other food but *tripe de roche.* In the course of this time
an Indian, with his wife and child, who were traveling in company
with us, were left in the rear, and are since supposed to have perished
through want, as no intelligence had been received of them at Fort
Providence in December last.   On the 7th day after I had joined the
Leader, &c, &c., and journeying on together, all the Indians excepting Petit, Pied and Bald-Head, left me to seek their families, and

In a subsequent conversation he stated to me, that the two Indians, who were actually with him at Fort Enterprize, whilst he remained there altering his ˙canoe, were prevented from hunting, one by an accidental lameness, the other by the fear of meeting alone some of the Dog-Rib Indians.

crossed Point Lake at the Crow's Nest, where Humpy had promised to meet his brother Ekehcho* with the families, but did not fulfill, nor did any of my party of Indians know where to find them : for we had frequently made fires to apprize them of our approach, yet none appeared in return as answers. This disappointment, as might be expected, served to increase the ill-humor of the Leader and party, the brooding of which (agreeably to Indian custom,) was liberally discharged on me in bitter reproach for having led them from their families, and exposed them to dangers and hardships, which but for my influence, they said, they might have spared themselves. Nevertheless, they still continued to profess the sincerest desire of meeting your wishes in making caches of provisions, and remaining until a late season on the road that leads from Fort Enterprize to Fort Providence, through which the Expedition-men had traveled so often the year before—remarking, however, at the same time, that they had not the least hopes of ever seeing one person return from the Expedition. These alarming fears I never could persuade them to dismiss from their minds; they always sneered at what they called 'my credulity,'—'If,' said the Gros Pied,† 'the Great Chief (meaning Captain Franklin,) or any of his party, should pass at my tents, he or they shall be welcome to all my provisions, or any thing else that I may have.' And I am sincerely happy to understand, by your communication, that in this he had kept his word—in sending you with

* *Akaitcho the Leader.*　　　　†*Also Akaitcho.*

We were here furnished with a canoe by Mr Smith,
and a bowman, to act as our guide ; and having left
Fort Chipewyan on the 5th, we arrived, on the 4th of
July, at Norway House.   Finding at this place, that
canoes were about to go down to Montreal, I gave all
our Canadian voyagers their discharges, and sent them
by those vessels, furnishing them with orders on the
Agent of the Hudson's Bay Company for the amount
of their wages.   We carried Augustus down to York

such promptitude and liberality the assistance your truly dreadful
situation required.   But the party of Indians, on whom I had placed
the utmost confidence and dependence, was Humpy and the White
Capot Guide, with their sons and several of the discharged Hunters from
the Expedition.   This party was well-disposed, and readily promised
to collect provisions for the possible return of the Expedition, provided they could get a supply of ammunition from Fort Providence ; for
when I came up with them, they were actually starving, and converting
old axes into ball, having no other substitute—this was unlucky. Yet
they were well inclined, and I expected to find means at Fort Providence to send them a supply, in which I was, however, disappointed, for
I found that establishment quite destitute of necessaries ; and then,
shortly after I had left them, they had the misfortune of losing three
of their hunters, who were drowned in Marten Lake ; this accident
was, of all others, the most fatal that could have happened—a truth
which no one, who has the least knowledge of the Indian character,
will deny ; and as they were nearly connected by relationship to the
Leader, Humpy, and White Capot Guide, the three leading men of this
part of the Copper Indian Tribe, it had the effect of unhinging (if I
may use the expression,) the minds of all these families, and finally
destroying all the fond hopes I had so sanguinely conceived of their

Factory, where we arrived on the 14th of July, and were received with every mark of attention and kindness by Mr. Simpson, the Governor, Mr. M'Tavish, and, indeed, by all the officers of the United Companies. And thus terminated our long, fatiguing, and disastrous travels in North America, having journeyed by water and by land (including our navigation of the Polar Sea,) five thousand five hundred and fifty miles.

assisting the expedition, should it come back by the Annadesse River, of which they were not certain.

" As to my not leaving a letter at Fort Enterprize, it was because by some mischance, you had forgot to give me paper when we parted.*

" I however wrote this news on a plank, in pencil, and placed it in the top of your former bedstead, where I left it. Since it has not been found there, some Indians must have gone to the house after my departure, and destroyed it. These details, Sir, I have been induced to enter into (rather unexpectedly,) in justification of myself, and hope it will be satisfactory."

* *I certainly offered Mr. Wentzel some paper when he quitted us, but he declined it, having then a note book ; and Mr. Back gave him a pencil.*

CHAPTER XIV.

FRANKLIN'S Second Great Expedition was made in 1825, and over much of the same ground as that traversed in his first. His preparations were more complete than on his first Expedition. His old friends Richardson and Back accompanied him, the whole party crossing the Atlantic in an American packet, and passing through the State of New York. At New York, Albany, and other places on their route receiving the enthusiastic attention of the people— to Canada and thence to Methoye River, north of Hudson's Bay, where they—the officers—joined the boats of the Expedition.

On the 30th of June, the party entered the Methoye River, and early in July crossed the lake of the same name. On the 12th, Capt. Franklin and Dr. Richardson set out in a canoe for Fort Chipewyan, to make preparations for the entire party. On the 15th they arrived at Athabasca Lake, and were by night at the Fort. By the end of the month Fort Resolution was reached, and all the portages on the road to Bear Lake crossed. The first week in August was spent on the Mackenzie River in getting to Fort Simpson. On the 8th of August a voyage to the sea was agreed upon for Capt. Franklin, while Dr. Richardson should coast above the northern shore of Bear Lake to the Copper-Mine River, while Lieutenant Back was to prepare winter quarters for the entire party. Capt. Franklin set off at noon, arriving in two days at Fort Good Hope, the lowest station of the Hudson Company. By the middle of August they reached latitude 69°, 14' N.,—longitude 135°, 57' W.,—the north-eastern entrance to the main channel of Mackenzie River, and 1045 miles from Slave Lake. Salt water was reached, and the party indulged in a little enthusiasm. The next day the boats were turned towards the Mackenzie on their way back to winter quarters. September 1st, the river Mackenzie was left for a stream which flows from Bear Lake, and on the 5th reached the winter quarters.

The winter of 1825–6 was passed by the company in comparative comfort. Buildings were erected and a plentiful supply of provisions stored in them, together with the expected supplies from fishing and hunting, to carry the party cozily through another year.

Amusements were also provided for the men, while

the officers made good use of a stock of books and quarterlies which they had brought with them.

The winter, though severe, passed rapidly away, and spring opened. We quote from Franklin's Journal.

^{Wednesday}
^{24th.} On the 24th of May, 1826, the mosquitoes appeared, feeble at first, but, after a few days, they became vigorous and tormenting. The first flower, a tussilago, was gathered on the 27th. Before the close of the month, several others were in bloom, of which the most abundant was the white anemone. The leaf-buds had not yet burst, though just ready to open.

The carpenters had now finished the new boat, which received the name of the Reliance. It was constructed of fir, with birch timbers, after the model of our largest boat, the Lion, but with a more full bow, and a finer run abaft. Its length was twenty-six feet, and breadth five feet eight inches. It was fastened in the same manner as the other boats, but with iron instead of copper, and to procure sufficient nails we were obliged to cut up all the spare axes, trenches, and ice-chisels. Being without tar, we substituted strips of water-proof canvas, soaked in some caoutchouc varnish, which we had brought out, to lay between the seams of the planks ; and for paint, we made use of resin, procured from the pine-trees, boiled and mixed with grease. The other boats were afterwards put in complete repair. The Lion required the most, in consequence of the accident in Bear Lake River. The defects in the other two principally arose from their having been repaired at Cumberland House with the elm that grows in its vicinity, and is very spongy. We now substituted white spruce fir, which, when grown in these high latitudes, is an excellent wood for boat-building. We were surprised to find, that, notwithstanding the many heavy blows these boats had received in their passage to this place, there was not a timber that required to be changed.

1826. May. In our bustle, we would gladly have dispensed with the presence of the Dog-Ribs (Indians) who now visited us in great numbers, without bringing any supplies. They continued hanging about the fort, and their daily drumming and singing over the sick, the squalling of the children, and bawling of the men and women, proved no small annoyance. We were pleased, however, at perceiving that the ammunition we had given to them in return for meat, had enabled them to provide themselves with leathern tents. Their only shelter from wind, snow, or rain, before this season, had been a rude barricade of pine branches. Fortunately, for our comfort, they were obliged to remove before the expiration of the month to a distant fishery to procure provision.

The preparations for the voyage along the
coast being now in a state of forwardness, my attention was directed to the providing for the return of
Dr. Richardson's party to this establishment in the
following autumn, and to the securing means of support for all the members of the Expedition at this
place, in the event of the western party being likewise compelled to return to it. Respecting the first
point, it was arranged that Beaulieu the interpreter,
and four Canadians, should quit Fort Franklin on the
6th of August, and proceed direct to Dease River
with a bateau, and wait there until the 20th of September, when, if Dr. Richardson did not appear,
they were to come back to the fort in canoes, and to
leave the boat, with provision and other necessaries,
for the use of the eastern detachment. All these
points were explained to Beaulieu, and he not only
understood every part of the arrangement, but seemed very desirous to perform the important duty en-
trusted to him.   I next drew up written instructions
for the guidance of Mr. Dease, during the absence of
the Expedition, directing his attention first to the
equipment and despatch of Beaulieu on the 6th of
August, and then to the keeping the establishment
well-stored with provision. He was aware of the
probability that the western party would meet his
Majesty's ship Blossom, and go to Canton in her.

But as unforeseen circumstances might compel us to winter on the coast, I considered it necessary to warn him against inferring, from our not returning in the following autumn, that we had reached the Blossom. He was, therefore, directed to keep Fort Franklin complete, as to provision, until the spring of 1828. Dr. Richardson was likewise instructed, before he left the fort in 1827, on his return to England, to see that Mr. Dease fully understood my motives for giving these orders, and that he was provided with the means of purchasing the necessary provision from the Indians.

Wed. 7th. The long reign of the east wind was at length terminated by a fresh N. W. breeze, and the ice yet remaining on the small lake soon disappeared, under the softening effects of this wind. This lake had been frozen eight months, wanting three days. A narrow channel being opened along the western border of Bear Lake, on the 14th Dr. Richardson took advantage of it, and went in a small canoe with two men to examine the mountains on the borders of Bear Lake River, and to collect specimens of the plants that were now in flower, intending to rejoin the party at Fort Norman. On the same day, in 1821, the former Expedition left Fort Enterprise for the sea.

Thurs. 15th. The equipments of the boats being now complete, they were launched on the small lake, and tried under oars and sails. In the afternoon the men were appointed to their respective° stations, and furnished with the sky-blue waterproof uniforms, and feathers, as well as with the warm clothing which had been provided for the voyage. I acquainted them fully with the object of the Expedition, and pointed out their various duties. They received these communications with satisfaction, were delighted with the prospect of the voyage, and expressed their readiness to commence it immediately. Fourteen men, including Augustus, were appointed to accompany myself and Lieutenant Back, in the Lion and Reliance, the two larger boats ; and ten, including Ooligbuck, to go with Dr. Richardson and Mr. Kendall, in the Dolphin and Union. In order to make up the complement of fourteen for the western party, I proposed to receive two volunteers from the Canadian voyagers ; and to the credit of Canadian enterprise, every man came forward. I chose Francois Felix and Alexis Vivier, because they were the first who offered their services, and this too without any stipulation as to increase of wages.

Spare blankets and everything that could be useful for the voyage, or as presents to the Esquimaux, which our stores could furnish, were divided between the eastern and western parties, and put up into bales of a size convenient ·for stowage. This interesting day was closed by the consumption of a small quantity of rum, reserved for the occasion, followed by a merry dance, in which all joined with great glee, in their working dresses. On the following Sunday the officers and men assembled at Divine service, dressed in their new uniforms ; and in addition to the ordinary service of the day, the special protection of Providence was implored on the enterprise we were about to commence. The guns were cleaned the next day, and stowed in the arm chests, which had been made to fit the boats. Tuesday and Wednesday were set apart for the officers and men to pack their own things. A strong western breeze occurred on the 21st, which removed the ice from the front of the house and opened a passage to the Bear Lake River. The men were sent with the boats and stores to the river in the evening, and were heartily cheered on quitting the beach. The officers remained to pack up the charts, drawings, and other documents, which were to be left at the fort ; and, in the event of none of the officers returning, Mr. Dease was directed to forward them to England. We quitted the house at half past ten, on Tuesday morning, leaving Coté, the fisherman, in charge, until Mr. Dease should return from Fort Norman. This worthy old man, sharing the enthusiasm that animated the whole party, would not allow us to depart without giving his hearty, though solitary cheer, which we returned in full chorus.

CHAPTER XV.

^{Thurs.}
^{22nd.} ON our arrival at the Bear Lake River, we were mortified to find the ice drifting down in large masses, with such rapidity as to render embarkation unsafe. The same cause detained us the whole of the following day ; and as we had brought no more provision from the house than sufficient for an uninterrupted passage to Fort Norman, we sent for a supply of fish. This was a very sultry day, the thermometer in the shade being 71° at noon, and 74° at three P. M.

The descent of the ice having ceased at eight in the morning of the 24th, we embarked. The heavy stores were put into a bateau, manned by Canadians, who were experienced in the passage through rapids, and the rest of the boats were ordered to follow in its wake, keeping at such a distance from each other as to allow of any evolution that might be necessary to avoid the stones. The boats struck several times, but received no injury. At the foot of the rapid we

met a canoe, manned by four of our Canadian voyagers, whom Dr. Richardson had sent with some letters
that had arrived at Fort Norman from the Athabasca
Lake ; and as the services of the men were wanted,
they were embarked in the boats, and the canoe was
left. Shortly afterwards we overtook Beaulieu, who
had just killed a young moose deer, which afforded the
party two substantial meals. At this spot, and generally along the river, we found abundance of wild
onions.

We entered the Mackenzie River at eight in the
evening, and the current being too strong for us to
advance against the stream with oars, we had recourse
to the tracking line, and traveled all night. It was
fatiguing, owing to large portions of the banks having
been overthrown by the disruption of the ice, and
from the ground being so soft that the men dragging
the rope sank up to the knees at every step ; but
these impediments were less regarded than the cease-
less torment of the musquitoes. We halted to sup at
the spot where Sir A. Mackenzie saw the flame rising
from the bank in 1789. The precipice was still on
fire, the smoke issuing through several apertures.
Specimens of the coal were procured.

^{Sunday} We reached Fort Norman at noon on the
25th. On the following morning the provision and
stores which had been left at this place were exam-

ined, and found to be in excellent order, except the powder in one of the magazines, which had become caked from damp. I had ordered a supply of iron-work, knives, and beads, for the sea voyage from Fort Simpson ; they had arrived some days before us, and with our stock thus augmented, we were well furnished with presents for the natives. The packages being finished on the 27th, the boats received their respective ladings, and we were rejoiced to find that each stowed her cargo well, and with her crew embarked floated as buoyantly as our most sanguine wishes had anticipated. The heavy stores, however, were afterwards removed into a bateau that was to be taken to the mouth of the river, to prevent the smaller boats from receiving injury in passing over the shoals.

We waited one day to make some pounded meat we had brought into pemmican. In the meantime the seamen enlarged the foresail of the Reliance.

The letters which I received from the Athabasca department informed me that the things I had required from the Company in February last, would be duly forwarded ; they likewise contained a very different version of the story which had led us to suppose that Captain Parry was passing the winter on the northern coast. We now learned that the Indians had only seen some pieces of wood recently cut, and a deer that had been killed by an arrow ; these things

we concluded were done by the Esquimaux. Three
men from Slave Lake, whom I had sent for to supply
the place of our Chipewyan hunters, who were very
inactive last winter, joined us at this place. They
were to accompany Mr. Dease and the Canadians to
Fort Franklin ; and that they, as well as the Indians,
might have every encouragement to exert themselves
in procuring provision during the summer, I directed
a supply of the goods they were likely to require, to
be sent from Fort Simpson, as soon as possible.

Wednesday 28th. Early this morning the boats were laden
and decorated with their ensigns and pendants, and
after breakfast we quitted the Fort, amidst the hearty
cheers of our friends Mr. Dease, Mr. Brisbois, and the
Canadians, and I am sure carried their best wishes for
our success. We halted at noon to obtain the latitude, which placed the entrance of Bear Lake River
in 64° 55' 37" N. ; and Dr. Richardson took advantage of this delay to visit the mountain at that point,
but his stay was short, in consequence of a favorable
breeze springing up. We perceived that the four
boats sailed at nearly an equal rate in light breezes,
but that in strong winds the two larger ones had the
advantage. When we landed to sup the musquitoes
beset us so furiously that we hastily despatched the
meal and re-embarked, to drive under easy sail before
the current. They continued, however, to pursue us,

and deprived us of all rest. On our arrival, next
morning, at the place of the first rapids, there was
scarcely any appearance of broken water, and the sand-
bank on which Augustus had been so perilously situated in the preceding autumn, was entirely covered.
This was, of course, to be ascribed to the spring floods ;
the increase of water to produce such a change, must
have exceeded six feet. In the afternoon we were
overtaken by a violent thunder-storm, with heavy
rain, which made us apprehensive for the pemmican,
that spoils on being wet. It unfortunately happened
that a convenient place for spreading out the bags
that were injured could not be found, until we reached
the Hare-Skin River, below the Rampart Defile, which
was at nine o'clock. They were spread out the next
morning, with the other perishable parts of the cargo,
and we remained until they were dry. We embarked
at ten, and, aided by a favorable breeze, made good
progress until six P.M., when the threatening appearance of the clouds induced us to put on shore, and we
had but just covered the baggage before heavy rain
fell, that continued throughout the night. Four
Hare Indians came to the encampment, to whom dried
meat and ammunition were given, as they were in
want of food from being unable to set their nets in
the present high state of the water. These were the
only natives seen since our departure from Fort Nor-

man ; they informed us, that, in consequence of not being able to procure a sufficiency of fish in the Mackenzie at this season, their companions had withdrawn to gain their subsistence from the small lakes in the interior.

July 1st. We embarked at half-past one on the morning of July. The sultry weather of the preceding day made us now feel more keenly the chill of a strong western breeze, and the mist which it brought on, about four hours after our departure. This wind, being contrary to the current, soon raised such high waves that the boats took in a great deal of water ; and as we made but little progress, and were very cold, we landed to kindle a fire, and prepare breakfast ; after which we continued the voyage to Fort Good Hope, without any of the interruptions from sand-banks that we had experienced in the autumn.

On our arrival we were saluted with a discharge of musketry by a large party of Loucheux, who had been some time waiting at the Fort, with their wives and families, for the purpose of seeing us. After a short conference with Mr. Bell, the master of the post, we were informed that these Indians had lately met a numerous party of Esquimaux at the Red River, by appointment, to purchase their furs ; and that in consequence of a misunderstanding respecting some bargain, a quarrel had ensued between them, which fortunately terminated without bloodshed. We could not, however, gain any satisfactory account of the movements of the Esquimaux. The only answers to our repeated questions on these points were, that the Esquimaux came in sixty canoes to Red River, and that they supposed them to have gone down the eastern channel, for the purpose of fishing near its mouth. The chief, however, informed us that he had mentioned our coming to their lands this spring, and that they had received the intelligence without comment; but from his not having alluded to this communication until the question was pressed upon him, and from the manner of his answering our inquiries, I thought it doubtful whether such a communication had really been made.

We had been led to expect much information from the Loucheux respecting the channels of the river, and the coast on the east and west side near its mouth, but we were greatly disappointed. They were ignorant of the channel we ought to follow in order to arrive at the western mouth of the river; and the only intelligence they gave us respecting the coast on that side was, that the Esquimaux represented it to be almost constantly beset by ice. They said also that they were unacquainted with the tribes who reside to the westward. Several of the party had been down the eastern channel, of which they made a rude sketch;

and their account of the coast on that side was, that, as far as they were acquainted with it, it was free from ice during the summer.

Having ascertained that the Esquimaux were likely to be seen in greater numbers than had been at first imagined, I increased the stock of presents from the store at this place, and exchanged two of our guns, which were defective, that the party might have entire confidence in their arms. And to provide against the casualty of either or both branches of the Expedition having to return this way, I requested Mr. Bell to store up as much meat as he could during the summer. We learned from this gentleman that the supply of meat at this post was very precarious, and that had we not left the five bags of pemmican in the autumn, the residents would have been reduced to great distress for food during the winter. These bags were now replaced. The arrangements being concluded, we spent the greater part of the night in writing to England. I addressed to the Colonial Secretary an account of our proceedings up to this time, and I felt happy to be able to state that we were equipped with every requisite for the Expedition.

Sunday 2d. We quitted Fort Good Hope at five on the 2nd. In the passage down the river we were visited by several Loucheux, who, the instant we appeared, launched their canoes, and came off to welcome us.

We landed, at their request, to purchase fish; yet,
after the bargain had been completed, an old woman
stepped forward, and would only allow of our receiving two fish : she maintained her point and carried off
the rest in spite of all remonstrance. The natives
were all clothed in new leathern dresses, and looked
much neater, and in better health, than last autumn.
Being anxious to reach the Red River, we continued
rowing against the wind until after midnight. On
reaching that place, the ground proved too wet for us
to encamp ; we, therefore, proceeded a short distance
lower down, and put up under some sandstone cliffs,
where there was but just room for the tents. As we
were now on the borders of the Esquimaux territory,
we devoted the following morning to cleaning the
arms ; and a gun, dagger, and ammunition, were issued to each person. We had no reason, indeed, to
apprehend hostility from the Esquimaux, after the
messages they had sent to Fort Franklin, but vigi-
lance and precaution are never to be omitted in intercourse with strange tribes.

Monday 3rd. Embarking at two in the afternoon of the 3rd,
we soon entered the expansion of the river whence the
different channels branch off, and steering along the
western shore, we came to the head of a branch that
flowed towards the Rocky Mountain range. Being
anxious not to take the eastern detachment out of

their course, I immediately encamped to make the necessary arrangements for the separation of the parties. The warm clothing, shoes, and articles for presents, had been previously put up in separate packages, but the provisions remained to be divided, which was done in due proportion. Twenty-six bags of pemmican, and two of grease, were set apart for the Dolphin and Union, with a supply of arrow-root, macaroni, flour, and portable soup, making in all eighty days' provision, with an allowance for waste. The Lion and Reliance received thirty-two bags of pemmican, and two of grease, with sufficient arrow-root, &c., to make their supply proportionate to that of the eastern party. Provided no accident occurred, neither party could be in absolute want for the whole summer, because at two-thirds allowance the pemmican could be made to last one hundred days ; and we had reason to expect to meet with deer occasionally. In the evening I delivered my instructions to Dr. Richardson.

As the parties entertained for each other sentiments of true friendship and regard, it will easily be imagined that the evening preceding our separation was spent in the most cordial and cheerful manner. We felt that we were only separating to be employed on services of equal interest ; and we looked forward with delight to our next meeting, when, after a successful termination, we might recount the incidents of our respective voyages. The best supper our means afforded was provided, and a bowl of punch crowned the parting feast.

We were joined by an elderly Loucheux, who gave us a better account of the eastern and western channels than we had hitherto obtained. "The west branch," he said, "would take us to the sea, and flowed the whole way at no great distance from the mountains." "The eastern was a good channel, and passed close to the hills on that side." He further informed us that the Esquimaux were generally to be found on an island in the eastern channel, but were seldom seen in the western branch. He was, however, unacquainted with the coast, and we found afterwards that he knew little about the movements of the Esquimaux.

Tuesday 4th. By six in the morning of the 4th the boats were all laden, and ready for departure. It was impossible not to be struck with the difference between our present complete state of equipment and that on which we had embarked on our former disastrous voyage. Instead of a frail bark canoe, and a scanty supply of food, we were now about to commence the sea voyage in excellent boats, stored with three months' provision. At Dr. Richardson's desire the western party embarked first. He and his companions saluted us with three hearty cheers, which were warmly returned ; and as we were passing round the point that was to hide them from our view, we perceived them also embarking. Augustus was rather melancholy, as might have been expected, on his parting from Ooligbuck, to proceed he knew not whither ; but he recovered his wonted flow of spirits by the evening.

Our course was directly towards the Rocky Mountain range, till we came near the low land that skirts its base ; where, following the deepest channel, we turned to the northward. I was desirous of coasting the main shore, but finding some of the westernmost branches too shallow, we kept on the outside of three islands for about twelve miles, when we entered the channel that washes the west side of Simpson's Island. It was winding, and its breadth seldom exceeded a quarter of a mile. During our progress we occasionally caught a glimpse of the Rocky Mountains, which was an agreeable relief to the very dull picture that the muddy islands in our neighborhood afforded. We halted to breakfast just before noon, and observed the latitude 67° 51' N.

In the afternoon one deer was seen, and many swans and geese ; we did not fire at them, for fear of alarming any Esquimaux that might be near. Encamped at eight P. M., opposite Simpson's Island. The boats were secured without discharging the cargoes, and two men were placed on guard, to be relieved every two hours.

18

^{Wed.}_{5th.} We set forward at four A. M., with a favorable breeze, and made good progress, though the river was very winding. At eight we entered a branch that turned to the westward round the point of Halkett Island into the channel washing the main shore. We soon afterwards arrived at a spot where a large body of Esquimaux had been encamped in the spring, and supposing that they might revisit this place, a present of an ice-chisel, kettle, and knife, was hung up in a conspicuous situation. Soon after we had entered the channel that flows by the main shore, we first perceived lop-sticks, or pine trees, divested of their lower branches, for the purpose of land-marks, and therefore concluded it was much frequented by the Esquimaux. Our course was then altered to N. W., and we soon passed the last of the well wooded islands. The spruce fir-trees terminated in latitude 68° 36′ N. ; and dwarf willows only grew below this part. A very picturesque view was obtained of the Rocky Mountains, and we saw the entire outline of their peaked hills, table-land, and quoin-shaped terminations. Two lofty ranges were fronted by a lower line of round-backed hills, in which we perceived the strata to be horizontal, and the stone of a yellow color. A few miles lower down we found hills of sand close to the west border of the river. We passed several deserted huts, and in one spot saw many chips and

pieces of split drift-wood, that appeared to have been recently cut. The channel varied in breadth from a half to three-quarters of a mile, but, except in the stream of the current, the water was so shallow as scarcely to float the boats, and its greatest depth did not exceed five feet. We landed at eight P. M., on Halkett Island, intending to encamp, but owing to the swampiness of the ground the tent could not be pitched. Having made a fire and cooked our supper, we retired to sleep under the coverings of the boats, which afforded us good shelter from a gale and heavy rain that came on before midnight. Latitude 68° 39′ N., longitude 135° 35′ W.

Thurs. 6th. The continuance of stormy weather detained us until two P.M. of the 6th, when, the rain ceasing, we embarked. After passing through the expansion of the river near the west extreme of Halkett Island, we turned into the narrower and more winding channel, between Colvill Island and the main. A fog coming on at eight P.M. we encamped. Several of the glaucous gulls were seen, and this circumstance, as well as a line of bright cloud to the N.W. resembling the ice-blink, convinced us that the sea was not far off. A rein-deer appearing near the encampment, two men were sent after it, who returned unsuccessful. Augustus obtained a goose for supper. Many geese, swans, and ducks, had been seen on the marshy shores of the island in the course of the day.

^{Friday.}_{7th.} The night was cold, and at day-light on the 7th the thermometer indicated 36°. Embarking at four A.M. we sailed down the river for two hours, when our progress was arrested by the shallowness of the water. Having endeavored, without effect, to drag the boats over the flat, we remounted the stream to examine an opening to the westward, which we had passed. On reaching the opening we found the current setting through it into the Mackenzie, by which we knew that it could not afford a passage to the sea, but we pulled up it a little way, in the hope of obtaining a view over the surrounding low grounds from the top of an Esquimaux house which we saw before us. A low fog, which had prevailed all the morning, cleared away, and we discovered that the stream we had now ascended issued from a chain of lakes lying betwixt us and the western hills, which were about six miles distant, the whole intervening country between the hills, and the Mackenzie being flat.

After obtaining an observation for longitude in 136° 19' W., and taking the bearing of several remarkable points of the Rocky Mountain range, we returned to the Mackenzie, and passing the shallows which had before impeded us, by taking only half the boats' cargoes over at a time, we came in sight of the mouth of the river. Whilst the crews were stowing the boats, I obtained an observation for latitude in 68° 53' N., and having walked towards the mouth of the river, discovered on an island, which formed the east side of the bay into which the river opened, a crowd of tents, with many Esquimaux strolling amongst them. I instantly hastened to the boats, to make preparations for opening a communication with them, agreeably to my instructions. A selection of articles for presents and trade being made, the rest of the lading was closely covered up ; the arms were inspected, and every man was directed to keep his gun ready for immediate use. I had previously informed Lieutenant Back of my intention of opening the communication with the Esquimaux by landing amongst them, accompanied only by Augustus ; and I now instructed him to keep the boats afloat, and the crews with their arms ready to support us in the event of the natives proving hostile ; but on no account to fire until he was convinced that our safety could be secured in no other way. Having received an impression from the narratives of different navigators that the sacrifices of life which had occurred in their interviews with savages, had been generally occasioned by the crews mistaking noise and violent gestures for decided hostility, I thought it necessary to explain my sentiments on this point to all the men, and peremptorily forbade their firing till I set the example, or till they were ordered to do so by Lieutenant Back. They were also forbidden to trade

with the natives on any pretence, and were ordered to
leave every thing of that kind to the officers.

On quitting the channel of the river we entered into
the bay, which was about six miles wide, with an unbounded prospect to seaward, and steered towards the
tents under easy sail, with the ensigns flying. The
water became shallow as we drew towards the island,
and the boats touched the ground when about a mile
from the beach ; we shouted, and made signs to the
Esquimaux to come off, and then pulled a short way
back to await their arrival in deeper water. Three
canoes instantly put off from the shore, and before
they could reach us others were launched in such quick
succession, that the whole space between the island
and the boats was covered by them. The Esquimaux
canoes contain only one person, and are named
kaiyacks ; but they have a kind of open boat capable
of holding six or eight people, which is named *oomiak*.
The men alone use the kaiyacks, and the oomiaks are
allotted to the women and children. We endeavored
to count their numbers as they approached, and had
proceeded as far as seventy-three canoes, and five
oomiaks, when the sea became so crowded by fresh
arrivals, that we could advance no farther in our
reckoning. The three headmost canoes were paddled
by elderly men, who, most probably, had been selected
to open the communication. They advanced towards

us with much caution, halting when just within speaking distance, until they had been assured of our friendship, and repeatedly invited by Augustus to approach and receive the present which I offered to them. Augustus next explained to them in detail the purport of our visit, and told them that if we succeeded in finding a navigable channel for large ships, a trade highly beneficial to them would be opened. They were delighted with this intelligence, and repeated it to their countrymen, who testified their joy by tossing their hands aloft, and raising the most deafening shout of applause I ever heard.

After the first present, I resolved to bestow no more gratuitously, but always to exact something, however small, in return ; the three elderly men readily offered the ornaments they wore in their cheeks, their arms, and knives, in exchange for the articles I gave them. Up to this time the first three were the only kaiyacks that had ventured near the' boats, but the natives around us had now increased to two hundred and fifty or three hundred persons, and they all became anxious to share in the lucrative trade which they saw established, and pressed eagerly upon us, offering for sale their bows, arrows, and spears, which they had hitherto kept concealed within their canoes. I endeavored in vain, amidst the clamor and bustle of trade, to obtain some information respecting the coast, but finding

the natives becoming more and more importunate and
troublesome, I determined to leave them, and, therefore, directed the boats' heads to be put to seaward.
Notwithstanding the forwardness of the Esquimaux,
which we attributed solely to the desire of a rude
people to obtain the novel articles they saw in our
possession, they had hitherto shown no unfriendly
disposition ; and when we told them of our intention
of going to sea. they expressed no desire to detain us,
but, on the contrary, when the Lion grounded in the
act of turning, they assisted us in the kindest manner
by dragging her round.   This manœuvre was not of
much advantage to us, for, from the rapid ebbing of
the tide, both boats lay aground ; and the Esquimaux
told us, through the medium of Augustus, that the
whole bay was alike flat, which we afterwards found
to be correct.

An accident happened at this time, which was
productive of unforeseen and very annoying consequences.   A kaiyack being overset by one of the
Lion's oars, its owner was plunged into the water with
his head in the mud, and apparently in danger of
being drowned.   We instantly extricated him from
his unpleasant situation, and took him into the boat
until the water could be thrown out of his kaiyack,
and Augustus, seeing him shivering with cold, wrapped
him up in his own great coat.   At first he was ex-

ceedingly angry, but soon became reconciled to his
situation, and looking about, discovered that we had
many bales, and other articles, in the boat, which had
been concealed from the people in the kaiyacks, by the
coverings being carefully spread over all. He soon
began to ask for every thing he saw, and expressed
much displeasure on our refusing to comply with his
demands ; he also, as we afterwards learned, excited
the cupidity of others by his account of the inex-
haustible riches in the Lion, and several of the younger
men endeavored to get into both our boats, but we
resisted all their attempts. Though we had not
hitherto observed any of them stealing, yet they
showed so much desire to obtain my flag, that I had
it furled and put out of sight, as well as every thing
else that I thought could prove a temptation to them.
They continued, however, to press upon us so closely,
and made so many efforts to get into the boats, that I
accepted the offer of two chiefs, who said that if they
were allowed to come in, they would keep the others
out. For a time they kept their word, and the crews
took advantage of the respite thus afforded, to endeavor to force the boats towards the river into deeper
water. The Reliance floated, but the Lion was im-
movable, and Lieutenant Back dropping astern again
made his boat fast to the Lion by a rope. At this
time one of the Lion's crew perceived that the man

whose kaiyack had been upset had a pistol under his shirt, and was about to take it from him, but I ordered him to desist, as I thought it might have been purchased from the Loucheux. It had been, in fact, stolen from Lieutenant Back, and the thief, perceiving our attention directed to it, leaped out of the boat, and joined his countrymen, carrying with him the great coat which Augustus had lent him.

The water had now ebbed so far, that it was not knee-deep at the boats, and the younger men wading in crowds around us, tried to steal every thing within their reach; slyly, however, and with so much dexterity, as almost to escape detection. The moment this disposition was manifested, I directed the crews not to suffer any one to come alongside, and desired Augustus to tell the two chiefs, who still remained seated in the Lion, that the noise and confusion occasioned by the crowd around the boats greatly impeded our exertions; and that if they would go on shore and leave us for the present, we would hereafter return from the ship which we expected to meet near this part of the coast, with a more abundant supply of goods. They received this communication with much apparent satisfaction, and jumping out of the boats repeated the speech aloud to their companions. From the general exclamation of "*teyma*," which followed, and from perceiving many of the elderly men retire to a distance, I conceived that they acquiesced in the propriety of the suggestion, and that they were going away, but I was much deceived. They only retired to concert a plan of attack, and returned in a short time shouting some words which Augustus could not make out. We soon, however, discovered their purport, by two of the three chiefs who were on board the Reliance, jumping out, and, with the others who hurried to their assistance, dragging her towards the south shore of the river. Lieutenant Back desired the chief who remained with him to tell them to desist, but he replied by pointing to the beach, and repeating the word *teyma, teyma,* with a good-natured smile. He said, however, something to those who were seated in the canoes that were alongside, on which they threw their long knives and arrows into the boat, taking care, in so doing, that the handles and feathered ends were turned towards the crew, as an indication of pacific intentions.

As soon as I perceived the Reliance moving under the efforts of the natives, I directed the Lion's crew to endeavor to follow her, but our boat remained fast until the Esquimaux lent their aid and dragged her after the Reliance. Two of the most powerful men, jumping on board at the same time, seized me by the wrists and forced me to sit between them ; and as I shook them loose two or three times, a third Esquimaux took his station in front to catch my arm whenever I attempted to lift my gun, or the broad dagger which hung by my side. The whole way to the shore they kept repeating the word " *teyma*," beating gently on my left breast with their hands, and pressing mine against their breasts. As we neared the beach, two oomiaks, full of women, arrived, and the "*teymas*' and vociferation were redoubled. The Reliance was first brought to the shore, and the Lion close to her a few seconds afterwards. The three men who held me now leaped ashore, and those who had remained in their canoes, taking them out of the water, carried them to a little distance. A numerous party then drawing their knives, and stripping themselves to the waist, ran to the Reliance, and having first hauled her as far up as they could, began a regular pillage, handing the articles to the women, who, ranged in a row behind, quickly conveyed them out of sight. Lieutenant Back and his crew strenuously, but good-humoredly, resisted the attack, and rescued many things from their grasp, but they were overpowered by numbers, and had even some difficulty in preserving their arms. One fellow had the audacity to snatch Vivier's knife from his breast, and to cut the buttons from his coat, whilst three stout Esquimaux surrounded Lieutenant Back with uplifted daggers, and were incessant in their demands for whatever attracted their attention, especially for the anchor buttons which he wore on his waistcoat. In this juncture a young chief coming to his aid, drove the assailants away. In their retreat they carried off a writing desk and cloak, which the chief rescued, and then seating himself on Lieutenant Back's knee, he endeavored to persuade his countrymen to desist by vociferating "*teyma teyma*," and was, indeed, very active in saving whatever he could from their depredations. The Lion had hitherto been beset by smaller numbers, and her crew, by firmly keeping their seats on the cover spread over the cargo, and by beating the natives off with the butt-ends of their muskets, had been able to prevent any article of importance from being carried away. But as soon as I perceived that the work of plunder was going on so actively in the Reliance, I went with Augustus to assist in repressing the tumult; and our bold and active little interpreter rushed among the crowd on shore, and harangued them on their treacherous conduct, until he was actually hoarse. In a short time, however, I was summoned back by Duncan, who called out to me that the Esquimaux had now commenced in earnest to plunder the Lion, and, on my return, I found the sides of the boat lined with men as thick as they could stand, brandishing their knives in the most furious manner, and attempting to seize everything that was movable; whilst another

party was ranged on the outside ready to bear away
the stolen goods. The Lion's crew still kept their
seats, but as it was impossible for so small a number
to keep off such a formidable and determined body,
several articles were carried off. Our principal object
was to prevent the loss of the arms, oars, or masts, or
any thing on which the continuance of the voyage, or
our personal safety, depended. Many attempts were
made to purloin the box containing the astronomical
instruments, and Duncan, after thrice rescuing it from
their hands, made it fast to his leg with a cord, determined that they should drag him away also if they
took it.

In the whole of this unequal contest, the self-posses-
sion of our men was not more conspicuous than the
coolness with which the Esquimaux received the heavy
blows dealt to them with the butts of the muskets.
But at length, irritated at being so often foiled in
their attempts, several of them jumped on board and
forcibly endeavored to take the daggers and shot-belts
that were about the men's persons ; and I myself was
engaged with three of them who were trying to disarm
me. Lieutenant Back perceiving our situation, and
fully appreciating my motives in not coming to extremities, had the kindness to send to my assistance
the young chief who had protected him, and who, on
his arrival, drove my antagonists out of the boat. I

then saw that my crew were nearly overpowered in the fore part of the boat, and hastening to their aid, I fortunately arrived in time to prevent George Wilson from discharging the contents of his musket into the body of an Esquimaux. He had received a provocation of which I was ignorant until the next day, for the fellow had struck at him with a knife, and cut through his coat and waistcoat ; and it was only after the affray was over that I learned that Gustavus Aird, the bowman of the Lion, and three of the Reliance's crew, had also narrowly escaped from being wounded, their clothes being cut by the blows made at them with knives. No sooner was the bow cleared of one set of marauders than another party commenced their operations at the stern. My gun was now the object of the struggle, which was beginning to assume a more serious complexion, when the whole of the Esquimaux suddenly fled, and hid themselves behind the drift timber and canoes on the beach. It appears that by the exertions of the crew, the Reliance was again afloat, and Lieutenant Back wisely judging that this was the proper moment for more active interference, directed his men to level their muskets, which had produced that sudden panic. The Lion happily floated soon after, and both were retiring from the beach, when the Esquimaux having recovered from their consternation, put their kaiyacks in the water,

and were preparing to follow us ; but I desired Au-
'gustus to say that I would shoot the first man who
came within range of our muskets, which prevented
them.

It was now about eight o'clock in the evening, and
we had been engaged in this harassing contest for
several hours, yet the only things of importance which
they had carried off were the mess canteen and kettles,
a tent, a bale containing blankets and shoes, one ot
the men's bags, and the jib-sails. The other articles
they took could well be spared, and they would, in
fact, have been distributed amongst them, had they
remained quiet. The place to which the boats wero
dragged is designated by the name of Pillage Point.
I cannot sufficiently praise the fortitude and obedience
of both the boats' crews in abstaining from the use of
their arms. In the first instance I had been influenced by the desire of preventing unnecessary bloodshed,
and afterwards, when the critical situation of my
party might have well warranted me in employing
more decided means for their defence, I still endeavored to temporize, being convinced that as long as the
boats lay aground, and we were beset by such numbers, armed with long knives, bows, arrows, and
spears, we could not use fire-arms to advantage. The
howling of the women, and the clamor of the men,
proved the high excitement to which they had wrought

themselves ; and I am still of opinion that, mingled as we were with them, the first blood we had shed would have been instantly revenged by the sacrifice of all our lives.

But to resume the narrative of the voyage. The breeze became moderate and fair ; the sails were set, and we passed along the coast in a W. N. W. direction, until eleven in the evening, when we halted on a low island, covered with drift wood, to repair the sails, and to put the boats in proper order for a sea voyage. The continuance and increase of the favorable wind urged us to make all possible despatch, and Sunday 9th at three in the morning of the 9th again embarking, we kept in three fathoms waters at the distance of two miles from the land. After sailing twelve miles, our progress was completely stopped by the ice adhering to the shore, and stretching beyond the limits of our view to seaward. We could not effect a landing until we had gone back some miles, as we had passed a sheet of ice which was fast to the shore ; but at length a convenient spot being found, the boats were hauled up on the beach. We quickly ascended to the top of the bank to look around, and from thence had the mortification to perceive that we had just arrived in time to witness the first rupture of the ice. The only lane of water in the direction of our course was that from which we had been forced to retreat :

in every other part the sea appeared as firmly frozen
as in winter ; and even close to our encampment the
masses of ice were piled up to the height of thirty
feet.   Discouraging as was this prospect, we had the
consolation to know that our store of provision was
sufficiently ample to allow of a few days' detention.

The coast in this part consists of black earth, un-
mixed with stones of any kind, and its general elevation is from sixty to eighty feet, though in some
places it swells into hills of two hundred and fifty
feet.   A level plain, abounding in small lakes, extends
from the top of these banks to the base of a line of
hills which lie in front of the Rocky Mountains.   The
plain was clothed with grass and plants, then in flower,
specimens of which were collected.   We recognized in
the nearest range of the Rocky Mountains, which I
have named after my much-esteemed companion Dr.
Richardson, the Fitton and Cupola Mountains, which
we had seen from Garry Island at the distance of
sixty miles.   Few patches of snow were visible on any
part of the range.

Having obtained observations for longitude and variation, we retired to bed about eight A. M., but had
only just fallen asleep when we were roused by the
men on guard calling out that a party of Esquimaux
were close to the tents ; and, on going out, we found
the whole of our party under arms.   Three Esqui-

maux had come upon us unawares, and in terror at seeing so many strangers, they were on the point of discharging their arrows, when Augustus's voice arrested them, and by explaining the purpose of our arrival, soon calmed their fears. Lieutenant Back and I having made each of them a present, and received in return some arrows, a very amicable conference followed, which was managed by Augustus with equal tact and judgment. It was gratifying to observe our visitors jumping for joy as he pointed out the advantages to be derived from an intercourse with the white people, to whom they were now introduced for the first time. We found that they belonged to a party whose tents were pitched about two miles from us; and as they were very desirous that their friends might also enjoy the gratification of seeing us, they begged that Augustus would return with them to convey the invitation; which request was granted at his desire.

Before their departure, marks being set up on the beach one hundred and fifty yards in front of the tent, and twice that distance from the boats, they were informed that this was the nearest approach which any of their party would be permitted to make; and that at this boundary only would gifts be made, and barter carried on. Augustus was likewise desired to explain to them the destructive power of our guns, and

to assure them that every person would be shot who
should pass the prescribed limit. This plan was
adopted in all succeeding interviews with the Esquimaux.   After five hours' absence Augustus returned,
accompanied by twenty men and two elderly women,
who halted at the boundary.   They had come without
bows or arrows, by the desire of Augustus, and, following his instruction, each gave Lieutenant Back
and myself a hearty shake of the hand. We made
presents to every one of beads, fish-hooks, awls, and
trinkets ; and that they might have entire confidence
in the whole party, our men were furnished with beads,
to present to them.   The men were directed to advance
singly, and in such a manner as to prevent the Esquimaux from counting our number, unless they paid
the greatest attention, which ·they were not likely to
do while their minds were occupied by a succession of
novelties.

Our visitors were soon quite at ease, and we were
preparing to question them respecting the coast, and
the time of removal of the ice, when Augustus begged
that he might put on his gayest dress, and his medals,
before the conference began.   This was the work of a
few seconds ; but when he returned, surprise and delight at his altered appearance, and numerous ornaments so engaged their minds, that their attention
could not be drawn to any other subject for the next

half hour. "Ah," said an old man, taking up his
medals, "these must have been made by such people
as you have been describing, for none that we have
seen could do any thing like it ;" then taking hold of
his coat, he asked, "what kind of animal do these
skins which you and the chiefs wear belong to ?
We have none such in our country." The anchor
buttons also excited their admiration. At length we
managed to gain their attention, and were informed
that, as soon as the wind should blow strong from the
land, the ice might be expected to remove from the
shore, so as to open a passage for boats, and that it
would remain in the offing until the reappearance of
the stars. "Further to the westward," they continued, "the ice often adheres to the land throughout
the summer ; and when it does break away, it is carried but a short distance to seaward, and is brought back
whenever a strong wind blows on the coast. If there
be any channels in those parts, they are unsafe for
boats, as the ice is continually tossing about. We
wonder, therefore," they said, "that you are not provided with sledges and dogs, as our men are, to travel
along the land, when these interruptions occur."
They concluded by warning us not to stay to the
westward after the stars could be seen, because the
winds would then blow strong from the sea, and pack
the ice on the shore. On further inquiry we learned

that this party is usually employed, during the summer, in catching whales and seals, in the vicinity of
the Mackenzie, and that they seldom travel to the
westward beyond a few days' journey.   We were,
therefore, not much distressed by intelligence which
we supposed might have originated in exaggerated
accounts received from others.   In the evening Augustus returned with them to their tents, and two of
the men undertook to fetch a specimen of the rock
from Mount Fitton, which was distant about twenty
miles.

The party assembled at divine service in the evening.   The wind blew in violent squalls during the
night, which brought such a heavy swell upon the ice,
that the larger masses near the encampment were
broken before the morning of the 10th, but there was
no change in the main body.

^{Monday,} The Esquimaux revisited us in the morning,
with their women and children ; the party consisted
of forty-eight persons.   They seated themselves as before, in a semicircle, the men being in front, and the
women behind.   Presents were made to those who
had not before received any ; and we afterwards purchased several pairs of seal-skin boots, a few pieces of
dressed seal-skin, and some deer-skin cut and twisted,
to be used as cords.   Beads, pins, needles, and ornamental articles, were most in request by the women,

to whom the goods principally belonged, but the men were eager to get any thing that was made of iron. They were supplied with hatchets, files, ice chisels, fire-steels, Indian awls, and fish-hooks. They were very anxious to procure knives, but as each was in possession of one, I reserved the few which we had for another occasion. The quarter from whence these knives were obtained, will appear in a subsequent part of the narrative. It was amusing to see the purposes to which they applied the different articles given to them; some of the men danced about with a large cod-fish hook dangling from the nose, others stuck an awl through the same part, and the women immediately decorated their dresses with the ear-rings, thimbles, or whatever trinkets they received. There was in the party a great proportion of elderly persons, who appeared in excellent health, and were very active. The men were stout and robust, and taller than Augustus, or than those seen on the east coast by Captain Parry. Their cheek-bones were less projecting than the representations given of the Esquimaux on the eastern coast, but they had the small eye, and broad nose, which ever distinguish that people. Except the young persons, the whole party were afflicted with sore eyes, arising from exposure to the glare of ice and snow, and two of the old men were nearly blind. They wore the hair on the upper lip and chin;

the latter, as well as that on their head, being permitted to grow long, though in some cases a circular
spot on the crown of the head was cut bare, like the
tonsure of the Roman catholic clergy.   Every man
had pieces of bone or shells thrust through the sep-
tum of his nose ; and holes were pierced on each side
of the under lip, in which were placed circular pieces
of ivory, with a large blue bead in the centre, similar
to those represented in the drawings of the natives on
the N.W. coast of America, in Kotzebue's Voyage.
These ornaments were so much valued, that they declined selling them ; and when not rich enough to procure beads or ivory, stones and pieces of bone were
substituted.   These perforations are made at the age
of puberty ; and one of the party, who appeared to be
about fourteen years old, was pointed out, with delight, by his parents, as having to undergo the operation in the following year.   He was a good-looking
boy, and we could not fancy his countenance would
be much improved by the insertion of the bones or
stones, which have the effect of depressing the under
lip, and keeping the mouth open.

   Their dress consisted of a jacket of rein-deer skin,
with a skirt behind and before, and a small hood ;
breeches of the same material, and boots of seal-skin.
Their weapons for the chase were bows and arrows,
very neatly made ; the latter being headed with bone

or iron ; and for fishing, spears tipped with bone. They also catch fish with nets and lines. All were armed with knives, which they either keep in their hand, or thrust up the sleeve of their shirt. They had received from the Loucheux Indians some account of the destructive effects of guns. The dress of the women differed from that of the men only in their wearing wide trowsers, and in the size of their hoods, which do not fit close to the head, but are made large, for the purpose of receiving their children. These are ornamented with stripes of different colored skins, and round the top is fastened a band of wolf's hair, made to stand erect. Their own black hair is very tastefully turned up from behind to the top of the head, and tied by strings of white and blue beads, or cords of white deerskin. It is divided in front, so as to form on each side a thick tail, to which are append- ed strings of beads that reach to the waist. The women were from four feet and a half to four and three-quarters high, and generally fat. Some of the younger females, and the children, were pretty. The lady whose portrait adorns this work, was mightily pleased at being selected by Lieutenant Back for his sketch, and testified her joy by smiles and many jumps. The men, when sitting for their portraits, were more sedate, though not less pleased, than the females ; some of them remarked that they were not handsome

enough to be taken to our country. It will be seen
from the engraving, that one of the men had a different cast of countenance from the rest ; we supposed
him to be descended from the Indians.

It would appear that the walrus does not visit this
part of the coast, as none of these people recognized a
sketch of one, which Lieutenant Back drew ; but
they at once knew the seal and reindeer. We learned
that the polar bear is seldom seen, and only in the
autumn ; and likewise that there are very few of the
brown bears, which we frequently saw on the coast
eastward of the Copper-Mine River. We had already
seen a few white whales, and we understood that they
would resort to this part of the coast in greater numbers with the following moon.

The habits of these people were similar, in every
respect, to those of the tribes described by Captain
Parry, and their dialect differed so little from that
used by Augustus, that he had no difficulty in understanding them. He was, therefore, able to give them
full particulars relative to the attack made by the
other party, and they expressed themselves much hurt
at their treacherous conduct. "Those are bad men,"
they said, "and never fail either to quarrel with us,
or steal from us, when we meet. They come, every
spring, from the eastern side of the Mackenzie, to fish
at the place where you saw them, and return as soon

as the ice opens. They are distinguished from us, who live to the westward of the river, by the men being tattoed across the face. Among our tribes the women only are tattoed ;" having five or six blue lines drawn perpendicularly from the under lip to the chin. The speaker added, " If you are obliged to return by this way, before these people remove, we, with a re-inforcement of young men, will be in the vicinity, and will willingly accompany you to assist in repelling any attack." Augustus returned with the Esquimaux to their tents, as there was not the least prospect of our getting forward, though the ice was somewhat broken.

Tuesday, 11th. A strong breeze from the westward during the night, contributed, with the swell, to the further reduction of the ice, in front of the encampment ; and on the morning of the 11th, the wind changed to the eastward, and removed the pieces a little way off shore, though they were tossing too violently for the boats to proceed. The swell having subsided in the afternoon, we embarked ; but at the end of a mile and a half were forced to land again, from the ice being fixed to the shore ; and as the wind had now become strong, and was driving the loose pieces on the land the boats were unloaded and landed on the beach. From the summit of an adjoining hill we perceived an unbroken field of ice to the west, and consequently, a barrier to our progress.

We encamped on the spot which our Esquimaux friends had left in the morning, to remove in their oomiaks and kaiyacks towards the Mackenzie, where they could set their fishing nets, and catch whales and seals. One of them showed his honesty, by returning some arrows, and a piece of a pemmican bag, that we had left at our last resting-place. The men also joined us here with specimens of rock from Mount Fitton.

The Esquimaux winter residences at this spot were constructed of drift timber, with the roots of the trees upwards, and contained from one to three small apartments, beside a cellar for their stores. There were generally two entrances, north and south, so low as to make it necessary to crawl through them. The only other aperture was a hole at the top for the smoke, which, as well as the doorways, could be filled up with a block of snow at pleasure. When covered with snow, and with lamps or fire burning within, these habitations must be extremely warm, though to our ideas rather comfortless. Lofty stages were erected near them for the purpose of receiving their canoes and bulky articles. The annexed engraving from Lieutenant Back's sketch of these habitations, renders further description unnecessary. A north-east gale came on in the evening, and rolled such a heavy surf on the beach, that twice, during the night, we were obliged to drag the boats and cargoes higher up.

Wed. 12th. About three the next morning a heavy rain commenced, and continued, without intermission, through the day ; at which we were delighted, however comfortless it made our situation, because we saw the ice gradually loosening from the land under its effects. We found the keeping a tide-pole fixed in the loose gravel beach impracticable here, as well as at the last resting-place, on account of the swell. It appeared to be high water this morning at half past one A. M., and that the rise of tide was about two feet. I need hardly observe that we had the sun constantly above the horizon, were it not for the purpose of mentioning the amusing mistakes which the men made as to the hour. In fact, when not employed, a question as to the time of day never failed to puzzle them, except about midnight, when the sun was near the northern horizon.

Lieutenant Back missing the protractor which he used for laying down his bearings on the map, Augustus set off in the rain early this forenoon to recover it from an Esquimaux woman, whom he had seen pick it up. The rain ceased in the afternoon, the wind gradually abated, and by eight in the evening it was calm. A south wind followed, which opened a passage for the boat, but Augustus was not in sight. At midnight we became greatly alarmed for his safety,

having now found that he had taken his gun, which
we supposed the natives might have endeavored to
wrest from him, and we were on the point of despatch-
ing a party in search of him, when he arrived at four
^{Thurs.}_{13th.} in the morning of the 13th much fatigued, ac-
companied by three of the natives. His journey had
been lengthened by the Esquimaux having gone farther to the eastward than he had expected, but he had
recovered the protractor, which had been kept in their
ignorance of its utility to us. His companions
brought five white fish, and some specimens of crystal
with other stones, from the mountains, which we purchased, and further rewarded them for their kindness
in not allowing Augustus to return alone.

The boats were immediately launched, and having
pulled a short distance from the land, we set the sails,
our course being directed to the outer point in view,
to avoid the sinuosities of the coast. We passed a
wide, though not deep bay, whose points were named
after my friends Captains Sabine and P. P. King ;
and we were drawing near the next projection, when a
compact body of ice was discovered, which was joined
to the land ahead. At the same time a dense fog
came on, that confined our view to a few yards ; it
was accompanied by a gale from the land, and heavy
rain. We had still hopes of getting round the point,
and approached the shore in that expectation, but

found the ice so closely packed that we could neither advance nor effect a landing. We, therefore, pulled to seaward, and turned the boat's head to the east-ward, to trace the outer border of the ice. In this situation we were exposed to great danger from the sudden change of wind to S. E., which raised a heavy swell, and brought down upon us masses of ice of a size that, tossed as they were by the waves, would have injured a ship. We could only catch occasional glimpses of the land through the fog, and were kept in the most anxious suspense, pulling in and out be-tween the floating masses of ice, for five hours, before we could get near the shore. We landed a little to the west of Point Sabine, and only found suffi-cient space for the boats and tents between the bank and the water. The rain ceased for a short time in the evening, and, during this interval, we per-ceived, from the top of the bank, that the whole space between us and the distant point, as well as the chan-nel by which we had advanced to the westward, were now completely blocked ; so that we had good reason to congratulate ourselves on having reached the shore in safety.

CHAPTER XVI

Friday,
July 14th.   ALTHOUGH it rained heavily during the night,
and the wind blew strong off the land for some hours,
there was no other change in the state of the ice on
the morning of the 14th, than that the smaller pieces
were driven a short way from the beach. The day
was foggy and rainy, but the evening fine. The bank
under which we were encamped is of the same earthy
kind as that described on the 9th, but rather higher
and steeper. It contains much wood-coal, similar to
that found in the Mackenzie River, and at Garry's Island. The beach and the beds of the rivulets that
flow through the ravines, consist of coarse gravel.
Specimens of its stones, of the coal, and of the plants
in flower, were added to the collection. We saw two
marmots, and two reindeer, which were too wary to
allow of our getting within shot of them. Between
noon and ten P.M., the loose ice was driving in front of
the encampment from the N.W. to S.E., and at the

latter hour it stopped. We could not detect any difference in the height of the water, and there was a calm the whole time. A light breeze from S.E. after midnight, brought the masses close to the beach. On the morning of the 15th, having perceived that the ice was loosened from the land near the outer point, to which I have given the name of Kay, after some much-esteemed relatives, we embarked, and in the course of a few hours succeeded in reaching it, by passing between the grounded masses of ice. On landing at Point Kay, we observed that our progress must again be stopped by a compact body of ice that was fast to the shore of a deep bay, and extended to our utmost view seaward; and that we could not advance farther than the mouth of a river which discharged its waters just round the point. The boats were, therefore, pulled to its entrance, and we encamped. Former checks had taught us to be patient, and we, therefore, commenced such employments as would best serve to beguile the time, consoling ourselves with the hope that a strong breeze would soon spring up from the land and open a passage. Astronomical observations were obtained, the map carried on, and Lieutenant Back sketched the beautiful scenery afforded by a view of the Rocky Mountains, while I was employed in collecting specimens of the plants in flower. The men amused themselves in various

ways, and Augustus went to visit an Esquimaux
family that were on an island contiguous to our encampment.

We now discovered that the Rocky Mountains do
not form a continuous chain, but that they run in detached ranges at unequal distances from the coast.
The Richardson chain commencing opposite the mouth
of the Mackenzie, terminates within view of our present situation.   Another range, which I have named
in honor of Professor Buckland, begins on the western side of Phillips Bay, and extending to the boundary of our view, is terminated by the Conybeare
Mountain.

It gave me great pleasure to affix the name of my
friend Mr. Babbage to the river we had discovered,
and that of Mr. Phillips, Professor of Painting at the
Royal Academy, to the bay into which its waters are
emptied.   We learned from the Esquimaux that this
river, which they call Cöök-Keaktok, or Rocky River,
descends from a very distant part of the interior,
though they are unacquainted with its course beyond
the mountains.   It appeared to us to flow between
the Cupola and Barn mountains of the Richardson
chain.   There are many banks of gravel near its
mouth, but above these obstructions the channel appeared deep, and to be about two miles broad.   There
were no rocks *in sitû,* or large stones, near the en-

campment ; the rolled pebbles on the beach were sandstone of red and light-brown colors, greenstone, and slaty limestone. We gathered a fine specimen of tertiary pitch-coal.

Augustus returned in the evening with a young Esquimaux and his wife, the only residents at the house he had visited. They had now quite recovered the panic into which they had been thrown on our first appearance, which was heightened by their being unable to escape from us owing to the want of a canoe. We made them happy by purchasing the fish they brought, and giving them a few presents ; they continued to skip and laugh as long as they staid. The man informed us that judging from the rapid decay of the ice in the few preceding days, we might soon expect it to break from the land, so as to allow of our reaching Herschel Island, which was in view ; but he represented the coast to the westward of the island as being low, and so generally beset with ice, that he was of opinion we should have great difficulty in getting along. This couple had been left here to collect fish for the use of their companions, who were to rejoin them for the purpose of killing whales, as soon as the ice should break up ; and they told us the black whales would soon come after its rupture took place. It would be interesting to ascertain where the whales retire in the winter, as they require to in-

hale the air frequently. Those of the white kind
make their appearance when there are but small spaces
of open water ; and we afterwards saw two black
whales in a similar situation. One might also infer
from these circumstances that they do not remove very
far. Is it probable that they go, at the close of the
autumn, to a warmer climate ? or can the sea be less
closely covered with ice in the high northern latitudes ?
The situation of our encampment was observed to be,
latitude 69° 19' N. ; longitude 138° 10½' W. ; variation 46° 16' E. ; and a rise and fall of nine inches in
the water. The wind blew from the west during the
night, and drove much ice near the boats ; but as the
masses took ground a little way from the shore, we
were spared the trouble of removing the boats higher
up the beach.

Sunday, 16th. We were favored in the forenoon of the 16th,
by a strong breeze from the land, which, in the course
of a few hours, drove away many of these pieces towards Point Kay, and opened a passage for boats.
We immediately embarked to sail over to the western
side of Phillips Bay, concluding, from the motion of
the ice, that it must now be detached from that shore.
On reaching it, we had the pleasure of finding an open
channel close to the beach, although the entrance was
barred by a stream of ice lying aground on a reef.
The boats being forced by poles over this obstruction,

we stood under sail along the coast to about five miles
beyond Point Stokes ; but there we were again compelled by the closeness of the ice to stop, and from the
top of a sand-hill we could not discover any water in
the direction of our course. The tents were therefore
pitched, and the boats unloaded, and hauled on the
beach. Heavy rain came on in the evening, by which
we indulged the hope that the ice might be loosened.
We were encamped on a low bank of gravel which
runs along the base of a chain of sand-hills about one
hundred and fifty feet high, and forms the coast line.
The bank was covered with drift timber, and is the
site of a deserted Esquimaux village. The snow still
remaining in the ravines was tinged with light red
spots. The night was calm, and the ice remained in
the same fixed state until six in the morning of the
17th, when, perceiving the pieces in the offing to be
in motion we launched the boats, and by breaking our
way at first with hatchets, and then forcing with the
poles through other streams of ice, we contrived to
reach some lanes of water, along which we navigated
for four hours. A strong breeze springing up from
seaward, caused the ice to close so fast upon the boat,
that we were obliged to put again to the shore, and
land on a low bank, similar to that on which we had
rested the night before. It was intersected, however,
by many pools and channels of water, which cut off

our communication with the land. As we could not
obtain, from our present station, any satisfactory view
of the state of the ice to the westward, I despatched
Duncan and Augustus to take a survey of it from
Point Catton, while Lieutenant Back and I made
some astronomical observations. They returned after
an absence of two hours, and reported that there was
water near Herschel Island, and a channel in the
offing that appeared to lead to it. We, therefore,
embarked ; and by pushing the boats between the
masses that lay aground, for some distance, we succeeded in reaching open water at the entrance of the
strait which lies between the island and the main, and
through which the loose pieces of ice were driving fast
to the westward. Having now the benefit of a strong
favorable breeze, we were enabled to keep clear of
them, and made good progress. Arriving opposite
the S. E. end of Herschel Island, we perceived a large
herd of reindeer just taking the water, and on approaching the shore to get within shot, discovered
three Esquimaux in pursuit. These men stood gazing
at the boats for some minutes, and after a short con-
sultation, we observed them to change the heads of
their arrows, and prepare their bows. They then
walked along the south shore, parallel to our course,
for the purpose, as we soon found, of rejoining their
wives. We reached the place at which the ladies

were before them, and though invited to land, we were
not able, on account of the surf. Augustus was
desired to assure them of our friendship, and of our
intention to stop at the first sheltered spot, to which
they and their husbands might come to receive a present. More than this our little friend could not be
prevailed upon to communicate, because they were
" old wives ;" and it was evident that he considered
any further conversation with women to be beneath
his dignity. On passing round the point we discovered
that the ice was closely packed to leeward, and such
a heavy swell setting upon it, that it was unsafe to
proceed. We, therefore, encamped, and Augustus
set off immediately to introduce himself to the Esquimaux. The tents were scarcely pitched, and the
sentinels placed, before he returned, accompanied by
twelve men and women, each bringing a piece of dried
meat, or fish, to present to us. We learned from
them that the boats, when at a distance, had been
taken for pieces of ice ; but when we drew near
enough for them to distinguish the crews, and they
perceived them clothed differently from any men they
had seen, they became alarmed, and made ready their
arrows, as we had observed. On receiving some presents, they raised a loud halloo, which brought five or
six others from an adjoining island, and in the evening
there was a further addition to the party of some

young men, who had been hunting, and who afterwards sent their wives to bring us a part of the spoils
of their chase. They remained near the tents the
greater part of the night, and testified their delight by
dancing and singing. An old woman, whose hair was
silvered by age, made a prominent figure in these
exhibitions.

The information we obtained from them confirmed
that which we had received from the last party, namely, that they procure the iron, knives, and beads,
^{Monday} through two channels, but principally from a
party of Esquimaux who reside a great distance to
the westward, and to meet whom they send their
young men every spring with furs, seal-skins, and oil,
to exchange for those articles ; and also from the Indians who come every year from the interior to trade
with them by a river that was directly opposite our
encampment ; which I have, therefore, named the
Mountain Indian River. These Indians leave their
families and canoes at two days' march from the mouth
of the river, and the men come alone, bringing no
more goods than they intend to barter. They were
represented to be tall stout men, clothed in deer-skins,
and speaking a language very dissimilar to their own.
They also said that the Esquimaux to the westward,
speak a dialect so different from theirs, that at the
first opening of the communication, which was so re-

cent as to be within the memory of two of our present
companions, they had great difficulty in understanding
them. Several quarrels took place at their first meet-
ings, in consequence of the western party attempting
to steal ; but latterly there has been a good understanding between them, and the exchanges have been
fairly made.

Our visitors did not know from what people either
the Indians or the Esquimaux obtained the goods,
but they supposed from some " Kabloonacht," (white
people,) who reside far to the west. As the articles
we saw were not of British manufacture, and were
very unlike those sold by the Hudson's Bay Company
to the Indians, it cannot be doubted that they are
furnished by the Russian Fur Traders, who receive in
return for them all the furs collected on this northern
coast. Part of the Russian iron-work is conveyed to
the Esquimaux dwelling on the coast east of the
Mackenzie. The western Esquimaux use tobacco,
and some of our visitors had smoked it, but thought
the flavor very disagreeable. Until I was aware of
their being acquainted with the use of it, I prohibited
my men from smoking in their presence, and afterwards from offering their pipes to the Esquimaux at
any time. At the conclusion of this conference, our
visitors assured us, that having now become acquainted with white people, and being conscious that the

trade with them would be beneficial, they would gladly
encourage a further intercourse, and do all in their
power to prevent future visitors from having such a
reception as we had on our arrival in these seas.   We
learned that this island, which has been distinguished
by the name of Herschel, is much frequented by the
natives at this season of the year, as it abounds with
deer, and its surrounding waters afford plenty of fish.
It is composed of black earth, rises, in its highest
point, to about one hundred feet, and at the time of
our visit was covered with verdure.   The straight between it and the main shore, is the only place that
we had seen, since quitting the Mackenzie, in which a
ship could find shelter ; but even this channel is much
interrupted by shoals.

Tuesday 18th. On the morning of the 18th the fog was so
thick that we could not see beyond the beach.   It
dispersed about noon, and we discovered that there
was a channel of open water near the main shore,
though in the centre of the strait the ice was heavy,
and driving rapidly to the north-west.   We embarked
at once, in the expectation of being able to penetrate
between the drift ice and the land, but the attempt
was frustrated by the shallowness of the water.; and
the fog again spreading as thick as before, we landed
on a sand-bank.   We were soon visited by another
party of the Esquimaux, who brought deer's meat for

sale ; and although the whole quantity did not amount to a deer, we had to purchase it in small pieces. This practice of dividing the meat among the party, we found to prevail throughout the voyage ; and they avowed as their reason for it, the desire that every one might obtain a share of the good things we distributed. One of the men drew on the sand a sketch of the coast to the westward, as far as he was acquainted with it ; from which it appeared that there was a line of reefs in front of the coast the whole way ; the water being deep on the outside of them, but on the inside too shallow even for their oomiacks to float. We subsequently found that his knowledge of the coast did not extend beyond a few days' march.

The atmosphere becoming more clear about two P. M., we again embarked, and endeavored to get to seaward. The boats, however, soon grounded ; and finding all our attempts to push through any of the channels between the reefs ineffectual, we pulled back close to Herschel Island. Following, then, the course of the drift ice, we passed near to its south-west point, which was found to be the only deep passage through the strait. We afterwards entered into a fine sheet of open water, the main body of the ice being about half a mile to seaward, and only a few bergs lying aground in the direction of our course.

The outer parts of the island appeared closely beset with ice. At the end of five miles we discerned another large party of Esquimaux, encamped on a reef; they waved their jackets as signals for us to land, which we declined doing, as we perceived the water to be shallow between us and them. They ran along the beech as far as the end of the reef, tempting us by holding up meat. Only two of the party were provided with canoes, and they followed us to a bluff point of the main shore, on which we landed. These proved to be persons whom we had seen at Herschel Island, and who had visited the Esquimaux in this quarter on purpose to make them acquainted with our arrival. We were happy to learn from them that we should not see any more of their countrymen for some time, because, while surrounded by them, the necessity of closely watching their motions, prevented us from paying due attention to other objects. Resuming our voyage, we pulled along the outer border of a gravel reef, about two hundred yards broad, that runs parallel to, and about half a mile from, the coast, having a line of drift ice on the outside of us. The wind being contrary, and the evening cold, temperature 40°, we encamped on the reef at eight P. M., where we found plenty of drift timber ; the water was brackish. The distance traveled this day was eight miles and a half. The main shore opposite the encampment was low to

a great distance from the coast ; it then appeared to
ascend gradually to the base of the Buckland chain of
mountains.

^{Wed.}_{19th.} The following morning being calm, and very
fine, the boats were launched at three A. M., and we
set off in high spirits ; but after pulling three miles,
we perceived the channel of open water becoming
narrow, and the pieces of ice heavier thàn any we had
before seen, some of them being aground in three
fathoms water. At six A. M., after having gone five
miles and a half, we were stopped by the ice which
adhered to the reef, and was unbroken to seaward.
Imagining we saw water at some distance beyond this
barrier, we were induced to drag the boats across the
reef, and launch them into the channel on the inside,
in the hope of reaching it. This proved to be a bay,
at the head of which we arrived in a short time. It
was then discovered that a fog hanging over the ice
had been mistaken for water. The boats were, therefore, reconveyed across the reef, the tents pitched,
and we had to draw largely on our nearly exhausted
stock of patience, as we contemplated the dreary view
of this compact icy field. A herd of rein-deer appeared very opportunely to afford some employment, and
most of the men were despatched on the chase, but
only one was successful. The following observations
were obtained :—Latitude 69° 36' N. ; longitude 139°

42' W. Being now abreast of Mount Conybeare, Lieutenant Back and I were on the point of setting out to visit its summit, when we were stopped by a very dense fog that accompanied a fresh breeze from the N. W., followed by heavy rain. The weather continued bad, until ten the following morning; the ice near the beach was broken into smaller pieces, but as yet too closely packed for our proceeding. The water being brackish in front of the reef, we despatched two men to bring some from the pools at a distance inland, which was found to have the same taste; from this circumstance, as well as from the piles of drift wood, thrown up far from the coast, one may infer that the sea occasionally washes over this low shore. The ice broken off from large masses, and permitted to drain before it was melted, did not furnish us with better water. A couple of pin-tailed ducks were shot, the only pair seen; the black kind were more numerous, but were not fired at, as they are fishing ducks, and, therefore, not good to eat. We also saw a few geese and swans.

^{Friday 21st.} The atmosphere was calm, and perfectly clear, on the morning of the 21st; and as there was not any change in the position of the ice, I visited Mount Conybeare, accompanied by Duncan and Stewart. Though its distance was not more than twelve miles from the coast, the journey proved to be very fatigu-

ing, owing to the swampiness of the ground between the mountain and the sea. We had also the discomfort of being tormented the whole way by myriads of musquitoes. The plain was intersected by a winding river, about forty yards broad, which we forded, and on its western side found a thicket of willows, none of which were above seven inches in circumference, and only five or six feet high. At the foot of the mountain were three parallel platforms or terraces, whose heights we estimated at fifty, eighty, and one hundred and thirty feet; composed of transition slate, the stone of the lowest being of the closest texture. We found the task of climbing above the upper terraces difficult, in consequence of the looseness of the stones, which did not afford a firm footing, but after an hour's labor, we succeeded in reaching the top. The mountain is also composed of slate, but so much weathered near the summit, as to appear a mere collection of stones. Its height above the sea we estimated at eight hundred feet. Two or three hardy plants were in flower, at the highest elevation, which we gathered, though they were of the same kind that had been collected in the lower lands; and during the whole march we did not meet with any plant different from the specimens we had already obtained. On arriving at the top of the mountain, we were refreshed by a strong south wind, which we fondly hoped might reach to the coast, and be of service by driving the ice from the land. This hope, however, lasted only a few minutes; for, on casting our eyes to seaward, there appeared no open water into which it could be moved, except near Herschel Island. The view into the interior possessed the charm of novelty, and attracted particular regard. We commanded a prospect over three ranges of mountains, lying parallel to the Buckland chain, but of less altitude. The view was bounded by a fourth range of high-peaked mountains, for the most part covered with snow. This distant range was afterwards distinguished by the name of the British Chain; and the mountains at its extremities were named in honor of the then Chancellor of the Exchequer, and President of the Board of Trade—the Right Honorable Mr. Robinson, now Lord Goderich, and Mr. Huskisson. When seen from the coast, the mountains of the Buckland chain appeared to form a continuous line, extending from N. W. by N., to S. E. by S.; but from our present situation we discovered that they were separated from each other by a deep valley, and a rivulet, and that their longest direction was N.N.E. and S.S.W. The same order prevailed in the three ranges behind the Buckland chain; and the highest of their mountains, like Mount Conybeare, were round and naked at the top; the vallies between them were grassy. We erected a pile of stones of sufficient height to be seen from the sea, and deposited underneath it a note, containing the latitude, longitude, and some particulars relative to the Expedition.

Saturday, 22nd. The 22nd was a calm, sultry day, the temperature varying between 58° and 63°, and we were tormented by musquitoes. The ice remained very close to the beach. Impatient of our long detention, we gladly availed ourselves, at three in the morning of the 23rd, of a small opening in the ice, to launch the boats, and push them forward as far as we could get them. We thus succeeded in reaching a lane of water, through which we made tolerable progress, though after two hours and a half of exertion, we were gradually hemmed in, and forced again to encamp at the mouth of a small stream westward of Sir Pulteney Malcolm River. We had, however, the satisfaction of finding, by the observations, that we had gained ten miles. The temperature of the water at the surface a quarter of a mile from the shore was 40°, that of the air being 49°. The water was two fathoms deep, ten yards from the beach.

The coast here was about fifteen feet high ; and from the top of the bank a level plain extended to the base of the mountains, which, though very swampy, was covered with verdure. At this place we first found boulder stones, which were deeply seated in the gravel of the beach. They consisted of greenstone, sandstone, and limestone ; the first mentioned being the largest, and the last the most numerous. Having seen several fish leaping in the river, a net was set across its mouth, though without success, owing to the meshes being too large. Two men were despatched to examine the state of the ice ; and on their return from a walk of several miles, they reported that, with the exception of a small spot close to the beach, it was quite compact. They had observed, about two miles from the encampment, stumps of drift wood fixed in the ground at certain distances, extending from the coast across the plain towards the Rocky Mountains, in the direction of two piles of stones, which were erected on the top of the latter. We were at a loss to conjecture what motive the Esquimaux could have had for taking so much trouble, unless these posts were intended to serve as decoys for the reindeer. The party assembled at divine service in the evening, as had been our practice every Sunday.

Monday 24th On the morning of the 24th we were able to make a further advance of two miles and three-quarters, by forcing the boats between the masses of ice, as far as the debouche of another rivulet. Under any other circumstance than that of being beset by ice, the beautifully calm and clear weather we then had would have been delightful ; but as our hope of being

released rested solely on a strong wind, we never
ceased to long for its occurrence. A breeze would
have been, at any rate, beneficial in driving away the
musquitoes, which were so numerous as to prevent
any enjoyment of the open air, and to keep us confined
to a tent filled with smoke, the only remedy against
their annoyance.

^{Tuesday 25th.} We were still detained the two following
days, and the only things we saw were a grey wolf,
some seals, and some ducks. More tedious hours than
those passed by us in the present situation, cannot
well be imagined. After the astronomical observations had been obtained and worked, the survey
brought up, a sketch made of the encampment, and
specimens of the plants and stones in the vicinity collected, there was, literally, nothing to do. The anxiety which was inseparable from such an enterprise as
ours, at such an advanced period of the season, left
but little disposition to read, even if there had been a
greater choice of books in our traveling library, and
still less composure to invent amusement. Even had
the musquitoes been less tormenting, the swampiness
of the ground, in which we sank ancle deep at every
step, deprived us of the pleasure of walking. A visit
to the Rocky Mountains was often talked of, but they
were now at a distance of two days' journey, and we
dared not to be absent from the boats so long, lest

the ice, in its fickle movements, should open for a
short time.   Notwithstanding the closeness of the ice,
we perceived a regular rise and fall of the water,
though it amounted only to seven inches, except on
the night of the 24th, when the rise was two feet;
but the direction of the flood was not yet ascertained.
We found a greater proportion of birch-wood, mixed
with the drift timber to the westward of the Babbage,
than we had done before; between the Mackenzie and
that river it had been so scarce, that we had to draw
upon our store of bark to light the fires.   Some lunar
observations were obtained in the afternoon of the 25th,
and their results assured us that the chronometers
were going steadily.   At midnight we were visited by
a strong S.W. breeze, accompanied by rain, thunder,
and lightning.   This weather was succeeded by calm,
and a fog that continued throughout the next day,
and confined our view to a few yards.   Temperature
from 41° to 43°.   On the atmosphere becoming clear
^{Wednesday} about nine in the evening of the 26th, we
discovered a lane of water, and immediately embarking,
we pulled, for an hour, without experiencing much interruption from the ice.   A fresh breeze then sprung
up from the N.W., which brought with it a very dense
fog, and likewise caused the ice to close so fast upon
us, that we were compelled to hasten to the shore.
We had just landed, when the channel was complete-

ly closed. We encamped on the western side of a river about two hundred yards broad, which, at the request of Lieutenant Back, was named after Mr. Backhouse, one of the under Secretaries of State for Foreign Affairs. It appeared that the water that flowed from this channel had caused the opening by which we had traveled from our last resting-place ; for beyond it, the ice was closely packed.

Thursday, 27th. Some heavy rain fell in the night, and the morning of the 27th was foggy ; but the sun, about noon, having dispersed the fog, we discovered an open channel, about half a mile from the shore.

Saturday, 29th. The morning of the 29th opened with heavy rain and fog ; the precursors of a strong gale from E.N.E., which brought back the ice we had already passed, and closely packed it along the beach, but we could not perceive that the wind had the slighest effect on the main body at a distance from the shore. This was a very cold, comfortless day, the temperature between 38° and 42°. On the following morning a brilliant sun contributed with the gale to the dispersion of the mist which had, for some days past, overhung the Rocky Mountains, and we had the gratification of seeing, for the first time, the whole length of the British Chain of Mountains, which are more peaked and irregular in their outline, and more picturesque than those of the Buckland Range. In exploring the bed of a rivulet we found several pieces of quartz, containing pyrites of a very bright color, which so much attracted the attention of the crews, that they spent several hours in examining every stone, expecting to have their labor rewarded by the discovery of some precious metal.

The gale having abated in the evening, we quickly loaded the boats, and pulled them into a lane of water that we had observed about half a mile from the shore. This, however, extended only a short way to the west, and at the end of a mile and a half inclined towards the beach, the ice beyond it being closely packed. Before the boats could be brought to the land, they received several heavy blows in passing through narrow channels, and over tongues of grounded ice. I walked to the extreme point that we had in view from the tent, and was rejoiced by the sight of a large space of water in the direction of our course; but up to the point the ice was still compact, and heavy. On my way I passed another Esquimaux village, where there were marks of recent visitors.

We witnessed the setting of the sun at eleven P.M., an unwelcome sight, which the gloomy weather had, till then, spared us; for it forced upon our minds the conviction that the favorable season for our operations was fast passing away, though we had, as yet, made so little progress. This was not the only uncomfortable circumstance that attended us this evening. Our friend Augustus was seized with a shivering fit, in consequence of having imprudently rushed, when in full perspiration, into a lake of cold water, to drag out a reindeer which he had killed. He was unable to walk on coming out of the water, and the consequence would have been more serious had it not been for the kindness of his companion, Wilson, who deprived himself of his flannels and waistcoat to clothe him. On their arrival at the tent, Augustus was put between blankets, and provided with warm chocolate, and the only inconvenience that he felt next morning was pain in his limbs.

Monday, 31st. We had several showers of rain during the night, with a steady S.W. breeze, and in the morning of the 31st were delighted by perceiving the ice loosening and driving off the land. We were afloat in a few minutes, and enjoyed the novelty of pulling through an uninterrupted channel as far as Point Demarcation, which has been so named from its being situated in longitude 141° W., the boundary between the British and Russian dominions, on the northern coast of America. This point seems to be much resorted to by the Esquimaux, as we found here many winter houses, and four large stages. On the latter were deposited several bundles of seal and deer skins, and several pair of snow-shoes. The snow-shoes were

netted with cords of deer-skin, and were shaped like
those used by the Indians near the Mackenzie. A
favorable breeze now sprang up ; and having ascertained, by mounting one of the Esquimaux stages,
that there was still a channel of open water between
a low island and the main shore, we set sail to follow
its course. At the end of three miles we found the
water gradually to decrease from three fathoms to as
many feet, and shortly afterwards the boats repeatedly
took the ground. In this situation we were enveloped
by a thick fog, which limited our view to a few yards.
We, therefore, dragged the boats to the land, until
we could see our way ; this did not happen before ten
in the evening, when it was discovered from the sub-
mit of an eminence about two miles distant, that
though the channel was of some extent, it was very
shallow, and seemed to be barred by ice to the westward. We also ascertained that it was bounded to
seaward by a long reef. The night proved very
stormy, and we were but scantily supplied with drift
wood.

^{Tuesday,} ^{1st.} Though the morning of the 1st of August
commenced with a heavy gale from E.N.E., and very
foggy weather, we proceeded to the reef, after much
fatigue in dragging the boats over the flats, under the
supposition that our best chance of getting forward
would be by passing on the outside of it. But there

finding heavy ice lying aground, and so closely packed
as to preclude the possibility of putting the boats into
the water, it was determined to examine the channel
by walking along the shore of the reef. An outlet to
the sea was discovered, but the channel was so flat
that gulls were, in most parts, wading across it; and
there was, therefore, no other course than to await
the separation of the ice from the reef. On the dispersion of the fog in the afternoon, we perceived that
some of the masses of ice were from twenty to thirty
feet high; and we derived little comfort from beholding, from the top of one of them, an unbroken surface
of ice to seaward.

Wednesday, 2nd. The gale blew without the least abatement
throughout the night, and until noon of the 2nd, when
it terminated in a violent gust, which overthrew the
tents. The field of ice was broken in the offing, and
the pieces put in motion; and in the evening there appeared a large space of open water, but we could not
take advantage of these favorable circumstances, in
consequence of the ice still closely besetting the reef.
Lieutenant Back occupied himself in sketching the
different views from the reef; from one of which the
annexed engraving has been selected, as conveying an
accurate delineation of our position on Icy Reef. We
remarked large heaps of gravel, fifteen feet above the
surface of the reef, on the largest iceberg, which must

have been caused by the pressure of the ice ; and from the top of this berg we had the satisfaction of discovering that a large herd of reindeer were marching in line towards the opposite side of the channel. Our party was instantly on the alert, and the best hunters were sent in the Reliance in chase of them. The boat grounded about midway across, and the eager sportsmen jumped overboard and hastened to the shore ; but such was their want of skill, that only three fawns were killed, out of a herd of three or four hundred. The supply, however, was sufficient for our present use, and the circumstances of the chase afforded amusing conversation for the evening.

Thursday, 3rd. On the morning of the 3rd a strong breeze set in from the east, which we were rejoiced to find caused a higher flood in the channel than we had yet seen, and the hope of effecting a passage by its course was revived ; as the ice was still fast to the reef, and likely to continue so, it was considered better to occupy ourselves in dragging the boats through the mud, than to continue longer in this irksome spot, where the wood was already scarce, and the water indifferent. The boats, therefore, proceeded with four men in each, while the rest of the crew walked along the shore, and rendered assistance wherever it was necessary, to drag them over the shallow parts. After four hours' labor, we reached the eastern part of the bay, which I have had the pleasure of naming after my friend Captain Beaufort, R.N., and which was then covered with ice. We had also the happiness of finding a channel that led to seaward, which enabled us to get on the outside of the reef; but as we pushed as close as we could to the border of the packed ice, our situation, for the next four hours, was attended with no little anxiety. The appearance of the clouds bespoke the return of fog, and we were sailing with a strong breeze through narrow channels, between heavy pieces of drift ice, on the outside of a chain of reefs that stretched across Beaufort Bay, which we knew could not be approached within a mile, owing to the shallowness of the water.

At six in the evening, the party passed the termination of the British chain of mountains, and the next day came in sight of the Romerzoff chain, continuing in boats along the shore. On the 7th of August, Filoxman Island was reached. In coasting along the Polar Sea, the Expedition was greatly troubled by the dense fogs, which almost put an end to traveling.

On the 16th day of August, the forces of the party were turned homeward to the winter quarter, at Fort Franklin, near Bear Lake River—which place they reached on Thursday, September 21—after traveling in three months, 2048 statute miles. Dr. Richardson had arrived with the Eastern detachment of the Expedition.   He had traveled 1980 miles—a sea voyage of 863 miles included—passing from Sacred Island to Fort Encounter, Fort Encounter to the Copper Mountains, and thence overland to Bear Lake.

The winter of 1826-7 was passed in comparative comfort, certainly without actual suffering ; and late in September, the party arrived in London.

CHAPTER XVII.

ON the 26th of May, 1845, Franklin—long since made Sir John Franklin—with the *" Erebus"* and *"Terror,"* two strong and well made vessels, with 140 men, set out on his *last* Arctic Expedition, and from which he has never returned.

A letter from Sir John Franklin, dated from the Whalefish Islands, Baffin's Bay, July 12, 1845, is the last communication from the Expedition ever received in England.

Dr. Rae, who prosecuted an overland journey in search of Franklin, gives the following particulars :

REPULSE BAY, July 29.

" SIR,—I have the honor to mention, for the information of my Lords Commissioners of the Admiralty, that during my journey over the ice and snow this spring, with the view of completing the survey of the west shore of Boothia, I met with Esquimaux in Pelly Bay, from one of whom I learned that a party of 'white men' (Kablounans) had perished from want of food some distance to the westward, and not far beyond a large river, containing many falls and rapids. Subsequently, further particulars were received, and a number of articles purchased, which places the fate of a portion, if not of all, of the then survivors of Sir John Franklin's long-lost party beyond a doubt—a fate terrible as the imagination can conceive.

"The substance of the information obtained at various times and from various sources was as follows—

"In the spring, four winters past (spring, 1850,) a party of 'white men,' amounting to about forty, were seen traveling southward over the ice and dragging a boat with them, by some Esquimaux, who were killing seals near the north shore of King Williams' Land, which is a large island. None of the party could speak the Esquimaux language intelligibly, but by signs the natives were made to understand that their ship, or ships, had been crushed by the ice, and that they were now going to where they expected to find deer to shoot. From the appearance of the men, all of whom except one officer, looked thin, they were then supposed to be getting short of provisions, and purchased a small seal from the natives. At a later date the same season, but previous to the breaking up of the ice, the bodies of some thirty persons were discovered on the continent, and five on an island near it, about a long day's journey to the N. W. of a large stream, which can be no other than Back's Great Fish River, (named by the Esquimaux Doot-ko-hi-calik,) as its description, and that of the low shore in the neighborhood of Point Ogle and Montreal Island, agree exactly with that of Sir George Back. Some of the bodies had been buried, (probably those of the first victims of famine,) some were in a tent or tents, others under the boat, which had been turned over to form a shelter, and several lay scattered about in different directions. Of those found on the island, one was supposed to have been an officer, as he had a telescope strapped over his shoulders, and his double-barrelled gun lay underneath him.

"From the mutilated state of many of the corpses, and the contents of the kettles, it is evident that our wretched countrymen had been driven to the last resource—cannibalism—as a means of prolonging existence.

"There appeared to have been an abundant stock of ammunition, as the powder was emptied in a heap on the ground by the natives out of the kegs or cases containing it; and a quantity of ball and shot was found below high-water mark, having probably been left on the ice close to the beach. There must have been a number of watches, compasses, telescopes, guns, (several double-barreled,) &c., all of which appear to have been broken up, as I saw pieces of those different articles with the Esquimaux, together with some silver spoons and forks. I purchased as many as I could get. A list of the most important of these I enclose, with a rough sketch of the crests and initials on the forks and spoons. The articles themselves shall be handed over to the Secretary of the Hudson's Bay Company on my arrival in London.

"None of the Esquimaux with whom I conversed had seen the 'whites,' nor had they ever been at the place where the bodies were found, but had their information from those who had been there, and who had seen the party when traveling.

"I offer no apology for taking the liberty of addressing you, as I do so from a belief that their lordships would be desirous of being put in possession, at as early a date as possible, of any tidings, however meagre and unexpectedly obtained, regarding this painfully interesting subject.

"I may add that, by means of our guns and nets, we obtained an ample supply of provisions last autumn, and my small party passed the winter in snow-houses in comparative comfort, the skins of the deer shot affording abundant warm clothing and bedding. My spring journey was a failure, in consequence of an accumulation of obstacles, several of which my former experience in arctic traveling had not taught me to expect. I have, &c.   JOHN RAE, C.F.,
"*Commanding Hudson's Bay Company's Arctic Expedition.*"

To such a tragic detail as this, little could be added, until the recent return of the screw yacht Fox, sent out by Lady Franklin, whose persistent devotedness of search for her husband is worthy of the highest praise. This vessel arrived off the Isle of Wight, Sept. 21, 1859. The following is the report submitted by Capt. McClintock to the Admiralty.

PROCEEDINGS OF THE YACHT FOX,
CONTINUED FROM MAY, 1858.

It will be remembered that the Fox effected her escape out of the main pack in Davis' Straits, in lat. 63¼ deg. N., on the 25th of April, 1858, after a winter's ice drift of 1,194 geographical miles.

The small settlement of Holsteinborg was reached on the 28th, and such very scanty supplies obtained as the place afforded.

On May 8th our voyage was recommenced; Godhaven and Upernivik visited, Melville Bay entered early in June, and crossed to Cape York by the 26th; here some natives were communicated with; they immediately recognized Mr. Peterson, our interpreter, formerly known to them in the Grinnell expedition under Dr. Kane. In reply to our inquiries for the Esquimaux dog driver "Hans" left behind from the Advance in 1848, they told us that he was residing at Whale Sound. Had he been there I would most gladly have embarked him, as his longing to return to South Greenland continues unabated.

On July 12th communicated with the Cape Warrender natives, near Cape Horsburg; they had not seen any ships since the visit of the Phœnix in 1854, nor have any wrecks ever drifted upon their shores.

It was not until 27th July that we reached Points Inlet, owing to a most unusual prevalence of ice in the northern portion of Baffin's Bay, and which rendered our progress since leaving Holsteinborg one of increasing struggle. Without steam power we could have done nothing. Here only one old woman and a boy were found, but they served to pilot us up the inlet for twenty-five miles, when we arrived at their village. For about a week we were in constant and most interesting communication with these friendly people. Briefly, the information obtained from them was, that nothing whatever respecting the Franklin expedition had come to their knowledge, nor had any wrecks within the last twenty or thirty years reached their shores.

The remains of three wrecked ships are known to them; two of these appear to have been the whalers Dexterity and Aurora, wrecked in August, 1821, some seventy or eighty miles southward of Pond's Inlet. The third vessel, now almost buried in the sand, lies a few miles east of Cape Hay. This people communicate overland every winter with the tribes at Igloolik; they all knew of Parry's ships having wintered there in 1822-3, and had heard of late years of Dr. Rae's visit to Repulse Bay, describing his boats as similar to our whale boat, and his party as living in tents, within snow houses, smoking pipes, shooting reindeer, &c., &c. None died. They remained there only one winter.

No rumor of the lost expedition has reached them. Within Pond's Inlet, the natives told us the ice decays away every year, but so long as any remains whales abound. Several large whales were seen by us, and we found amongst the natives a considerable quantity of whalebone and many norwhale's horns, which they were anxious to barter for knives, files, saws, rifles, and wool; they drew us some rude charts of the inlet, showing that it expands into an extensive channel looking westward into Prince Regent's Inlet. We could not but regret that none of our own whaling friends—from whom we had recently received so much kindness—were here to profit by so favorable an opportunity. Leaving Pond's Inlet on the 6th August, we reached Beechy Island on the 11th, and landed a handsome marble tablet, sent on board for this purpose by Lady Franklin, bearing an appropriate inscription to the memory of our lost countrymen in the Erebus and Terror.

The provisions and stores seemed in perfect order, but a small boat was much damaged from having been turned over and rolled along the beach by a storm. The roof of the house received some necessary repairs. Having embarked some coals and stores we stood in need of and touched at Cape Hotham on the 16th, we sailed down Peel Strait for 25 miles on the 17th, but finding the remainder of this channel covered by unbroken ice, I determined to make for Bellot's Strait on 19th of August, examined into supplies remaining at Port Leopold, and left there a whale-boat which we brought away from Cape Hotham for the purpose, so as to aid us in our retreat should we be obliged eventually to abandon the Fox. The steam launch had been forced higher up on the beach, and somewhat damaged by the ice. Prince Regent's Inlet was unusually free from ice, but very little was seen during our run down to Brentford Bay, which we reached on the 20th August. Bellot's Strait, which communicates with the Western sea, averages one mile in width, by 17 or 18 miles in length. At this time it was filled with drift ice, but as the season advanced became perfectly clear; its shores are in many places faced with lofty granite cliffs, and some of the adjacent hills rise 1,600 feet; the tides are very strong, running six or seven knots at the springs. On the 6th of September we passed through Bellot's Strait without obstruction, and secured the ship to fixed ice across its western outlet. From here, until the 27th, when I deemed it necessary to retreat into winter quarters, we constantly watched the movements of the ice in the western sea or channel. In mid-channel it was broken up and drifting about; gradually the proportion of water increased, until at length the ice which intervened was reduced to three or four miles in width. But this was firmly held fast by numerous islets, and withstood the violence of the autumn gales. It was tantalising beyond description thus to watch from day to day the free water which we could not reach, and which washed the rocky shore a few miles to the southward of us!

During the autumn attempts were made to carry our depots of provisions towards the magnetic pole, but these almost entirely failed in consequence of the disruption of the ice to the southward. Lieutenant Hobson returned with his sledge parties in November, after much suffering from severe weather, and imminent peril on one occasion, when the ice upon which they were encamped became detached from the shore, and drifted off to leeward with them.

Our wintering position was at the east entrance to Bellot's Strait in a snug harbor, which I have named Port Kennedy, after my predecessor in these waters, the commander of one of Lady Franklin's former searching expeditions. Although vegetation was tolerably abundant, and our two Esquimaux hunters, Mr. Peterson, and several sportsmen were constantly on the alert, yet the resources of the country during eleven months and a half, only yielded us eight reindeer, two bears, eighteen seals and a few water fowl and ptarmigan.

The winter was unusually cold and stormy. Arrangements were completed during the winter for carrying out our intended plan of search; I felt it to be my duty personally to visit Marshal Island, and in so doing purposed to complete the circuit of King William's Island. To Lieut. Hobson I alloted the search of the western shore of Boothia to the magnetic pole, and from Gateshead Island westward to Wynniatt's farthest. Captain Allen Young, our sailing master, was to trace the shore of Prince of Wales's Land, from Lieut. Browne's farthest; and also to examine the coast from Bellot's Strait northward, to Sir James Ross's farthest.

Early spring journeys were commenced on the 17th Feb., 1859, by Capt. Young and myself, Capt. Young carrying his depot across to Prince of Wales's Land, whilst I went southward, towards the magnetic pole in the hope of communicating with the Esquimaux, and obtaining such information as might lead us at once to the object of our search.

I was accompanied by Mr. Peterson, our interpreter, and Alexander Thomson, quarter-master. We had with us two sledges drawn by dogs. On the 28th of Feb., when near Cape Victoria, we had the good fortune to meet a small party of natives, and were subsequently visited by about forty-five individuals.

For four days we remained in communication with them, obtaining many relics, and the information that several years ago a ship was crushed by the ice off the north shore, off King William's Island, but that all her people landed safely, and went away to the Great Fish River, where they died. This tribe was well supplied with wood, obtained, they said, from a boat left by the white men on the great river.

We reached our vessel after twenty-five days' absence, in good health but somewhat reduced by sharp marching and the unusually severe weather to which we had been exposed. For several days after starting the mercury continued frozen.

On the 2nd of April our long projected spring journeys were commenced; Lieutenant Hobson accompanied me as far as Cape Victoria, each of us had a sledge drawn by four men, and an auxiliary sledge drawn by six dogs. This was all the force we could muster.

Before separating, we saw two Esquimaux families living out upon the ice in snow huts; from them we learned that a second ship had been seen off King William's Island, and that she drifted ashore on the fall of the same year. From this ship they had obtained a vast deal of wood and iron.

I now gave Lieut. Hobson directions to search for the wreck, and follow up any traces he might find upon King William's Island.

Accompanied by my own party and Mr. Peterson, I marched along the east shore of King William's Island, occasionally passing deserted snow huts, but without meeting natives till the 8th of May, when off Cape Norton we arrived at a snow village containing about thirty inhabitants. They gathered about us without the slightest appearance of fear or shyness, although none had ever seen living white people before. They were most willing to communicate all their knowledge, and barter all their goods, but would have stolen everything had they not been very closely watched. Many more relics of our countrymen were obtained—we could not carry away all we might have purchased.

They pointed to the inlet we had crossed the day before, and told us that one day's march up it, and from thence four days overland, brought them to the wreck.

None of these people had been there since 1857-8, at which time they said but little remained, their countrymen having carried away almost everything.

Most of our information was received from an intelligent old woman ; she said that it was on the fall of the year that the ship was forced ashore ; many of the white men dropped by the way as they went towards the Great River ; but this was only known to them in the winter following, when their bodies were discovered. They all assured us that we would find natives upon the south shore, at the Great River, and some few at the wreck ; but unfortunately this was not the case. Only one family was met with off Point Booth, and none at Montreal Island, or any place subsequently visited.

Point Ogle, Montreal Island, and Barrow Island, were searched without finding anything except a few scraps of copper and iron in an Esquimaux hiding-place.

Recrossing the Strait to King William's Island, we continued the examination of its southern shore without success until the 24th of May, when about ten miles eastward of Cape Herschel a bleached skeleton was found, around which lay fragments of European clothing. Upon carefully removing the snow a small pocket book was found containing a few letters—these, although much decayed, may yet be deciphered. Judging from the remains of his dress, this unfortunate young man was a steward or officer's servant, and his position exactly verified the Esquimaux's assertion that they dropped as they walked along.

On reaching Cape Herschel next day, he examined Simpson's Cairn, or rather what remains of it, which is only four feet high, and the central stores had been removed, as if by men seeking something within it. My impression at the time, and which I still retain, is that records were deposited there by the retreating crews, and subsequently removed by the natives.

After parting from me at Cape Victoria on the 28th April, Lieutenant Hobson made for Cape Felix ; at a short distance westward of it he found a very large cairn, and close to it three small tents, with blankets, old clothes, and other relics of a shooting or a magnetic station ; but although the cairn was dug under, and a trench dug all round it at a distance of ten feet, no record was discovered. A piece of blank paper folded up was found in the cairn, and two broken bottles which may perhaps have contained records, lay beside it amongst some stones which had fallen from off the top. The most interesting of the articles discovered here, including a boat's ensign, were brought away by Mr. Hobson. About two miles farther to the S. W. a small cairn was found, but neither records nor relics obtained. About three miles north of Point Victory a second small cairn was examined, but only a broken pickaxe and empty canister found.

On 6th May, Lieut. Hobson pitched his tent beside a large cairn upon Point Victory. Lying amongst some loose stones which had fallen from the top of this cairn was found a small tin case containing a record, the substance of which is briefly as follows:—This cairn was built by the Franklin Expedition upon the assumed site of James Ross's pillar, which had not been found. The Erebus and Terror spent their first winter at Beechy Island, after having ascended Wellington Channel to lat. 77 deg. N., and returned by the west side of Cornwallis Island. On the 12th of September, 1846, they were beset in lat. 70 05 N. and lon. 98 23 W.

Sir J. Franklin died on the 11th June, 1847. On the 22nd April, 1848, the ships were abandoned five leagues to the N.N.W. of Point Victory, and the survivors, a hundred and five in number, landed here under the command of Captain Crozier. This paper was dated 25th April, 1848, and upon the following day they intended to start for the Great Fish River. The total loss by deaths in the expedition up to this date was nine officers and fifteen men. A vast quantity of clothing and stores of all sorts lay strewed about, as if here every article was thrown away which could possibly be dispensed with ; pickaxes, shovels, boats, cooking utensils. iron work, rope, blocks, canvass, a dip circle, a sextant engraved " Frederic Hornby," R. N., a small medicine chest, oars, &c.

A few miles southward across Black Bay, a second record was found, having been deposited by Lieutenant Gore and M. des Vœux in May, 1847. It afforded no additional information.

Lieut. Hobson continued his search until within a few days' march of Cape Herschel, without finding any trace of the wreck or of natives. He left full information of his important discoveries for me ; therefore, when returning northward by the west shore of King William's Island, I had the advantage of knowing what had already been found.

Soon after leaving Cape Herschel the traces of natives became less numerous and less recent, and after rounding the west point of the island, they ceased altogether. This shore is extremely low, and almost utterly destitute of vegetation. Numerous banks of shingle and low islets lie off it, and beyond these, Victoria Strait is covered with heavy and impenetrable packed ice.

When in lat. 69 deg. 09 N., and long. 99 deg. 27 W., we came to a large boat, discovered by Lieutenant Hobson a few days previously, as his notice informed me. It appears that this boat had been intended for the ascent of the Fish River, but was abandoned apparently upon a return journey to the ships, the sledge upon which she was mounted being pointed in that direction. She was 28 feet in length, by 7½ feet wide, was most carefully fitted, and made as light as possible, but the sledge was of solid oak, and almost as heavy as the boat.

A large quantity of clothing was found within her, also two human skeletons. One of these lay in the after part of the boat, under a pile of clothing; the other, which was much more disturbed, probably by animals, was found in the bow. Five pocket watches, a quantity of silver spoons and forks, and a few religious books, were also found, but no journals, pocket-books, or even names upon any articles of clothing. Two double-barrelled guns stood upright against the boat's side precisely as they had been placed eleven years before. One barrel in each was loaded and cocked; there was ammunition in abundance, also 30 lbs. or 40 lbs. of chocolate, some tea and tobacco. Fuel was not wanting; a drift tree lay within 100 yards of the boat.

Many very interesting relics were brought away by Lieutenant Hobson, and some few by myself. On the 5th of June I reached Point Victory, without having found anything further. The clothing, &c., was again examined for documents, note-books, &c., without success, a record placed in the cairn, and another quired ten feet true north of it.

Nothing worthy of remark occurred upon my return journey to the ship, which we reached on the 19th of June, five days after Lieutenant Hobson.

The shore of King William's Island between its north and west extremes, Capes Felix and Crozier, has not been visited by Esquimaux since the abandonment of the Erebus and Terror, as the cairns and articles lying strewed about, which are in their eyes of priceless value, remain untouched.

If the wreck still remains visible, it is probable she lies upon some of the off-lying islets to the southward between Capes Crozier and Herschel.

On the 28th of June, Capt. Young and his party returned, having completed their portion of the search, by which the insularity of Prince of Wales's Land was determined, and the coastline intervening between the extreme points reached by Lieuts. Osborne and Browne discovered; also between Bellot's Strait and Sir James Ross's farthest in 1849, at Four River Bay.

Fearing that his provisions might not last out the requisite period, Capt. Young sent back four of his men, and for forty days journeyed on through fogs and gales with but one man and the dogs, building a snow hut each night; but few men could stand so long a continuance of labor and privation, and its effect upon Capt. Young was painfully evident.

Lieut. Hobson was unable to stand without assistance upon his return on board; he was not in good health when he commenced his long journey, and the sudden severe exposure brought on a serious attack of scurvy; yet he also most ably completed his work: and such facts will more clearly evince the unflinching spirit with which the object of our voyage has been pursued in these detached duties, than any praise of mine.

We were now, at length, all on board again. As there were some slight cases of scurvy all our treasured resources of Burton ale, lemon juice, and fresh animal food were put into requisition, so that in a comparatively short time all were restored to sound health.

During our sojourn in Port Kennedy, we were twice called upon to follow a shipmate to the grave. Mr. George Brands, engineer, died of apoplexy, on the 6th of November, 1858; he had been out deer-shooting for several hours that day and appeared in excellent health.

On the 14th June, 1859, Thomas Blackwall, ship's steward, dind of scurvy; this man had served in two of the former searching expeditions. The summer proved a warm one; we were able to start on our homeward voyage on the 9th of August, and although the engine-driver in 1857, and the engineer in 1858, left us with only two stokers, yet with their assistance I was able to control the engines and steam the ship up to Fury Point.

For six days we lay there closely beset, when a change of wind removing the ice, our voyage was continued almost without further interruption, to Godhaven, in Disco, where we arrived on the 27th August, and were received with great kindness by Mr. Olick, inspector of North Greenland, and the local authorities, who obligingly supplied our few wants.

The two Esquimaux dog drivers were now discharged, and on the 1st September we sailed for England.

From all that can be gleaned from the record paper, and the evidence afforded by the boat, and various articles of clothing and equipment discovered, it appears that the abandonment of the Erebus and Terror had been deliberately arranged, and every effort exerted during the third winter to render the traveling equipments complete.

It is much to be apprehended that disease had greatly reduced the strength of all on board—far more, perhaps, than they themselves were aware of.

The distance by sledge route, from the position of the ships when abandoned, is 65 geographical miles; and from the ships to Montreal Island, 220 miles.

The most perfect order seems to have existed throughout.

In order to extend as much as possible the public utility of this voyage, magnetical, meteorological, and other observations, subservient to scientific purposes, and for which instruments were supplied through the liberality of the Royal Society, have been continually and carefully taken, and every opportunity has been embraced by the surgeon, D. Walker, M.D., of forming complete collections in all the various branches of natural history.

This report would be incomplete, did I not mention the obligations I have been under to the companions of my voyage, both officers and men, by their zealous and unvarying support throughout.

A feeling of entire devotion to the cause which Lady Franklin has so nobly sustained, and a firm determination to effect all that men could do, seem to have supported them through every difficulty. With less of this enthusiastic spirit, and cheerful obedience to every command, our small number—twenty-three in all—would not have sufficed for the successful performance of so great a work.

F. L. M'CLINTOCK, Captain, R. N.,
Commanding the Final Searching Expedition.
The Yacht Fox, R.Y.S., off Isle of Wight,
Sept. 21, 1859.

This letter is followed by a very minute detail of the relics, &c., discovered at various points of search ; some of these were brought home, and others were left. Our readers will be enabled to judge of the nature of these relics by the few appended examples :—

Relics brought from the Boat found in lat. 69 deg. 8 43 N., lon. 99 deg. 24 42 W., upon the West Coast of King William's Island, May 30, 1859.

Two double-barrelled guns—one barrel in each is loaded. Found standing up against the side in the after-part of the boat.

In one parcel.—A small Prayer-book, cover of a small book of " Family Prayers ;" " Christian Melodies," an inscription within the cover to " G. G.," (Graham Gore ?) ; " Vicar of Wakefield ;" a small Bible, interlined in many places, and with numerous references written in the margin ; a New Testament in the French language.

Tied together.—Two table knives with white handles—one is marked " W. R. ;" a gimlet, an awl, two iron stancheons, nine inches long, for supporting a weather cloth, which was round the boat.

Tied together.—Twenty-six pieces of silver plate—eleven spoons, eleven forks, and four tea-spoons, three pieces of thin elm board (tingles) for repairing the boat, and measuring eleven by six inches, and three-tenths inch thick.

All wrapped up in a piece of canvas.—Bristles for shoemakers' use, bullets, short clay pipe, roll of waxed twine, a wooden button, small piece of a port fire, two charges of shot, tied up in the finger of a kid glove, tied up in a fragment of a seaman's blue surge frock, &c., &c.

Relics found about Ross Cairn, on Point Victory, May and June, 1859, brought away.

A six-inch diss circle, by Robinson, marked " I 22." A case of medicines, consisting of twenty-five small bottles, canister of pills, ointment, plaster, oiled silk, &c. A two-foot rule, two joints of the cleaning-rod of a gun, and a small copper spindle, probably for dog-vanes of boats. The circular brass plate broke out of a wooden gun case, and engraved " C. H. Ormer, R.N." The field glass and German silver top of a two-foot telescope, a coffee canister, a piece of a brass curtain rod. The record tin—the record dated 25th April, 1848, has been taken out. A six-inch double frame sextant, on which the owner's name is engraved, " Frederic Hornby, R.N."

Seen about Ross Cairn, Point Victory, not brought away.

Four sets of boat-cooking apparatus complete, iron hoops, four feet of a copper lightning conductor. Hollow brass curtain rod three-quarters of an inch in diameter, three pickaxes, one shovel, old canvas, a pile of warm clothing, blankets two feet high, two tin canteens stamped " 89 Co., Wm. Hedge, 88 Co., Wm. Heather," and a third one not marked. A small panniken made on board out of a 2lbs. preserved meat-tin (and marked " W. Mark,") a small deal box for gun-wadding. The heavy iron-work of a large boat, part of a canvas tent, part of an oar sawed longitudinally, and a blanket nailed to its flat side, three boat hook staves, strips of copper, a 9-inch single block strapped, a piece of rope and spun yarn. Amongst the clothing was found a stocking marked " W," green, and a fragment of one marked " W. S."

Relics obtained from the Boothian Esquimaux, near the Magnetic Pole, in March and April, 1859.

Seven knives made by the natives out of materials obtained from the last expedition, one knife without a handle, one spearhead and staff (the latter was broken off), two files, a large spoon or scoop, the handle of pine or bone, the bowl of musk or ox horn, six silver spoons and forks, the property of Sir John Franklin, Lieutenants H. de Vescomte, and Fairholme, A. M'Donald, Assistant Surgeon, and Lieut. E. Couch, (supposed from the initial letter T and crest a lion's head), a small portion of a gold watch chain, a broken piece of ornamental work, apparently silver gilt, a few small naval and other metal buttons, a silver medal obtained by Mr. M'Donald as a prize for superior attainments at a medical examination in Edinburgh, April, 1838, some bows and arrows, in which wood, iron, or copper has been used in the construction—of no other interest.

Relics obtained from the Esquimaux near Cape Norton, upon the East Coast of King William's Island, in May, 1859.

Two table-spoons, upon one is scratched W W, on the other W G; these bear the Franklin crest. Two table-forks, one bearing the Franklin crest; the other is also crested, probably Captain Crozier's; silversmith's name is I. West. Two teaspoons, one engraved A. M. D. (A. McDonald); the other bears the Fairholme crest and motto ; handle of a desert knife, into which had been inserted a razor (since broken off) by Millikin, Strand ; buttons, wood, and iron were in abundance ; but as enough of these had already been obtained, no more were purchased.

Found lying about the skeleton, nine miles eastward of Cape Herschel, May, 1859.—The tie of a black silk handkerchief, fragments of a double-breasted blue cloth waistcoat with covered silk buttons, and edged with braid ; a scrap of a colored cotton shirt, silk covered buttons of blue cloth great coat, a small clothes, brush, a horn pocket-comb, a leather pocket-book, which fell to pieces when thawed and dried ; it contained nine or ten letters, a few leaves apparently blank. A sixpence, date 1831, and a half-sovereign, date 1844.

Enclosed are Copies of Original Papers found by Captain M'Clintock on Prince of Wales's Island.

" — of May, 1847.

" Her Majesty's ships Erebus and Terror wintered in the ice in lat. 70 deg. 5 min., lon. 98 deg. 23 min. W.

" Having wintered in 1845-6 at Beechey Island, in lat. 74 deg. 43 min. 28 sec. N., lon. 91 deg. 39 min. 15 sec. W., after ascending Wellington Channel to lat. 77 deg., and returning by the west side of Cornwallis Island.

" SIR JOHN FRANKLIN, Commanding the Expedition.

" All well.

" Whoever finds this paper is requested to forward it to the Secretary of the Admiralty, London, with a note of the time and place at which it was found, or, if more convenient, to deliver it for that purpose to the British consul at the nearest port."

(The same in French, Spanish, Dutch, Danish, and German.)

" Left the ships on Monday, the 24th of May, 1847, the party consisting of two officers and six men.

" G. M. GORE, Lieutenant.
"CHAS. F. DES VŒUX, Mate."

It will thus be seen that, though in some points contradictory to Dr. Rae's accounts, in the main a remarkable confirmation is obtained. It is evident that the fate of Sir John Franklin has been ascertained. This is the means of relieving many minds from the uncertainty which, hitherto, appertained to the Expedition; while the pertinacity with which the search was continued, will have its influence on those who may be called to go forth on perilous undertakings. It has been made evident, alike by England and America, that those who go forth in a public service, shall not be abandoned, and thus moral courage is strengthened for future enterprises.

The recent expedition of Capt. M'Clintock has done more than bring records and relics of Franklin's company. Our geographical knowledge is enlarged by the examination of eight hundred miles of coast, and this connected with previous surveys. In short, while steadfastly pursuing the noble service to which the Fox was primarily devoted, her officers and crew found opportunity to add a large quota to our information of the globe we inhabit.